JACOB'S LADDER

JACOB'S LADDER

On Angels

Sergius Bulgakov

*Translated
and with an Introduction by*

Thomas Allan Smith

WILLIAM B. EERDMANS PUBLISHING COMPANY
GRAND RAPIDS, MICHIGAN / CAMBRIDGE, U.K.

Originally published in Paris in 1929 under the title *Lestvitsa Iakovlia. Ob angelakh.*

English translation © 2010 Wm. B. Eerdmans Publishing Company

Published 2010 by
Wm. B. Eerdmans Publishing Co.
2140 Oak Industrial Drive N.E., Grand Rapids, Michigan 49505 /
P.O. Box 163, Cambridge CB3 9PU U.K.

Printed in the United States of America

16 15 14 13 12 11 10   7 6 5 4 3 2 1

Library of Congress Cataloging-in-Publication Data

Bulgakov, Sergei Nikolaevich, 1871-1944.
[Lestvitsa Iakovlia. English]
Jacob's ladder: on angels / Sergius Bulgakov;
translated and with an introduction by Thomas Allan Smith.
p.   cm.
ISBN 978-0-8028-6516-8 (pbk.: alk. paper)
1. Angels. I. Smith, T. Allan. II. Title.

BT966.3.B8513 2010

235'.3 — dc22

2010010182

www.eerdmans.com

Contents

Translator's Introduction

With a powerful meditation on the meaning of love, penned in the midst of an era when European society was least characterized by this cardinal Christian virtue, Sergius Bulgakov (1871-1944) introduces his theological exploration of the doctrine of Angels. Few of Bulgakov's professional writings attain such lyrical heights as the present volume, the third of his first dogmatic trilogy[1] dealing with Divine Sophia and creation. *Jacob's Ladder* completes the word picture of divinized and Sophianic creation begun in *The Burning Bush* and *The Friend of the Bridegroom*. It is, as he says, a written exposition of the icon of the Deesis, the intercession of the preeminent representatives of humankind and angels before the throne of God.[2] Mary, the ever-Virgin Mother of God and John the Forerunner and Angel-Man, female and male, represent the visible creation; they are surrounded by the noetic heaven, the angels, who represent invisible creation.

---

1. Scholarly literature has unhappily settled on the phrases "minor trilogy" and "major trilogy" when referring to Bulgakov's principal theological writings. I am using the phrase coined by his initial interpreter Lev Zander in *Bog i mir (God and the World)*, 2 volumes (Paris: YMCA Press, 1948), 1:62. With the appearance of this volume, Bulgakov's first trilogy is now available in English: *The Burning Bush,* translated with an introduction by Thomas Allan Smith (Grand Rapids, MI, and Cambridge, UK: Wm. B. Eerdmans Publishing Co., 2009); *The Friend of the Bridegroom,* translated with an introduction by Boris Jakim (Grand Rapids, MI, and Cambridge, UK: Wm. B. Eerdmans Publishing Co., 2003). The second dogmatic trilogy is also available in English, all ably translated by Boris Jakim: *The Lamb of God* (2008), *The Comforter* (2004), *The Bride of the Lamb* (2002), all published by Wm. B. Eerdmans Publishing Co.

2. See the author's preface of this translation.

Together they proclaim the Wisdom of God in creation, Sophia as the ground of existence for the world of creatures.[3]

Bulgakov accepts the existence of angels as unquestioningly as he does the physical world: angels are simply part of the reality in which humans live. His bold affirmation of a traditional if at times neglected part of Christian doctrine came at a crucial moment in European and world history and is a reminder that the theologian attuned to his or her vocation speaks not what the world wants to hear but what it needs to hear. Europe drained of its youth was rebuilding after the first World War; pandemic influenza had swept away millions of people around the globe; Communism was imposing a cold materialist socialism in the newly created Soviet Union; uncontrolled economic growth and spiralling inflation would lead to the Great Depression and even more misery, and the dual barbarity of Fascism and National Socialism were already casting their siren's spell on a bewildered citizenry. In such a context is a book on angels necessary? Bulgakov was not asked this question but would undoubtedly have responded in the affirmative. A strong statement on the reality of the invisible, non-material dimension of the universe such as one finds in *Jacob's Ladder* seems especially necessary when the human being is reduced to a sum of chemical processes and life itself is stripped of meaning. To be reminded that the universe, all that is visible and invisible, is not ultimately a vast storehouse for exploitation and material gain or a platform for tyrannical oppression but a reflection of Divine Beauty and a partner in its own glorious transformation is to be given hope — the final gift of Bulgakov's first dogmatic trilogy itself.

Sergius Bulgakov was the son of a poor parish priest who served a cemetery church in the provincial town of Livny. He entered the seminary to train for the priesthood as generations of Bulgakov sons had done before him; but just before his final year, he left the seminary, having lost faith in God. In 1890 he was admitted to the Law Faculty at Moscow University and studied political economy, by now a convinced Marxist. In 1900 he published his dissertation, *Capitalism and Agriculture*. From 1901 to 1906 he taught political economy at the Polytechnical Institute of Kiev and then at Moscow University. He resigned in protest over government policy towards the university in 1911. In the course of researching and writing his dissertation, Bulgakov became convinced that Marxism offered a

3. For an accessible explanation of Bulgakov's controversial theological method, Sophiology, see Sergei Bulgakov, *Sophia. The Wisdom of God* (1937, New York; revised edition, Hudson, NY: Lindisfarne Press, 1993).

fatally flawed interpretation of economy, particularly agriculture. Disillusionment with Marxism opened him to German idealist philosophy and Russian religious philosophy. He associated with leading members of the intelligentsia in their quest for a religious renewal and reformation of Russian society and helped found the Moscow Religious-Philosophical Society. His two most significant works to emerge from this period of personal reconstruction are *Philosophy of Economy* (1911) and *Unfading Light* (1916).[4] In them he elaborates in philosophical terms his intellectual project of Sophiology.

Bulgakov participated actively in the political life of Russia and was elected to the Second Duma (parliament) in 1907, but his political career ended abruptly in June that same year when the parliament was suppressed. His social activism and interest in religious matters led him to take a more public role in the transformation of the Russian Church and in 1917 he was a delegate to the All-Russian Council of the Orthodox Church. His return to his ancestral faith was completed in 1918 when he was ordained to the priesthood. From then on, Bulgakov would devote most of his intellectual energies to employing Sophiology in the field of dogmatic theology. He held a professorship in the Crimea from 1918 until 1922, when he and hundreds of others were expelled from the Soviet Union. Travelling by way of Constantinople and Prague, he ended up in Paris in 1925. Bulgakov's early activism continued in exile, where he became involved in the ecumenical movement. Attending the Lausanne Conference in 1927 he spoke provocatively on the Church and the Theotokos, urging Protestants to rediscover devotion to the Mother of God. He was instrumental in the creation of the Fellowship of St. Alban and St. Sergius in England, which brought Anglican and Orthodox Christians together as a means of mutual self-discovery and ecumenical cooperation. In 1939 Bulgakov was operated on for throat cancer which left him with only limited use of his vocal chords. Death came in 1944.

His Paris years saw the production of his first and second dogmatic trilogies dealing with Divine Wisdom in creation and the humanity of God respectively. Though much admired in Paris for his theological work, Bulgakov's commitment to Sophiology would cause charges of pantheism to be raised against him. His own ecclesiastical superior, Metropolitan Evlogii, steadfastly defended Bulgakov when he fell under the con-

4. Sergei Bulgakov, *Philosophy of Economy,* translated, edited, and with an introduction by Catherine Evtuhov (New Haven and London: Yale University Press, 2000); *Svet nevechernii* (Moscow, 1916).

demnation of the two other Russian Orthodox jurisdictions, the one centered in Moscow and the other in Karlovsti, Serbia. He defended himself against the accusations, but it was only at the end of the twentieth century that his name began to emerge from the undeserved oblivion to which it had been consigned.

Writing about love naturally invites personal investment in the theme; Bulgakov's introduction is no exception. His reflections on the nature of love and love's constitutive purpose in characterizing authentic humanity, his yearning for an intimate other and friend recall the passionate thinking of St Augustine of Hippo, equally poised on the brink of a disintegrating world.[5] Like his early Christian counterpart, Bulgakov knows by experience that love is not ultimately satisfied in its physical expression (though unlike Augustine, he remains optimistic about the sexual dimension of human life) and that a love which ends with time is no love at all. His reflections on the varieties of human love — from our love for God, to our love of others, familial and parental love, marital love, and friendship — determine that authentic love is sacrificial, self-offering, in imitation of the inner Trinitarian kenotic love underlying all reality. The spiritual dimension of human love which seeks a friend or other who is never divorced from us is anchored in the angelic world, specifically in the guardian angel assigned to each human being as a perpetual, loving companion and friend and whose entire being is a self-offering in service to the human counterpart.

Bulgakov constructs his introduction and indeed the entire book out of biblical, dogmatic, liturgical, and iconographical material, but his work is by no means an abstract or coolly rational treatise — and that despite its typically philosophical and theological language and categories. Bulgakov writes of angels from personal experience, and he relates a moving episode when his guardian angel came to him and brought him back from near-death to life. It is an episode that he returns to in other writings and it clearly made a profound, life-altering impression on him.[6] The events occurred in 1926 roughly one year after Bulgakov had taken up residence in Paris and assumed the duties of professor of dogmatic theology

---

5. That Bulgakov was a serious reader of Augustine has been shown by Myroslaw Tataryn in *Augustine and Russian Orthodoxy. Russian Orthodox Theologians and Augustine of Hippo, a Twentieth Century Dialogue* (Lanham, MD: International Scholars Publications, 2000), esp. pp. 74-84, 90-95.

6. Sergei Bulgakov, "Sofiologija smerti (A Sophiology of Death)," *Tikhie Dumy* (Moscow: Izd. "Respublika," 1996), pp. 291-93.

at the newly founded Orthodox Theological Institute of St. Sergius. As he lay in a state between life and death, reflecting on his family and friends and sensing God's overwhelming presence, Bulgakov was suddenly called back to consciousness by his guardian angel. He writes,

> At that time the voice of a *companion* sounded within — I was not alone but together with my own other I; it was my guardian angel. He told me that we had gone too far ahead and it was necessary to return . . . to life. I understood and heard with my inner hearing that the Lord was bringing me back to life, and I was recovering. One and the same call which released me from this world and from life, simultaneously and with the same word returned me to it. Interiorly I already knew that I would recover although I was still not any better. I returned to life from death. And I knew all this time that I was not alone, that with me was a friend, the most near, tender and quiet. I did not see him with my eyes, he hid himself from them, but I sensed and was aware of his presence. . . .[7]

In other words, the angel's love worked to restore him to life and undoubtedly illuminated Bulgakov's mind about the nature of these unseen spiritual beings. Evidently, the decision to introduce a theological study of angels with a reflection on love is not a sentimental indulgence. Love is a way of knowing, perhaps *the* way of knowing another person, whether that other is a human being, an angelic being, or God. By beginning, then, with these words on love, Bulgakov sets the interpretive method for himself and for those who read his words. Here too he seems to be operating in a manner not unlike what one finds in Augustine's *De doctrina christiana* which also begins with a discourse on love and establishes it as the hermeneutical key to unlock the meaning of Scripture.[8] Rigorous thinking enriched by personal experience is the hallmark of Bulgakov's theological and philosophical corpus, and the reader will not be disappointed as the pages of *Jacob's Ladder* pass in review.

With the introduction setting the parameters for what follows like the overture to a great opera, Bulgakov turns to examine various theological questions pertaining to angels: their creation, their function as guardians, their nature and life, their appearances to humans through the ages,

---

7. Infra, p. 19.

8. Saint Augustine, *Teaching Christianity*, introduction, translation, and notes, Edmund Hill, O.P. (Hyde Park, NY: New City Press, 1996), pp. 106-26.

their incorporeality and their knowledge of and share in the incarnation. These topics are those of a common Christian reflection on angels stretching from the patristic era to the contemporary period.[9] Bulgakov's own reflections then fit into the broad stream of tradition. His aim, however, is novel: to provide a theological interpretation of the doctrine of Angels. That is, by using scriptural, doctrinal, liturgical, artistic, and experiential data, Bulgakov will expound the meaning of Christianity's belief in angels within a unified, coherent, theological whole.

Two scriptural passages stand out as signal texts for Bulgakov's appropriation of the doctrinal tradition concerning angels: "In the beginning God created *heaven and earth*" (Gen. 1:1), and "He measured its wall as one hundred and forty-four cubits *with a human measure, which is also the angel's measure*" (Rev. 21:17). His book interprets these two verses exhaustively in order to demonstrate the correlativity of angels and human beings. He had already broached this theme with an excursus in his second book of the first trilogy, *The Friend of the Bridegroom*,[10] but there he tied his thought to the overarching theme of that book, St. John the Forerunner, known to Orthodox tradition as the Angel-Man. The present volume focuses in particular on the guardian angels who more than anything else are presented as friends of the human race and each human being. The intimate relationship angels enjoy with human beings allows Bulgakov to pursue another important theme, theological anthropology. A correct understanding of human nature informs a correct understanding of angels and vice-versa. He thus explores the meaning of corporeality, birth, and sexuality for humans and how heavenly angels participate in these seemingly very earthly realities of human existence. The book closes as it opened, with a reiteration of Bulgakov's understanding of love.

9. See for example George Tavard, *Die Engel* (Freiburg im Breisgau: Herder, 1968), French translation *Les Anges* (Paris: Cerf, 1971); Jean Daniélou, *The Angels and Their Mission*, trans. David Heimann (Westminster, MD: The Newman Press, 1957).

10. *Friend of the Bridegroom*, pp. 156-70.

From the Author

The subject of the present work is the doctrine of angels. Although it is presented as an entirely independent whole, it nevertheless is directly connected with two recently published works, *The Burning Bush* (1927) and *The Friend of the Bridegroom* (1928). These three parts together form one dogmatic trilogy which is defined by the unity of its Sophiological theme, *concerning the Wisdom of God in creation,* which the Most Pure and the Forerunner make known in the human world, and the angels, in the heavenly world. Were one to express this theme iconographically, it would correspond to the central part of the Deesis rank in an iconostasis: the Deesis (the Most Pure and the Forerunner praying to Christ) surrounded by angels, i.e., "the noetic heaven." The doctrine of angels in itself, perhaps, does not need a new investigation: it is set forth fully and in general uniformly in dogmatic handbooks, with no particular differences between Orthodox and Catholic dogmatics. However, the theological interpretation of this doctrine, which properly constitutes the chief task of the proposed work, does not correspond at all in an equal measure to its dogmatic definiteness. Here theologizing must sometimes proceed gropingly, have recourse to hypotheses, and at times be limited by certain inquiries which already contain in themselves the seed of an answer. It is precisely in the theological incompleteness of angelology that the present work finds its justification. In constructing this work, as previously, the author has made use of data not only from biblical and patristic theology but also from liturgical and iconographic theology. It goes without saying that the doctrine of angels is not only of scientific-theological but also of religious-practical interest for every Christian. Would that what the author was given to experience in the course of this work was passed on to the reader — not only the joy of comprehension but also great spiritual consolation. May our prayer be directed to them, our heavenly protectors and comforters, on this the day of their festival:

> You, arch-commanders of the heavenly hosts, do we unworthy ones ever pray, that by your prayers you will protect us with the cover of the immaterial wings of your glory.

The Synaxis of the holy Arch-Commander Michael and all the heavenly powers
8/21 November 1928
Paris. Sergiev Podvor'e

INTRODUCTION

On a Heavenly Friend

God-Love created human beings for love. The human heart wants to love and thirsts to be loved. It suffers when it does not love and when it is deprived of love. It wants to expand, to make room in itself, in its own life, for other lives, for many lives, for all lives; going out of itself it seeks to melt, to lose itself in the other, to become *the other* for its own self, to drown in the ocean of universal love. To lose its own soul in order to save it — such is the law of love as it is shown by the Word who established this law. To discover abundant wealth in spiritual poverty, to live not for oneself but with all and for all, to become in all of one's life the other for one's own self, to become in oneself the not-self, in one's own, the not-own, in emptying oneself to become filled, in humbling oneself to be exalted, to live in love, to become love according to the image of the Holy Trihypostatic and Consubstantial Undivided Trinity — such is the frontier for human nature. Being-closed-in-on-oneself, limitedness, self-love, self-desire, and self-worship are unnatural for a human being. That is the lot of sinful, fallen, perverted human nature, and not that of nature's law in its power and glory. For both as the generic being — Adam and Eve — that received a blessing from the Creator to go out of itself for the increase of descendants, and as the sovereign lord of all creation, capable of loving it in its own nature and comprehending it in love, the human being was created by God — a microcosm in a macrocosm, a small world "propertied" with the ability of turning not to itself but to the other, to humanity and to the whole world, and above all and in all — to the Lord God. A human being lives only to the degree and by how much it loves, and it dies to the extent and by how much it does not love. The one who loves is rich, for one becomes rich in God-Love. Created after the image of God, who created everything by love and who embraced everything by love, the human being is called to make room in its own love for everyone and everything. It only *begins* the first lessons of love; before it lies the life of the future age, all of eternity, which can be filled only by love, for there is no life and there is no eternity in non-love.

The power of love is the ability to become other, to accommodate what is other, to be filled with universal life. However, this is only one image of love — *natural,* essential, ousia, a predicate, that which is predicated. If the power of love were exhausted by it alone, then the person would dissolve without a trace in *cosmic* love, and drowning in it, it would perish. The paths of expansion of "cosmic self-awareness" lead to just such depersonalization through the extinguishing of the personal principle: the ecstasy of Plotinus, the Buddhist nirvana, and the pantheistic merging with the world. But humans cannot and must not be depersonalized in their love; the loss of the soul is necessary in order to save it, and humans must love their neighbor *as their very self* — perhaps there is a certain form of legitimate self-love established by God. This is love *for oneself and not for one's own,* love for the hypostatic person. The hypostatic I in a human is the irreducible, absolute point of God-likeness: the hypostatic creaturely I looks at itself in the hypostatic, trihypostatic image of Divinity, finds itself and is firmly established in it. It will never die out and never dissolve; it loves, for it is *one who loves,* just as God is Love, not non-hypostatic but hypostatic, trihypostatic Love of the One Loving and of the Ones Loving. The power of love, its resilience, is concentrated in *a personal* center from which it proceeds and to which it returns. The blessedness of love is in this ceaseless dying and resurrecting of the personal I.

The person is a noetic sun, which gives off rays of love and its warmth. It needs not only to give itself away but also to find itself, to love and be loved, "to love one's neighbor as one's very self," to love *mutually.* Such a love is usually called *personal* love in distinction from *liking* as a general relation to everything. But this expression is to a certain extent a pleonasm, because all love is personal, and goes from person to person or persons. It does not destroy the person, by dissolving it, but makes it more sensitive, demanding, increasing the possibilities of love. In the love of the divine trihypostasis all is personal, through and through saturated with personal properties: the Father has His *everything* as the hypostatic Son and lives by Him in the hypostatic Spirit; the Son has His *everything* as the Father's Word being revived by the Holy Spirit; the Spirit has His life in the Father, speaking the hypostatic Word. The divine fullness, divine self-revelation, divine Sophia-Love contains in itself the revelation of the divine world, the Idea or Prototype of *everything*. But it does not exist in original extra-hypostaseity or impersonality. It is pre-eternally hypostatized in the Holy Trinity, in its hypostases. In creation it is hypostatized in created spirits as bearers of the image of God and above all having hypostatic being. Everything truly existing is personal, because love is personal and therefore reciprocal. God loves His Very Self in the holy Trinity *with a personal* love in a pre-eternal act of love-reciprocity. He loves His creation — the human being in whom He wants to have *a friend,* that is, the reciprocation of love. And through love for God every "feeling" of love in the human being becomes love, that is, personal love-reciprocity.

But can there be reciprocity of love between the supermundane God and creaturely nothingness? Is not human love for God a reverential worship of Divinity in Its "properties," in Its revelation, and not personal, reciprocal love? God created the world, however, in such a way that He did not spare his Only Begotten Son so that in Him He shows Himself conformable to us and accessible to our love. The Lord calls the apostles His friends and in their person summons every soul to co-friendship, to reciprocal personal love with Him. God descends from His supermundane state by becoming human and uniting Himself with the world. He becomes accessible to reciprocal love. It is given to each to love Christ with a personal love and in Him to find reciprocal love. Christ is the all-human, the second Adam: in Him is actually contained all humanity; consequently every being finds itself in fullness and its own universal significance. In His person it discovers its own proper I as a ray of the Divine I. Christ's humanity contains in itself every human being (excepting sin) and every human person with its personal characteristics. It is the universal, all-human, all-personal I. Therefore each loves Christ in one's own manner in conformity with one's own individual person, and yet in the manner of Christ, for each one is also in Christ who accommodates everyone and everything in Himself. Here is the mystery *of the one* Adam, the second Adam, the mono-hypostatic and pan-hypostatic divine-human multi-unity.

Through Christ and in Christ we receive the ability to love our neighbor: "I give you a *new* commandment, that you love one another." "Love your neighbor as your very self" — this is a still more ancient command, although confirmed by Him. But the *new* command about love is about love *in a new way,* in keeping with a co-humanity not in Adam (to which the Old Testament commandment referred) but in Christ, and Christ's questions at the Last Judgment will be evidence of this, where His pan-humanity will be revealed. For here each human being is identified with Christ who is for us the all-encompassing "neighbor." Christ in His human nature as the new Adam grounds the possibility of pan-human love.

But there still remains love for oneself. It is permitted by God, or, more truly, it is the foundation and outcome of love for one's neighbor: love your neighbor *as your very self.* This love of self is not animal egoism, representing the negation or absence of love, self-love, as limitedness. No, it is also *love* or at least it can become love. Every creation of God *is worthy* of love in God's plan for it, and one cannot love all people and all things, one cannot honor and esteem the whole of God's creation only to despise and hate one's own self. The loss of the soul for the sake of its salvation signifies something else entirely. Here sacrifice is understood only by its limited self-love, the surmounting of the negative boundaries of one's own personality, which has in itself the positive core of its own existence, God's idea and God's love. It shines for us in our neighbors, but exists in every separate human being as such.

The need for *personal* love — to love and be loved, is placed in the human being as its ontological property. The human cannot know itself, see itself, and consequently love itself in its positive nature *itself,* without being reflected in an other, and this quest for itself *of the other* is the quest for *the friend* (according to the evidence of the genius of the Slavo-Russian language).[1]

Love is the divine power of every life, overcoming personal limitedness and giving being to all and in all, but a personal principle is also found in it, in love for one's own self in one's proper person. Ontologically correct self-love is the discovery of oneself in the other, by the other, through the other, the finding of one's I in the other as one's own image and likeness, an abiding in a certain essential duality, a syzygy. In the first, divine sense, love is *a gracious* gift of God, by the power of which a human being surpasses its own self on its individual path, becomes personally super-personal in the image of the Holy Trinity, living by its own hypostasis *outside* itself, in others and with others, losing itself without noticing. In the second meaning love is a natural power of personal life, which, however, irrepressibly strives to be realized also outside itself, in an other — in a friend, to have the friend for itself and in itself as its other I, even though renouncing itself for the friend's sake, affirming and finding precisely its own self in that self-renunciation. This is *creaturely* love and in that sense natural love.

Omnis individuatio est negatio, individuality is not only essential rich-

---

1. In Greek, *philos* derives from *phileo,* I love, as in Latin *amicus* derives from *amo.*

ness of content but also limitedness, exclusiveness. Creaturely awareness, having arisen out of nothingness, cannot realize itself, comprise its content other than by means of limitedness, exclusiveness, repellent self-defense. In divinization, in graced love the creature as it were loses its creatureliness and with it its limitedness, dissolving in divine love. But in this love there is no place for metaphysical depersonalization, the death of the hypostasis. On the contrary, similar to the union of both natures, divine and human, undivided and unmingled, in the Lord Jesus Christ, so too in a human who is being divinized, the creaturely nature and in it the creaturely hypostasis or individuality are preserved and confirmed in the creature's own originality, even though they are being expanded in divinization to universal love. As a hypostatic I, it is the absolute center, albeit it of creaturely life. And along with superpersonal love, therefore, personal love remains and confirms itself by striving not only to repudiate itself but also to return to the self, through love for the other and through that other. The chain of worldly love is composed of rings of syzygic love — a dyad and various other dyadic combinations — a metaphysical *hen dia duoin.*

So-called personal love is precisely this metaphysical self-love, because love for one's own self, as blind animal egoism, is not love at all which exists only *between (metaxu)* or according to the expression of the blessed Augustine as *amor unitivus amborum.* Generally speaking, for the human being egoism is an unnatural condition bordering in its extreme manifestations on moral madness or in any case moral underdevelopment. In the case of full egoism the capacity for love would remain undisclosed and unrealized; it is therefore rather a certain abstraction for the human as a being generic by nature. Normal self-love — in the ontological and hence also empirical sense — is expressed in personal love, in the irrepressible yearning to love — a definite person or persons — and to be loved, to become the other for oneself and *to become oneself in others.*[2] "Jonathan loved David *as his own soul.*" This image of amicable Old Testament love combines with another Old Testament image: "on my bed at night I sought him whom my soul loved," . . . "I sleep but my heart keeps vigil"

2. The biblical image of this personal love-friendship is given in the relations of David and Jonathan, the son of Saul: "the soul of Jonathan was bound to his soul and Jonathan loved him as his own soul" (1 Samuel 18:1, 19:1; here and elsewhere Bulgakov's biblical references have been corrected). "And they kissed each other and both wept together, but David wept more" (1 Samuel 20:41). In his song on the death of Saul and Jonathan David says, "I grieve for you, my brother Jonathan; you were very dear to me; for me your love was better than the love of women" (2 Samuel 1:26).

(Song of Songs 3:1). The fiery power and mystery of love is expressed in the following words of the Song of Songs: "Place me as a seal on your heart, as a signet-ring on your hand, for strong as death is love, cruel as infernal jealousy; her arrows are fiery arrows; she is a very powerful (var., Divine) flame" (Song of Songs 8:6). Personal love, its quest, which has a fateful character, like a type of divine *fatum*, contains in itself the self-revelation of the person and it is necessary to examine it in its ontological essence. It is not a caprice or whim, it is not only a state or accident, but belongs to the very essence of the person. In its secrecy the person has a need to see, to know, and to love itself in the spiritual mirror of the other, to find its image through its likeness.

Our I, though our most inalienable property, does not belong to us individually, but is strangely divided in two and goes out beyond itself in order to identify itself only through coming back from that procession. The I seems to exist as two, as a pair, as a syzygy, having its own double, and this double is for it the general postulate of love, a kind of metaphysical "place of points." It can be filled by one human essence or many, in a different way at a different time. It is as it were an algebraic quantity, correlative with the personal I, in place of which various concrete arithmetic quantities can be substituted. It is an axiom of love that *I* is not single, not solitary, but paired, syzygic-correlative, that it knows and possesses itself only in connection with its double, in a duality, which can display itself in an indefinite plurality when it is realized; but it can also be entirely unrealized in life owing to a mysterious *fatum amoris*, as well as evil or good will, failure or self-renunciation. The I finds a place for itself in being where it is confirmed and where it is convinced once and for all, only in syzygy, by holding on to the hand of the other. Through this metaphysical hand-shake it comes out of the gloom of half-being; it discovers its own power and reality in the world. There are two forms and paths of love: one — through the loss of the self, self-renunciation in love for God — is the ascent out of the self to the heights; and there is another form — the self-affirmation of the self through procession from the self — which is love in the world. Both of these forms are inalienably inherent in creaturely nature, and on both paths it is saved from non-being and participates in reality. There is a difference between them, but not a contradiction, for the second commandment about love of "neighbor" *is similar to* the first about love of God. However, the very form of this union of both paths remains for us mysterious as does God's idea about our human godlike essence. The general and the particular have the same force, as do self-renunciation and self-affirmation, universality and individuality, person and essence, I and thou, and thou and we and they.[3] . . . Therefore human love is not only *impersonal* (or *pan-personal*), but also personal. Its realization does not go from the general to the particular, but the reverse — from the concrete to the universal. In other words, not only the human being, a human as such, or humanity itself, is loved in general, but the given, unrepeatable person, the hypostasis itself is loved; not only *something, but someone* is loved. And such *personal* love seeks without fail to become responsive, mutual, syzygic. Such love, if it exists alone and unrequited, represents the unnatural sacrifice of a love which is not incarnated and is thus the source of sufferings.

Humanity knows various forms of personal love: paternal, maternal, spousal, filial, daughterly, brotherly, sisterly, familial, and finally, friendship, although love in the proper sense refers to the love between man and woman, husband and wife, which is accompanied or can be accompanied by carnal union. In general although human love has a spiritual basis, it cannot be separated from a bodily form. It is always spiritual-sensual or spiritual-corporeal and such is all *human* love, not only that between different sexes. The human is a spiritual-corporeal entity; in this is the fullness, the ontological norm of its being. A purely spiritual understanding of human love is not sublimity but an abstraction or something contrary to nature. Only God do we love with a spiritual love; but by coming near to us, clothing Himself in flesh and becoming like us, God was made accessible to the fullness of our love: "what we have heard, what we have seen with our own eyes, what we examined, what we touched with our hands" (1 John 1:1). In a word, the Theologian bears witness to the sensual-corporeal perception of the Theos-Logos, as

---

3. It is deserving of attention that in the Lord Jesus Christ in whom uncorrupted human nature was fully revealed it is possible to see not only perfect love for the Father and God and for the whole fallen human race, but also for individual persons. The Lord in keeping with his humanity had personal love or friendship, personal relations: "Lazarus our friend," "Lazarus, Martha, and Mary whom Jesus loved," as well as the disciple John the Theologian, "whom Jesus loved." . . . But does he not also say that whoever wants to follow Him must hate his father and mother and children and brothers and sisters (Luke 14:26) and come after Him, that is, by opposing every form of personal love to love for Him? Yes, to the extent that both forms of love are in mutual conflict on their paths. And yet in other circumstances the Lord did not in any way deny the right of existence for every sort of human love, established by God when humans were created; likewise the apostles in their epistles were as distant as possible from this rejection. With the words about hatred one must compare the words "husbands, love your wives as Christ loves the church."

in the future age all nations "*will see* the Lord revealed in glory in the air," after which "we shall be with the Lord" (I Thessalonians 4:17). If we love the soul let us also love the corporeal form, the individual-corporeal image of the human in its real corporeality and in its unrepeatable originality together with its personal attributes: the voice, laughter, the whole thing.

Love is nourished and manifested not only by spiritual intercourse but also by corporeal perception, by tender, loving contemplation. In the beloved are loved not only the soul and its attributes but also the body and its features. Thus we kneel and embrace holy relics and equally we venerate tombs: spiritual respect and love for the departed is not enough; corporeal approach to them remains unavoidable. The dogma of icon veneration responds to this by making room for the fundamental possibility of the embodiment of love, so to speak: the church legitimates and blesses the loving contemplation of physical images of the saints, and by this rejects a false, abstract spiritualism. In this sense all human love is not only spiritual but also sensual, and it is entirely possible for this *sensuality* not to have the particular carnal quality which is inherent in the relation between the different sexes. In the latter case the stated *concrete* character of love is revealed only with the greatest acuteness and exclusiveness, and sometimes with a breach of spiritual equilibrium. Of course, by virtue of its complexity this two-in-one norm of love hides in itself the possibility of constant violation and limitation. Rather than revealing the spiritual, it can turn out that the corporeal conceals it. This violation of equilibrium, this deviation from the ontological norm happened once and for all for the whole human race through original sin, where the human became not spiritual-fleshly, but fleshly-spiritual, and the flesh received an undue primacy over the spirit. This undue primacy is manifested all the more acutely in the relations between the sexes. Physical sexual attraction attains to such tension and independence that it enslaves and leads the spirit after itself: spiritual-physical love (for even in fallen humanity it is not entirely physical) becomes as it were independent from the spiritual and subjugates it to itself. "Love" is the usual name given to that passionate spiritual-physical attraction which is captivity for the spirit. In it there can be no place at all for spiritual love. Such passionate states and flames (of passion) are notable for their subjugating power when they take possession of a human being, but their spiritual emptiness is displayed when they depart or are extinguished through gratification. In Christian marriage the original norm is re-established by grace but even

8

here it still usually remains far from the proper equilibrium, owing to the feebleness of nature caused by original sin.[4]

Other forms of love, even if they are free of desire, retain their concrete spiritual-sensual character. When we love, we love the whole human in its spiritual-physical form, indissoluble because primordial.

The concreteness of love, which binds it with space and time, simultaneously introduces into love all of the limitedness that is inherent in that bond. Everything spatial and temporal is transient in the form of its being. Although its ontological essence is preserved and perpetuated (on which is based the determination of eternal human fate as the consequence of temporal earthly life), nonetheless this essence is other and will be revealed to us beyond the threshold of existence other than it is revealed in this life. Here one needs to exclude beforehand the numerous, even innumerable cases of discrepancy in spiritual and physical relations: thus physical generation is not infrequently not accompanied by spiritual generation, but on the other hand spiritual generation ("spiritual birth") is possible without being connected with the flesh; likewise one must exclude the so numerous flare-ups of carnal passion which terminate in extinction and futility, without leaving any place for whatever sort of spiritual bonds. But even if one were to exclude this obvious discrepancy, the stamp of limitedness and relativity remains in any earthly human love, for although it has its foundation in eternity, it can nevertheless depart from its norms to such a degree that it becomes impossible to speak about its preservation in its own concreteness.

When asked by the Sadducees to which of the seven husbands the woman who had them would belong in the resurrection, the Lord replied, "In the resurrection they are neither married nor given in marriage but they live as angels of God in the heavens" (Matthew 22:30). This obvious negation of the perpetuity of the marital bond beyond the limits of this life, which is accompanied by the mysterious reference to the life of the angels of God, of course, must *a fortiori* be extended also to all other human relations of love and generation. Of course, this *does not* declare all of them to be eternally insignificant; rather, bound to the carnal life of the psychic body, they are not immediately extended to the future life in the spiritual body.[5] The seal *of relativity* is thus placed on all relations of hu-

---

4. Is this not indirectly attested to by the fact that the divinely elect births of the Virgin Mary and John the Forerunner were accomplished by very elderly parents with a naturally extinguished passion of the flesh?

5. "It is sown a psychic body, it rises a spiritual body. . . . But the spiritual is not

man love. It contains in itself the admixture of the temporal to the eternal, the corruptible to the incorruptible which for us remains irreducible and even vaguely discernible, and which, however, will be removed by God's power beyond the limit of temporal being. It contains in itself the seal of fateful incompleteness, covered by the exaggeration of the partial at the expense of the integral. *The other I* splinters into *other I's,* in the many relations of love (similarly in marriage, about which the Sadducees tested the Lord, the church herself permits a second and a third marriage). This love is not only relative, but also *co-relative* in its diversity. But the latter not only realizes love's fullness, it also breaks it into pieces, makes it incomplete and relative in each of its partial manifestations.

All is *love:* parental love for children, children's love for parents, spousal love, friendship's love, and familial love. This whole gamut of love or the many-colored spectrum of the white beam of a single love, in being reflected reciprocally when it is fractured, is realized like a series of possibilities of love, a series *of other I's* for one universal *I.* By this means not only is the fullness of diversity introduced but also the limitedness of each separate form of love which always strives to be absolute. This relativity in realization in a sense relativizes the value itself of every sort of human love to such a degree that a principled refusal of it appears possible without causing damage to the fullness of personal being, and consequently, to the fullness of divine love — *in monasticism.* Examined from this perspective, the idea of monasticism consists in renouncing, by means of an ascetical opposition to the innate nature that demands personal, human love, this relative love in the name of a personal absolute love for God in which there is no relativity. Monasticism is in this sense a kind of absolutism in love, which cannot be reconciled with any relativity and hence renounces all earthly *personal* love. It is a kind of negative absolutism of the means in the name of an absolute goal, whereby this absolutism is expressed in ascetical struggle against all relativity of love. In this sense monasticism is the acceptance "of the angelic image." But this *relativity* is perceptible to each human in the measure of their awareness, and in this perceptibility their own particular voice rings, and their own revelation is contained. Everything relative comes to be known by us as such only in the light of the absolute, just as all colors and tones exist only in the presence of light and sound. And the call and yearning, the quest for absolute, eternal, and full love bears witness not about its unfeasibility in this world

---

first, rather the psychic is first, then the spiritual. . . . But I tell you, brothers, that flesh and blood cannot inherit the kingdom of God" (1 Corinthians 15:44-50).

but precisely about its existence, for the given is always presupposed by the proposed. By means of this quest evidence is given about *the knowledge* of love as a kind of absolute fact. God's love for us and our love for God is just such an absolute fact of love, being united with knowledge of the self in God. This absolute love is realized in creation, not, however, in human love, but in spiritual love. For at its very creation the human being receives not only the divine gift of love, but also *the possibility* of love; not only for its own self, but also for its friend, and not only for human friends but also for a spiritual friend. This *other* of each human, this friend, unique and personal, proper to each human being, is *the guardian angel,* a being not from here, not of the human world.

> When the noise of life subsides and its dissonant voices fall silent,
> When the soul is washed in quiet and filled with silence,
> When its childhood element is laid bare and removed are the
>   shrouds weighing it down,
> When the soul is freed from the captivity of this world and stays
>   one on one with God,
> When the fetters of earthly nature are dissolved, and the soul finds
>   its own self,
> When it is separated from the earthly shell and finds itself in a new
>   world,
> When it is filled with light and washed with the rays of immortality,
> Then does it feel bending over it with inexpressible love a being,

so near, so similar, so tender, so calm, so loving, so faithful, so mild, so affectionate, so bright — that joy, peace, blessedness, things unknown on earth, bubble up in the soul. It feels then its non-solitude, and rushes to meet the unknown and near friend. For the soul will come to know that friend about whom its whole life it dreamt and for whom it pined, seeking to flow together with the other to the end, to surrender to him wholeheartedly, to find its other I in him. This *other* for each human being, this friend, is given by God and fashioned for each, is each one's guardian angel, who is ever keeping watch over each one, living with each *one life.* He is most near, although also far, for he is unseen, unheard, inaccessible to every bodily and even psychic perception. So silent and gentle is his spiritual touch that his very presence for a human is unnoticed. But language bears witness to us that we notice him unconsciously. For unwittingly we call our neighbors who are full of love, affection, gentleness, and concern our "guardian angels" without understanding the meaning of our words. They comprise for us light and air but like those indiscernible things, they are known by us in their whole significance only when we lose them. Similarly, while always being overshadowed by the guardian angel's wing, we do not distinguish this overshadowing in our consciousness; it is as if we do not notice it, even though it is always with us. The guardian angel, dweller of the celestial fleshless world, does not have *direct* access to our material world, to our fleshly nature. Of course he could shake it or even destroy this fleeting nature of ours by his dread appearance (whence springs the Old Testament horror before the appearance of an angel: it is impossible to look at him face to face and not die). But for this appearance the express will of God is necessary, and without it there is no foundation for this in the quiet gentleness of the angel. As "the guardian of our souls and bodies" he is terrible and insuperable in interceding for us against the impure and wicked spirits which overwhelm us. In a spiritual battle our nature would be destroyed and poisoned, corrupted and annihilated without this defender. This commander, this spiritual warrior always protects us from that. In this he is actively energetic, unceasingly taut; he acts with all his power. But he does not coerce the earthly friend, the human protected by him, and he does not want to nor can he coerce. He nurses and cherishes the human's soul, his whisper in audible silence blows blessed thoughts to it, which are born in it, but in such quiet and gentleness that the soul does not notice the insufflation. Silence is prescribed for him, for "silence is the secret of the future age" according to the saying of Isaac the Syrian, and the guardian angel speaks to us only with silence. He *looks* into our soul and sees us, and this is sufficient for this mysterious mute conversation of the soul with its higher I.[6] When we surrender to the influence of the tender and dear being, he never directly teaches us but by his very own existence and presence around us he arouses in us our better powers which are unknown to us without him, as if they were poured into us by him. This "inpouring" is beyond all calculation, not because of weakness but because of its depth and tender intimacy. It is like the inspiration through which one's own depth is revealed to a human being.

6. "When the feelings are locked by silence, they are not permitted to be directed outwards and with the aid of silence remembrances fade away; then you will see what the *natural thoughts of the soul* are, what the very nature of the soul is, and what kind of treasure it has hidden within. *This treasure constitutes knowledge of the bodiless powers,* it arises in the soul by itself without a preliminary notion of it and without effort. A man does not even know that such thoughts arise in human nature. For who was his teacher, or how did he reach that which cannot be explained for others, even though it is intelligible? *Or who was his tutor in that which he did not learn from another at all?*" (Isaac the Syrian, *Ascetical Sayings* [Moscow, 1854] Saying 3).

There is a higher task for education and pedagogical tact — to awaken and guard a good initiative, to act so that every boon in a human being should not be inspired from outside but arise in the human itself, giving birth to and displaying one's own self for oneself. Otherwise the very goal of education will not be attained, which is for the one being educated to become an agent and not an obedient tool in the hands of the educator. The task of the latter is to become entirely imperceptible, to disappear, by merging with the will of the one being educated. To this task corresponds the manner of the influences of the guardian angel who awakens in us our higher I. This heavenly pedagogy is complex and multiform, inexhaustible and bottomless. As a very tender mother follows the awakening of dark and light movements in the soul of her child, in his life shaken by hostile elements, so a guardian angel keeps watch over us always, but he does nothing *without* us or *apart* from us: "waiting for our voluntary correction and not compelling" (from the prayerful canon to the guardian angel); "having gained you, a guardian, companion, associate, protecting, accompanying, and offering saving things to me always" (from the same). This is an unceasing creative act, the guardian angel's unceasing labor over ungrateful and disobedient material in the midst of a world infected by sin. But this labor carries on unceasingly. Each one of us lives not alone but as a pair, together, inseparably. Friendly help is always with us, and over us are always outstretched angel wings. In conceiving of the nature of the relations between angels and humans one needs to be freed completely from an external, simplified mechanical interpretation. According to the latter, a guardian angel protects a given person because like an obedient instrument he has been sent to this post and installed in it by God; this is his service which he fulfills like any other. To this external fulfillment correspond straightforwardness, simplicity, and unerringness in the application of corresponding means. Such a conception of spiritual functionaries or guards stationed in their places in good time and executing every order indifferently is completely irresponsible. Any spiritual service is imposed not from without but from within; it flows out of the very essence of the servitor, of his life, calling, nature. God's commands are imperative, for they are ontological. Hence the service of a guardian angel is for him not his external assignment to this or that human being; rather it is his *cause* in creation, and in so far it expresses his proper essence.

The guardian angel is a friend; he *loves* the one who is entrusted to him, and this love is even for him *personal* love, possessing the qualities known to us although exceeding any earthly love in degree and purity and, what is important, in its absoluteness. He looks into our soul with a loving, gentle, tender, bright, and joyful gaze in which the whole power of love shines. He never lowers this gaze from us; he does not grow weak in his love. In this love is concealed not only our salvation but as in any love, his own life too. It has a power; it is vital not only for us but for him as well. There is in the spiritual world a being which lives with us *one* life, shares our fate, seeks our reciprocity. The guardian angel is that friend, who loves us and hence lives with us. His relation to us is determined not by external service but by the inner bond of love, which already bears witness to the ontological unity. Of course, this service is mediatory in the fulfillment of God's will. *Angels* are called to it in their creation, that is, they are messengers, heralds, executors, in the proper sense. Likewise the hierarchical heights of the angelic rank and the vision of the face of God give him the heights of knowledge, wisdom, and sanctity inaccessible for us. But for all this, the guardian angel is turned towards us. With his *creaturely* nature he is joined to us in his proper life and work. The guardian angel's care for us is *labor*, filled with vigilant concern, effort, anxious and caring love; it is suffused with its own joys and sorrows. About all of this the holy Church directly bears witness in its prayerful addresses to the guardian angel. This is an indisputable dogmatic fact which one must only accept and interpret in all its force.

The guardian angel is called "*the indefatigable guardian* of my soul," and "the preceptor and superintendent of life," "the faithful preceptor, guardian of our souls and bodies." An angel is not God with respect to his knowledge, wisdom, and power. He is only a creature, *limited in all things*, no matter how lofty he is, and likewise he is not a blind instrument of God's will. A creative task is given to an angel. Although corresponding to the eminence of the angelic nature it exceeds every human possibility and achievement, nonetheless it remains within the bounds of creaturely, limited creative work. And this creative work flows in time, in which successes unite with failures, sorrows dissolve with joys. Thus the labor of love and the creative work of angelic love for humans naturally contains for angels themselves the source of particular joys with humans and for humans which they share with the human world. "The holy angels by their proximity to holy men," says venerable Isaac the Syrian, "are in communion with their sufferings and sorrows."[7] But they rejoice not only over holy men, but also over sinners and their salvation, and they grieve over their fall.[8] "*At night and in the day I sorely aggrieve you with my evil deeds*

---

7. Isaac the Syrian, *Saying* 58.

8. Cf. the tale about the weeping guardian angel in the vision of blessed Andrew, the fool for Christ's sake.

and I offend and irritate you" (Canon, Ode 3, troparion 2). "I have not ceased *to aggrieve* my defender with my lawless words and deeds: *but do not become embittered,* but rather wait a little" (Ode 4, troparion 2). "Foreseeing the torments and tortures which await me . . . you groan in showing pardon and lament and grieve, filled with dejection" (Ode 5, prayer 3) "and not for one hour, not for a moment or a brief portion thereof have I let you re-joice and be glad over me and leap for joy, who am forever being corrupted by sin" (Ode 5, Glory). In the hour of death "brightly stand before me *with smiling face and joyful regard*" (Ode 7, prayer 3) "so that *I may see you* stand-ing *at the right hand of* my *accursed* soul, *bright and calm,* my defender and su-perintendent" (Ode 9, troparion 1). At the Last Judgment "stand before me then *calm and joyful,* removing my fear with the hope of salvation" (Ode 8, Glory).

These sorrows and joys, successes and failures, the smile ("with smil-ing face") and the tears of the guardian angels for our sake, about which the holy Church tells us, themselves bear witness that the direction of our life and its preservation are both a labor and a creative task for the holy angels. It is unceasingly resolved by their love and creative work, and al-though not entirely identical, it is similar to what happens in human cre-ative work, including its ups and downs. The Apostle Paul utters these very mysterious and significant words in 1 Corinthians 6:3: *"Do you not know that we are to judge the angels?"* Does not this human judgment upon angels bear witness that in the labor of the angels themselves on humans there can be a *more or less?* Even for them creaturely limitedness excludes absolute correctness and infallibility. In this way, guardian angels do not behold our life from unattainable heights and inaccessibility; rather, they live with us, they make our life, and they themselves live by it. For them it is their proper life. As ones who have participated in eternity in the bless-edness of their divine knowledge, they are subject to mutability in their relation to the life that elapses in time. In us and through us they are bound to human life and perhaps also to our whole world; our life is also their life. Only God, supermundane and exalted above all creatures, cre-ates, preserves, saves, and loves His creation without changing anything in His eternal self-identity and all-blessedness, receiving nothing from the life of the creature, remaining exalted above every temporal becoming, be it change or increment. An angel is not like that, even though he is higher than creation because of his proximity to God. From the beginning he is subject to changeableness with respect to nature, as the fall of a portion of the angels reveals. According to the teaching of the Church, the angels who stood firm in the good, did battle with Satan and cast him down out of heaven, were once and for all confirmed in the rightness of their path, and consequently in the blessedness of their divine knowledge. Inasmuch as they are unwavering, their life is already illumined with eternity. But as much as they are linked with the human world, the life of the world is also their life, and its destinies are their destinies. Of course this dependence does not extend so far that it alters the angels' own definitive self-determination, but it is capable of determining the form of their being in relation to our world. And the power that establishes the link between both worlds is *love.*

Angels serve the world for they are sent into it by God, but angels also love the world which they serve, just as a guardian angel loves his human double. And if there is no love without sacrifice, in which is the power of love, then the love of the guardian angel for us is sacrificial love. It includes not only the involuntary kenosis of angelic nature by the command of God but also voluntary kenosis by the power of angelic consent and obedience. This love represents a certain abandonment of the blessedness of the angelic world through a union with the life and destinies of bodily, plump, fleshly nature. There is here for an incorporeal spirit a metaphysical self-impoverishment, an ontological kenosis, thanks to which his life is united through love with the life of a fleshly human. This kenosis has for itself a likeness (and at the same time an ultimate foundation) in the kenosis of the God-Word, who for our sake became poor and took on the likeness of human nature — being incarnated and become human. Along with Him and following on Him is angelic nature which does not become human but becomes co-human and is united by the bonds of love with humans. The guardian angel is deprived of the fullness and imperturbability of its vision of God for the sake of the human being so that he can lead the human to a higher calling, but so that he too may walk together with him as if discovering anew what is already given to him (which, of course, does not remove his simultaneous heavenly blessedness). This kenosis of the angelic nature for the sake of human nature is a voluntary self-limitation which, like any sacrifice of love, raises new higher possibilities and interrelations. Together with this natural kenosis is united personal service, ascesis, selflessness, and, above all, patience. For to endure our sinfulness and dullness, our persistence in evil and opposition to good, our animality and satanification, and our interminable laziness and spiritual sleepiness, requires an intensity of compassionate love such that we are incapable of conceiving for ourselves. All the forms of the patience of love which we know — the mother who forgives everything and gives up everything for her worthless prodigal son, the wife who bears everything from her unworthy husband, the friend or brother or sister who save a spiritually self-destructive person — are the forms of *that* patience, that love, which the guardian angel shows us. Similarly the suffering from the wounds of love that are inflicted by one person on another is a form *of that* wound by which we unceasingly wound the incorporeal Friend, whereby these injuries sometimes consist in that ultimate wound which is inflicted on him by the unworthy end of human life in sin or suicide. Suicide is an intentional sin against the guardian angel, a profanation of his love. A suicide, pushing his guardian angel away from himself, throws himself into the demon's embrace. And in this effort of patience, angelic love, like all true love, *does not seek its own*. What can we give to an angel? For him it is "more blessed to give than to receive," according to the Lord's saying. The gifts of this love are similar to how a mother lavishes her love and tenderness on her child without requiring anything for it but only rejoicing in her love for the child. And the sole thing with which we can respond to angels and by which we can reward their love is to give them the possibility of rejoicing on our account as a mother rejoices at every success and smile of her child. But just as maternal love *precedes* every possibility of reciprocal love or joy, so too angelic love waits for and protects us earlier than we are able to respond to it.

And so, an angel participates as far as it is able in the creative work of human life and its salvation by protecting, by admonishing, and by praying.[9] Nothing in our life is completed without his vigilance and participation, excepting only if we ourselves impede or make impossible our communion with him through our evil and criminal will by wallowing in sin, and send our guardian angel away. But even when we have sent him away, while grieving and weeping over us he prayerfully keeps vigil over us, not taking his eyes off us and waits for the first evident opportunity to assist us, to toil for us. His love never abandons us and immeasurable is the all-suffering tenderness of this love. This labor of angels over us and with us is not immediately known to us, because as fleshly beings we cannot grasp experientially the life of a fleshless spirit. But we know that even for us fleshly ones labor is not always only physical exertion and expenditure of power but also a certain spiritual effort. And this spiritual labor is com-

---

9. "For I have you as my defender in my whole life, my preceptor and guardian, given to me by God for ever" (Canon of the Guardian Angel, ode 7, tr. 1). "Guardian of my soul and body chosen for me by God, divine angel," "I have won you, O holy angel, as my guardian, companion, and ally, who watches, travels with, accompanies and offers saving words to me always" (ode 5, tr. 1).

pleted by the guardian angel as evidence of the operation of his love. How is one to identify this love, this gentleness, this concern, this endurance, this humility, this selflessness of the guardian angel's love for us? With eyes filled with love he looks into our soul and it dimly senses this gaze and this love. But at the limits of this life the soul will learn that this friend integrally and always belongs to it, that all his love and concern was only on its account. And then the most burning inescapable thirst of the human being will be satisfied, the longing for mutual love. This is one's own friend who belongs inseparably to a human, who never will be taken away from one, for he is that one's *other higher I.* There was never a time in the life of a man when the friend would not be with him: "you have appointed him a guardian for me from my youth, because you love humankind" (Canon of the Guardian Angel, ode 9, tr. 5), "given to me for ever." At the initial boundary of life, at birth, the guardian angel meets us and at life's final boundary, in death, he meets our soul and accompanies it. They say that on one's death bed a person is left alone, and this is true with respect to people, to our confreres according to humanity, but one is not alone in this separation, for one's angel is present. By looking at him, the soul grasps and sees itself and its own life, no longer with earthly eyes but in eternity, to which the friend belongs. He is the mediator, the guide, and teacher for eternity.

> . . . for long hours and days I found myself in a fiery furnace. For the first time I understood why and in what sense the Church so loved this image of a furnace burning. For I myself was burning with my sins; they burned me and at the same time were consumed in the fire. By the great mercy of God I myself was burning, but I was not consumed although it was natural that I be consumed and perish, and it seemed, it was even impossible that I not perish. In that fiery furnace a certain coolness was sent to me — *the guardian angel* who appeared to the three youths in the furnace also came down to me, refreshed me, and saved me. It is impossible to explain this with words but from then on I knew that it is possible to be consumed in a fiery furnace without being consumed. . . .
>
> And suddenly — after this burning — coolness and consolation penetrated the fiery furnace of my heart. . . . Suddenly my sin stopped burning me, it stopped existing, it was no more and with my whole heart I sensed *forgiveness,* its measureless lightness and joy. The *guardian angel,* who was with me without interruption, placed this in my heart. I felt that all was forgiven, that God's wrath was no longer upon

me, that nothing separated me from the Lord, for I was redeemed by my Lord.

But this mystery of forgiveness was revealed to me only in connection with the mystery of death, for simultaneously with this I felt that my life had ended, that I was dying. Where was it, the fear of death? There was none, there was only the joy of death, joy in the Lord. Heavenly joy inexpressible in human language filled my entire being. . . . I was conscious of myself beyond the limit of the world. I was aware that everything was equally alive and near, both the living and the dead. I spiritually sensed *everyone* with me, and at the same time I realized that all the same my physical sufferings did not permit me to communicate with those attending my bed. I was calling loved ones to myself, as if I was touching them spiritually, those long dead as well as the living, one after the other. I was being moved where I wanted to go. And over everything the presence of God reigned. . . . Then by some sort of interior command, I moved forward, from this world to there — to God. I floated quickly and freely, stripped of all heaviness. I knew by means of some sort of trustworthy interior feeling that I had already passed beyond our time, that I had passed through the next generation, and that beyond it, in the midst of the following one the end had already started to dawn. The ineffable lights of God's approach began to blaze, the horizon grew brighter, the joy even more indescribable: "it is not for a human to say." At that time the voice of a *companion* sounded within — I was not alone but together with my own other I; it was my guardian angel. He told me that we had gone too far ahead and it was necessary to return . . . to life. I understood and heard with my inner hearing that the Lord was bringing me back to life, and I was recovering. One and the same call which released me from this world and from life, simultaneously and with the same word returned me to it. Interiorly I already knew that I would recover although I was still not any better. I returned to life from death. And I knew all this time that I was not alone, that with me was a friend, the most near, tender and quiet. I did not see him with my eyes, he hid himself from them, but I sensed and was aware of his presence. . . . (From a note)[10]

---

10. Bulgakov recounts an experience from 1926, the full account of which is contained in his treatise, "Sofiologija smerti," in *Tikhie dumy* (Moscow: Izd. "Respublika," 1996), pp. 291-93. Translator's note.

But if in the days of our life from birth until death our friend remains inseparably with us, who is "appointed," "chosen," "given," and "received" from God then what was his life like *before* our birth and what will it be like *after* our death? Did he belong to us and we to him in the eternal angelic love when we as yet did not exist, and on the other hand is this bond dissolved and severed when we are no longer on earth? Does our guardian angel then receive another designation, another soul, another friend? Will his love and friendship for us be severed, having been replaced by another service? Does a new and final loss await us beyond the limit of this world and will we turn out to be abandoned by the friend in some metaphysical solitude? Of course it is enough merely to pose such a question in order to see straight away that it can only be answered in the negative. Humans enter the world through birth and their life *begins* in time, for each human being in their own time. But their guardian angel is not born along with them; he exists before their birth, or more precisely, he *pre-exists* them. What is his relationship to this very birth, to the entry into the world of a new human being? Is it active or passive, positive or indifferent? But if it is impossible to understand the sending of a guardian angel to a human being as an external designation or command, given so to speak to the angel next in line for service without an interior correlation of the one being sent with the one to whom he is sent, then one must consider this correlation to be predetermined. In what is this predetermination?

Furthermore, the guardian angel does not die along with the human being, for angels do not know death. But a dead man or woman is only "departed," i.e., fallen asleep. Although they experience a temporary separation of body and soul, they still live; true, they live not a full life, but like souls deprived of their bodies, in the expectation of the general resurrection and a new union with them. And so, is death separation from the guardian angel as well, who is thus released from his service such that the temporal bond with the earthly life of a human being departs into the past and in the same manner is handed over to oblivion? Or, on the contrary, does the bond remain indissoluble and is it preserved even beyond the limits of this life, in the world beyond the grave, beyond the limits even of this age, in the life of the future age, in the resurrection?

In other words, does the bond of the guardian angel with the human being entrusted to him, which is *angelic love* in all its force and glory, possess only an instrumental, auxiliary, and hence temporary conditional meaning? Or as love is it a personal bond, for love is personal, is it an individual election and thus absolute-individual, for it is not subject to any limitation of time and location, as are other human relations, even the most personal ones? Perhaps even such a puzzling question will arise: does not the guardian angel after the death of the human being receive so to say a new designation, a new service to another human being and then to yet another one and so forth? There is no direct answer to this question in Scripture or in church teaching. But one must have in view that in Scripture there is not even the slightest indication of this possibility: everywhere that it speaks about angels in relation to a human being only personal relationship is intended — especially Matthew 18:10. Neither is there any indirect foundation for this in the correlation of the numbers of the human and angelic worlds. According to the generally received teaching of the Church, the number of angels *exceeds* the number of people many times over (the parable about the ninety-nine sheep abandoned for the sake of finding one — Matthew 18:12-13 — is sometimes applied — although not without a stretch — to determining the correlation of the number of angels and humans). Incidentally, the decisive objections against such an assumption flow most of all from the general correlation of humans and angels, as will be explained below. But even if one were to agree conditionally to such an assumption that guardian angels receive a new service, this does not annul or even weaken the *personal* character of the relationship between humans and guardian angels, which is the most important consideration here. Angelic love is personal but not exclusive; it includes or rather co-includes in itself whole circles of being, by extending into all the world, into all humanity and into all creation. Therefore if it were even possible to contemplate that one guardian angel is sent to protect many humans, this would merely indicate that their souls and fates are run through by a common thread which gathers them together, that they find themselves in a deliberate mystical bond with each other. But even apart from such intentionality the bond of angelic love penetrates and unites all humanity among themselves. Thus, so as not to complicate our discussion with this vain and improbable assumption, which additionally does not alter the question essentially, but only complicates it, we shall proceed from the proposition that to each human being is given one's own proper guardian angel. But one ought to interpret this particular correlation only by proceeding from the general interrelation of the angelic and human worlds.

CHAPTER 1

Heaven and Earth

"In the beginning God created heaven *and* earth" (Genesis 1:1). The generally accepted understanding of this sacred text, in which the most general outline of the whole creaturely world appears, is that the text speaks here about the creation of a noetic *heaven,* or the angelic world of bodiless spirits, and of *the earth* as the prime substance and simultaneously the universal substance of our world, which has as its head and focus the human being. A certain parallelism is established between the creation of heaven and the creation of earth — a positive correlation expressed by the word *and.* This word of the Word of God contains in itself a doctrine concerning the correlation of the angelic and human world, heaven and earth,[1] and we ought first of all to stop here to disclose it. The Word of God gives a clear indication that angels are created *before* the final creation of the human world, before the termination of the six days, and in any case before the creation of the human being; on this the faith of the Church is based. "The divine mind, having conceived *the angelic ranks first of all,* established mirrors which receive in themselves, as much as may be comprehended, the radiance of the thearchic light and three-sunned candle." The question of when exactly the angels were created finds no direct answer in the Word of God (here we recognize, according to Job 38:7, only a *terminus ad quem,* namely, before the creation of the stars, i.e., the fourth day) and

---

1. This idea about the creation of heaven and earth is expressed more extensively in the prayer of Esdras (Nehemiah 9:6): "And Esdras said: You yourself are the Lord alone, You created heaven and the heaven of heavens and all their hosts, the earth and all that is on it, the seas and what is in them, and You animate everything, and the heavenly hosts bow down before You."

further it has no uniform answer in ecclesiastical literature. According to blessed Augustine the creation of the angels refers to the first day: *let there be light*, understood to be the shining not only of physical but also of noetic light, i.e., "of second lights," of angels. For other fathers (Saints Basil the Great, Gregory the Theologian, John Chrysostom, Ambrose of Milan, John Damascene, blessed Jerome, and others) it refers to a time preceding even the first day of creation, and this opinion seems to correspond best to Genesis 1:1. It also seems to be the most natural on the basis of the general correlation between the spiritual and human world, expressed in the significant word *and*.

The angelic world is turned in a *two-fold* manner: as *second lights, as theophoric coal, kindled by the dawn of Your essence*[2] they are saturated with divine light, "divinized by Divinity." Their life in God is "a participation in ineffable glory" and praise of God. They are immersed in the ocean of divine life and rise from light to light, instructed and illuminated through the nine-level hierarchy, from highest to lowest. But at the same time the bodiless powers are *angels* and only under this name do we humans know them, and this name already contains in itself the disclosure of that mysterious *and*, by which heaven and earth are united. *Heaven*, i.e., the world of noetic powers and bodiless spirits, is created not separately and independently but *together with the earth and in relation to the earth*. The bodiless spirits are defined in their being not for themselves but as angel envoys, heralds, i.e., in *relation* to the earth. The angelic world is created with the idea of angelic service, of this envoy-like participation in the destinies of the world, in other words, with the idea of the human world. By their service the angels are united with the human world in one indivisible whole, so that the world does not exist without angels or angels without the world, and both together constitute one creation: *heaven and earth*.

This proximity and bond of the angelic and human worlds is outlined in the Word of God in various respects. Angels are the keepers of the forces of nature: fire, heavenly bodies (according to ancient belief), and in general the inanimate world. Analogously one can conclude that they are the keepers of the plant and animal worlds. They are the executors of God's commands upon human beings, as guardian angels of individual people and whole nations, of kingdoms, separate churches, and generally speaking of the whole human race in the beginning, in the middle and at the end of this age, at the harvest of time. In the Word of God only some aspects of angelic service are indicated, not all; however, there is no basis

2. Service of the Bodiless Powers, tone 2, canon ode 1, tr. 1.

for understanding this incomplete enumeration in a limited sense (for example, from the fact that it speaks about an angel of waters, fire, and winds but not about an angel of earth or the plant or animal worlds one may not conclude that these domains are foreign to the protection of angels). Rather, this enumeration is exemplary and not exhaustive. In a similar vein, on the basis of indications about the existence of particular angels for the Persian and Jewish kingdoms or of angels for the seven churches of Asia Minor no one comes to the conclusion that angelic protection is proper to them alone; on the contrary, their protection is extended to all churches, kingdoms, peoples, and even monasteries, cities, locales, etc. In a word it will be no exaggeration to say that our whole world in its entirety and in its parts comprises the domain of angelic service, and the angel hosts include in their number the guardian angels not only of individual human beings but also of the whole earthly creation.

Everything in the world is preserved by angels, and everything has *its* angel and its *correlation* in the angelic world. This proposition, although not explicitly expressed in church teaching about angels, is satisfactorily supported by it and this is made sufficiently clear by the impossibility of asserting the opposite. In fact what can one show in creation that would not be under angelic care, or that would bear the stamp of being ontologically outcast? But then it would simply not exist. One can infer a certain limitation, which is rather a precision, only in the case when deformed entities or conditions that have no direct ontological justification arise in a world distorted by sin, in an improper state of creation; this is the fruit of the negative working of the devil in a world taken prisoner by him. Concerning these ontological deformities one can say that they are extra-Sophianic or anti-Sophianic; or to express it in the language of Platonic idealism, they are entities outside or contrary to ideas. However, it is impossible for them to be completely extra-Sophianic or anti-ideal, for then they would not exist at all. Thus if one is to admit such a limitation, it can be accepted only in a restricted sense. The devil cannot create anything; he can only distort what already exits and is created by God. Thus the positive ontic force even of these distortions has its support only in the foundations of being given by God and preserved by angels (similar to the way that parasites or malignant formations can exist only in a living organism and therefore by its force, not by their own). On the other hand, even the offspring of the kingdom of Abaddon, like a locust possessing the authority of scorpions (Rev. 9:3-11), is found under the control of angels, inasmuch as it is an instrument of God's wrath. On the whole this comes to light in the Apocalypse in the appearance of the seven trumpets (8:10) and the seven cups of divine wrath (8:16), which are poured out likewise by angels (the result of which are repulsive festering wounds on the body and the transformation of water into blood, excessive burning heat, mortal anguish). In other cases angels are destructive instruments of God's wrath, like the angel who destroyed the sons of Israel with pestilence for David's sin (2 Samuel 24) or the army of Sennacherib (2 Kings 19:35). On the basis of these cases[3] one ought to conclude that even in its infirm sinful states the world is not left deprived of angelic watchfulness in the fulfillment of God's plan for it. But the operation of God's providence is accomplished through angels.[4] Hence it is possible to establish as a general proposition that nothing in the life of this world except sin remains foreign to the world of angels, and that nothing in this world is accomplished without the participation of angels. Of course in our present state we know little about this on the basis of experience, which undoubtedly explains why the dogma on angels is generally lacking elucidation and is meager in its knowledge of them. As always, in her life, in her practical veneration of God and her liturgy the Church knows much more than what enters into her dogmatic consciousness and theologizing. She triumphantly bears witness to the angels' constant communion with us: with respect to iconography, the presence of icons of angels in church buildings is evidence of their actual presence, and with respect to hymnography, the attestations of the prayerful accompaniment of angels in the temple are constantly repeated. From this depth of the Church's knowledge doctrinal truths are raised to the surface of dogmatic erudition, new and at the same time old, for nothing new that is not contained in this depth can be brought to light in the ecclesial consciousness; but at the same time this consciousness never contains this depth in its fullness.

Knowledge of the angelic world, vague and obscure, was not unfa-

---

3. In Psalm 77/78:49 it even says: "He sent against us the flame of His wrath, indignation and fury and calamity and the *embassy of wicked angels*." It is possible to understand this expression both as referring to angel-heralds of wrath and God's punishments, and as referring in fact to evil spirits who are permitted to demonstrate their action (e.g., in the tempting by Satan of Job) and are instruments of God's providential power all the same.

4. This general idea is expressed in the "Canon of Bodiless Powers" through a comparison of angels with horses whose bridles the Lord holds in his hands while mounted in a chariot for the salvation of the world. "You have mounted angels like a horse, O lover of humankind, and taken in Your hand their reins, and salvation is Your circuit, truly to You do we sing: glory to Your power, Lord" (Tone 8, ode 4, tr. 1). This comparison is applied also to the apostles, as is known.

miliar even to pagan devotion. The very appearance of a doctrine about angels in the Bible is now attributed by scientific criticism to Persian and Assyro-Babylonian influence. This opinion recognizes as correct only that some knowledge of the angelic world is accessible to the natural religious consciousness outside the bounds of Revelation just as is observed with respect to many other religious truths. The ancients in their immediacy *heard* angels, knew their presence, and expressed this knowledge in the general conviction that *panta plere theon* — everything is filled with gods, i.e., with personal manifestations of divine power, the angels of God. Each human being has their own "demon" (*daimonion*), which was known with such marvellous clarity by Socrates, and every place has its *genius loci*. Divine power flows and is manifested everywhere: trees have their Dryads and rivers and seas their gods, towns their protectors and even sacred objects have their spirits (fetishism). Polytheism knew spiritual hierarchies but never knew how *to distinguish and contrast* the Creator and the creation. Knowledge of the angelic world appears with greater force and clarity in it than knowledge about divinity itself. Though separated from true divine knowledge, pagans were not abandoned by angels.

Out of the general correlation between the angelic and human world springs a series of further questions. How is participation in this service distributed among the various ranks of angels? Do all of them participate in it? On the other hand, in which regions of the life of the world and in what form does this participation appear? But before all these particular questions a general question arises concerning the ontological foundations of this selfsame correlation, concerning the very meaning of the doctrine of heaven *and* earth.

The world of bodiless spirits is created as *angels* for the service of this world. The mediating place of angels between God and the world is depicted in Psalm 17:10-11 (18:9-10): "He lowered the heavens and came down; darkness was under His feet. *And He mounted the cherubim and took flight* and was borne on the wings of the wind." Compare Psalm 79:2 (80:1). The image of sitting on cherubim (proper also to Ezekiel's vision of the chariot) contains the idea that God draws near to creation, is correlated with it through the angels. The angels' service assumes the existence of an ontological link between the angelic and human worlds. The angels' ascent and descent is accomplished on a ladder that exists between earth and heaven and was seen by Jacob. Not only is a guardian angel found in a personal correlation with the one whom it protects, but angels of fire, winds, and water are also found in an analogous correlation with a given region of creation. Angels are sent to one or another service not indifferently but in conformity with their own idea or personal nature, and this correlation of course has a higher expediency and concreteness. In its nature, although *by its own* particular manner, the angelic world possesses the whole structure, which is to say, the whole content of our world and only by virtue of such a correlation can angelic service be accomplished. Heaven *and* earth represent as it were two forms of being of the one world, the one creation: *ano* and *kato,* the ideal and the real world, the empyreal and the terrestrial, which look at themselves one in the other and are correlated one to the other. The first words of the book of *Genesis*[5] express the most secret foundation of creation in its two forms, in two worlds, but of the *one* divine creation: *God (Elohim) created (bara) heaven and earth,* creating them *in the beginning,* i.e., originally and primordially. *Heaven and earth* as the totality of all *possibilities* of creation *precede* in their origination all further creation, the Hexaemeron,[6] and already include it as a possibility. Separate acts of creation need not be understood as some entirely new creative work out of nothing, equal "to the initial one" or as some ontological constraint that thrusts on the earth something hitherto strange and unusual to it. On the contrary, they contain the direct command to manifest their might to the earth: let the earth bring forth vegetation (Genesis 1:11), let the waters produce reptiles, a living soul (Genesis 1:20), let the earth produce a living soul each according to its species (Genesis 1:24). The earth looks at itself in heaven, carrying in its womb the whole creation already outlined in the heavens, and obedient to the command of God brings it about. But on principle nothing new is created in the six days which would not have been created *in the beginning*[7] up to the six days, or, so to say, *above* the six days. Nothing more is said *about heaven,* signalling that it is created by a single act in the fullness of its perfection (cf. Genesis 2:1: "and so heaven and earth were created and all their host"[8]) but *about earth* is added: "the earth was formless and void, and darkness was over the abyss, and the Spirit of God floated above the water" (Genesis 1:2). And it is brought forth from the formlessness and emptiness only in the six days. But heaven and earth were created "in the beginning," i.e.,

---

5. Bulgakov writes "the book of the *Genesis* of the world." Translator's note.

6. Bulgakov uses here a patristic and liturgical term meaning "the six days" which tradition understood as a discrete period in the act of divine creation. Translator's note.

7. Blessed Augustine taught that the world was created by a single act, immediately, and that the days of creation correspond only *to the manifestation* in creation of the seeds of being planted in it.

8. Psalm 88:12-13/89:11: "Yours are the heavens, Yours the earth: You have founded the universe and what fills it."

not only initially but also primordially, *out of or on the foundation* of a single underlying, world-creating principle — the Wisdom of God. The world is created by Wisdom: "You have created all things by Wisdom." The Wisdom of God, the self-revelation of the Holy Trinity, of the Father in the Son by the Holy Spirit, contains the idea or prototype of creation — the divine world, pre-eternally existing in God. The tri-hypostatic God has a single essence or nature, a single life and self-revelation, and this self-revelation of Divinity, as existing in itself, is the Glory of God and His Wisdom. This Wisdom is the foundation and goal of creation. "The Lord had me as the beginning of His paths from the outset" (Proverbs 8:22). All that God makes is contained in His Wisdom and cannot dwell outside of her ("remaining in pitch darkness, the outer dark," outside being). With respect to God himself His Wisdom is the pre-eternal content of the Word of God, the word of the Word, and eternal Life, the reality of this word through the Holy Spirit. She is God Himself in His self-revelation.[9] With respect to the creaturely world she is the word before creation, *kosmos noetos,* the Divine world, the prototypical containing in itself the sufficient and exhaustive foundation for all that is. In the beginning *(en arche)* — once more the first word of the book of Genesis is repeated by the Evangelist Theologian — *was the Word and the Word was with God and the Word was God:* in the Beginning, i.e., in the Wisdom of God the Word of God, the Word of the Father, *was,* i.e., it had being and life pre-eternally ("in Him was life") through the Life-giving Spirit. In this initial text of the Gospel of John is contained the revelation not only of the Word but also of the whole Holy Trinity. And this cannot be otherwise because by means of the revelation of the Son the revelation of the Father is already introduced, and it cannot stop at Duality but of necessity brings in the Trinity. Therefore it is necessary to interpret *was* not in the sense of a simple copula verb (which, evidently, is inappropriate and insufficient in a text of such high theological content) but in the sense of a mysterious, concealed indication about the life-giving Holy Spirit who unites the Father and the Son as *amor unitivus amborum* ("and the Word was with God . . . He was from the beginning with God"). This *was,* as well as this *with God (pros ton theon),* where clearly the Father is to be understood, is nothing other than an indication of the Holy Spirit. And this notion is even more definitely expressed in verse 4: "in Him was life, and the life *(he zoe)* was the light of

---

9. Concerning this see Sergius Bulgakov, *The Burning Bush,* trans. with an introduction by Thomas Allan Smith (Grand Rapids, MI: William B. Eerdmans Publishing Company, 2009).

humans." Here *life* clearly designates the Life-Creating Spirit who rests on the Son, who illuminates the world through the Holy Spirit. The prologue of the Gospel of John understood in this Trinitarian sense contains in itself the doctrine not only of the Word of God, the Son of the Father, but also of the Holy Spirit the Comforter, which is natural for the prologue of a Gospel that is pre-eminently pneumatological. But the prologue of John's Gospel has not only a Trinitarian significance but even more so a Sophiological one. Above all, the first word of the prologue *in the beginning* is the same as that in Genesis (and of course in Proverbs 8:22). Obviously it cannot signify here *time* in respect to the pre-eternal life of the Holy Trinity, but has a general ontological meaning. If the "*in the beginning*" of Genesis 1:1 can still be understood *also* in a temporal sense, inasmuch as it refers to the origin of the world, then in the prologue where *the origination* of the Word in whatsoever manner is *implicitly* rejected, but His primordial, i.e., everlasting being is affirmed, this temporal understanding of *en arche* is quite inappropriate and contradictory. *En arche* signifies here not "in the beginning of time" but "in the eternity of God," and the first meaning of *beginning* is therefore *eternity*. But what else does the eternity of God signify than His Wisdom and Glory?

The Sophiological meaning of the prologue is further clear from the fact that the doctrine of the Holy Trinity is set forth here in direct relation to the creation of the world: "everything came to be through Him," "the light shines in Him," "the Word became flesh." Here the doctrine of the pre-eternal life of God in Himself, in the Holy Trinity, is compared and brought into connection with the doctrine of God-the Creator who proceeds from Himself towards the creation, who illumines with His light the "pitch" darkness, that is, non-being, creaturely nothing before creation. In this context Sophia the Wisdom of God is the *beginning* that unites God with the world:[10] "The Lord had me (wisdom) *as the beginning* of His paths." In this way it is possible to say that *the beginning (arche)* of the prologue of the Gospel of John is the pre-eternal Wisdom of God, the divine world before creation, as the basis of creation. Turned towards Divinity she contains in herself the life of the Holy Trinity: *Houtos ēn en arche pros ton theon* — this is the Trinitarian formula in a Sophiological aspect. The *beginning* contains in itself the revelation of the Father which is addressed to the Son and is effected by the Holy Spirit. *The beginning* in the book of

---

10. The identical force of the expressions *beginning* and *wisdom* is established by the book of the Proverbs of Solomon 8:22f., where both expressions are fixed exactly in their equivalency.

Genesis contains the revelation of the same Wisdom but already in her turning towards creation as the foundation of that creation: "in the beginning God created heaven and earth." Here the phrase *in the beginning* means "by the beginning," "through the beginning," "in conformity with the beginning," and "on the basis of the beginning." Pre-eternal Wisdom is in God and as the beginning of the creation of the world she is not two different beginnings but one and the same beginning *(arche)*, turned to God and to the world: in the first sense she is the world as the divine uncreated proto-basis of creation; in the second sense she is the world as something arising from nothing by the will of God, creaturely Wisdom,[11] all creation, where obviously the world angelic and human enters.

And so the general foundation of creation for the *whole* created world, heaven and earth, is contained in the Wisdom of God. And one must be cognizant of this — the Sophianic unity of the angelic and human worlds — in all its import when it is brought to bear on the question under examination. Angels without a doubt are related to this *whole* — *panta*, i.e., to the prototypal ideas of creation, which arises through the Word in the Wisdom of God. What place does the angelic world occupy in all creation? Is it a particular world alongside of the human world and so to say apart from it? Was there manifested in its creation the inexhaustibility of God's creative work, thanks to which God, who was not satisfied with the visible world, fabricates an invisible world apart from it?[12] This consideration, prompted more by piety than by theology, does not pose the question in its entire scope. True, it contains the indisputable idea that the angelic world represents an independent region of creation, dif-

11. The particular Christological or more precisely logological emphasis placed here on the Second hypostasis by the evangelist in conformity with his particular aim does not contradict this Sophiological meaning of the prologue of the Gospel of John. The intentional turning to the world of precisely this cosmourgic hypostasis comes to the fore: "All came to be through Him [the Word], and without Him nothing came to be that comes to be" (although in the word "came to be" it is already possible to understand the life-creating operation of the Holy Spirit in creation).

12. "Since it was not sufficient for God's goodness to be occupied solely with contemplation of His own self but it was incumbent that good should overflow, going further and further such that the number of beneficiaries should be as great as possible, because this is characteristic of the highest good; God conceived of the angelic heavenly powers before all else; and the idea became fact, which was carried out by the Word and completed by the Spirit. . . . In as much as the first creatures were pleasing to Him, He conceived of a second world, material and visible, or what is the same, the harmonious structure of heaven and earth, and that which is between them." St. Gregory the Theologian, Sermon 38.

ferent from our world and in this sense not dependent on it. However, this idea about the independence of the angelic world from the human world which is valid within its own limits cannot be ultimately upheld. Otherwise it directly contradicts that connection in which the Word of God places both worlds, heaven and earth, and compels us to forget the *angelic* predetermination of the bodiless spirits. The naming of angels points to their *service* and the latter presupposes the direct connection and correlativeness of both worlds.

We already said that the service of angels to the human world cannot be understood externally, as something not flowing out of their own nature but must be explained on the foundation of the internal connection of both worlds, which is based on the ontological unity of creation. Angels serve the world and humans because they are related to it and in a sense are identical in their fundamental ontological theme or, so to say, in the motif of creation. The angel of fire himself is fiery in the sense that he carries in his nature the noetic element of fire, just as the angel of waters has an aqueous nature, etc. Guardian angels of people, nations, and societies are found in intentional spiritual affinity precisely with the given spiritual individualities. The general foundation of this connection of heaven and earth, of both worlds, is that both are created equally in the same *beginning*, mono-principledly, and this mono-principled beginning *of all* creation is Sophia the Wisdom of God in whom pre-eternally the prototypes *(paradeigmata)* of everything created are outlined. The angelic world and the human world are distinguished *by the form* of their being, but have a unity of creative foundation and a community of ontological theme. Divine prototypes, the ideas of the world, are realized in creation in two ways: in heaven — spiritually, non-incarnately, and on earth in incarnation. The one divine Wisdom gives being to both worlds and connects them. Of course, one ought not to understand this notion in a narrow and straightforward way. Originality in the realization of a single creative theme is peculiar to each of the worlds. In particular the form of being of the angelic world has its own distinctions that one can express briefly in this way: in the angelic world there is no place at all for particular non-hypostatic, natural being, and even in general there is no place for nature or especially for the world, the cosmos, in which and out of which and for which the human being is created. The angelic world, as a spiritual or bodiless world, is thoroughly hypostatic, and there is nothing in it which would not have personal being, as by the way in our world the whole pre-human, i.e., inorganic and organic, world is impersonal; it is hypostatized only in and through the human, and hypostatic being is only proper to the human. Further, the angelic world has its own hierarchical structure flowing out of the distinction of the angels' proximity to God and therefore a particular interior life within its bounds. Finally, the angels' own life in their turning to God is defined by their standing before the throne of God and receives from this its particular strength. In a word, the angelic world is not a simple repetition of our world in the spiritual domain, for in general there can be no repetition whatever in God's creation. The unity of the ontological beginning in no way presupposes such repetition. However, in it is contained the foundation for the positive correlation or unity between both worlds by virtue of which they also live one common life, despite all their differences. One cannot understand the creation of both worlds by the one Wisdom of God to mean that two independent beginnings are distinguished in her, one for the spiritual and the other for the physical world. No, the beginning is one. Moved to create the world, however, God *begins* with the spiritual, angelic, bodiless[13] world and concludes with the earthly world. Why precisely that order of creation and not the reverse? It is impossible not to see the explanation for this in the natural hierarchy of creation. The Lord initially realizes the creative forms of His Wisdom in the making of the bodiless angelic world, and he summons to being creaturely hypostatic figures in which are imprinted all the forms of being, its "ideas." The Wisdom of God receives a personal, multi-hypostatic reflection in "the second lights" of the angelic world which are found in immediate proximity to the Godhead in their hierarchic assembly. Present in its own way to the angelic world is the whole fullness *(pleroma)* of creation; this is not *a part* of the world but the *entire* world, only in its particular hypostatic-spiritual form of being. The Lord has the Wisdom of God as the Beginning of His paths in which He created heaven and earth. Of course, it is reflected in all its fullness in the angelic world as the sum total of ideas, themes, and paradigms of the world in the hypostatic form of being. In this sense the angelic world participates in *all* that is created by the Word and contains in itself this *all.* This fullness of creative ideas, inserted in the creation of the angelic world, flows from the fact that the angelic world just as the human world is created by the Word of God, is headed equally by Him and in Him has the beginning and end, the origin and goal of its being. "By Him is created all that is in the heavens and on the earth, visible and invisible: thrones, lordships, principles, powers, all are created by Him and for Him. And He is before everything, and everything stands by Him" (Colossians 1:16-17), "in

13. Bulgakov provides no information for this note.

the arranging of the fullness of time so that everything heavenly and earthly may unite under the head of Christ" (Ephesians 1:10). An angel differs from a human in a sense other than do separate ranks of creation, diverse "according to their species," like greenery, grasses, trees (Genesis 1:12), birds and crawling things, reptiles, cattle and wild animals of the earth (24-25). Angels are not *a species* of creation alongside of the human being and diverse forms of creation which are headed and united by the human. Angels are heavenly *co-humans;* they are of the same world but in a different form of being: heaven *and* earth.

And yet the angelic world with all its creaturely fullness is not *all* in the sense of the form of realization; it is only the initial, first step of a creation which is not exhausted by the angelic world but continues beyond it and further than it — to the earth and the human world. The angelic world is not the end but the beginning of creation; it occupies an intermediate position between God and the world like a personal *metaxu,* a living instrument. God creates angels as *angels,* i.e., with the idea of a subsequent creation which they will serve, namely, the human world. Of course, as hypostatic spirits angels in themselves have independent existence and the meaning of their own being even apart from our world; they form in themselves their own domain of being through their participation in God. All the same, the fullness of the form of angelic being remains subordinated to our world. Angels are predetermined for its service; they have in this sense an auxiliary, instrumental significance; they exist *for* our world. This world, on the contrary, is created not for the sake of some other world but for itself and in itself, although it looks at itself in the angelic world as in its heavenly mirror, and presupposes it.

Revelation says nothing about *how* precisely the auxiliary participation of angels in the very origination of our world is expressed. The church does not accept the Gnostic idea that the world was created by angels (this idea is reflected in contemporary theosophical doctrines about the origin of the world through the active participation of "hierarchies" as for example in Steiner[14]). However, this rejection in no way excludes the idea that angels are the *executors* of the creative word of God, i.e., that their service to the world commences already with its very creation. On the contrary, this notion is fully natural. So too is the idea that appropriate angelic orders labor on the parts of the universe predestined to their care —

14. Rudolph Steiner (1861-1925) was an influential Austrian thinker and founder of the Anthroposophy movement through which he sought to create a synthesis of mysticism and science. Translator's note.

33

for the corresponding days of creation. This idea is suggested to us by the fact that service in relation to definite facets of the universe is assigned to different angels (in particular Lucifer is understood precisely as the supreme guardian angel of the world, who converted himself into "the prince of this world" and its god only by theft). In any case it is impossible not to relate the beginning of the creature's safeguarding and service to the first days of creation, since the presence of guardians already constitutes as it were the condition of the very possibility of creation.[15] Just as in the world formed by God there was nothing accursed and rejected by God but rather God's blessing, "it is very good," was over all of it, so too this whole world was placed under the protection and service of the angelic ranks which for this purpose must have had in themselves correlatively all the fullness of the universe. In this general sense it must be said that the angelic world contains in itself the ideal analogue of the universe in *all* its parts: all ideas or creative themes of this world are present in the angelic world and are realized only when it is present. In this the angelic world is really *the intermediary* between God and the world, the ladder from earth to the heavens without which our world could not endure the immediate proximity of God. It both unites and separates the creature from God. Such is the first ontological meaning of the vision of Jacob's ladder: the angelic world as a *medium* between God and human beings: "and [Jacob] dreamt: behold a ladder is standing on earth and its top touches heaven. And behold the angels of God are ascending and descending on it" (Genesis 28:12-13).[16] In this sense the angelic world contains in itself the hypostatized prototypes of all worldly being. That world of the ideas, prototypes of being, which Plato gained sight of, only vaguely discerning its real place in God and even mixing it with Divinity, is in reality the angelic world in its relation to being, *Jacob's ladder.* Such is the true sense of Platonic idealism.

This does not resolve beforehand the question about whether all the

---

15. Is this not confirmed by the text of Revelation 9:14-15 where it speaks about angels *made ready,* although for destruction? "I heard a voice that spoke to the sixth angel who was holding a trumpet: release the four angels bound by the mighty river Euphrates. And the four angels were set free, *made ready for the hour and day and month and year* in order to slay a third part of the people."

16. This text must be interpreted in connection with Genesis 1:1, "In the beginning God created heaven and earth," since precisely the same comparison is used here: "earth" as the base for the ladder and "heaven" as its upper base ("it touches heaven"), this living ladder consisting of angels ascending and descending on it (an image of the constant participation of angels in the life of the world).

ranks and choirs of angels are turned immediately to the world and appear *as angels* to it or whether the loftiest hierarchies, standing before God's throne, remain in heavenly worship and are free from this direct turning to the world. However, this very distinction in the services of separate angelic choirs does not alter the fundamental ontological correlation between the worlds: although some choirs do not immediately take part in service to the human world, they do so intermediately inasmuch as the life of the angelic assembly represents a true unity and all of it is turned to the earth by means of its creaturely aspect; it is Jacob's ladder — ascent and descent. Though with its very top this ladder stretches into the heavens, it still rests on the earth with its base. And in this sense one can say about *the entire* angelic world that it is found in a positive and essential relationship to our world. All bodiless spirits are *angels,* i.e., servants of this world united with it by the bonds of creaturely nature. Therefore even if it is assumed that there are higher ranks of angels which always stand before God and hence are completely free from immediate association with the human world, all the same they remain connected with it. But the series of examples of higher angels does not speak in favor of this assumption: Gabriel who stands before God's throne, the archangel Michael himself, "the prince" of the Hebrew people, further Raphael from the story of Tobit, and finally the seraph who touches Isaiah's lips with coal (Isaiah 6:6-7). A fact firmly established by the Church attests to this common bond and the correlativity of the angelic and human world — not only guardian angels but also all angelic ranks pray to the Lord for the human race, and the Church instructs us to pray for this "advocacy of the honorable heavenly bodiless powers," without any limitation (cf. the Dismissal of the Monday service), on a level with prayer to the Mother of God and all the saints: "holy archangels and angels, pray for us to God."[17] (In some ancient orders of the Preparation of the Gifts, a particle for angels is taken from the nine-ranked prosphora together with particles for all the saints; in any case this remains even today on feast days of the angels, i.e., first of all on 8 November, 26 November, 26 March, and 6 September.)

But the earthly world in its collectiveness and totality is the human world. It is the human who as an individual being is a microcosm, "a world acquired"; as a generic entity the human encompasses the whole macrocosm, which is why it was created on the sixth day, in the fullness of creation. As evidence of its lordship the human was told: "Fill the earth

17. See the Canon to the Bodiless Powers, 8th tone, the Canons to all the Saints, and many others.

and have possession of it and exercise dominion over all living creatures" (Genesis 1:28). This *possession and dominion* arises from an inner correlation between humans and the world — the whole six days can be regarded as the gradual creation of the human and the preparation of the world for the human. It follows from this that everything relating to this human world is in a certain sense also *human* or more precisely, co-human, conformed to the human. "The human is the measure of things" — in a new and unexpected sense Protagoras's saying returns to us. The co-humanity of the angelic world follows from this as well. Angels are sent to humankind inasmuch as they exist with humankind and for humankind; in its turn humankind is bound to the angelic world and in a certain sense is conformed to it, is co-angelic. Humankind, however, comprises an end in itself, the summit of creation; and it cannot be said that humankind exists *for* the angelic world. Although humankind receives service from the angelic world, it does not serve it. And in response to this idea the starry words of Revelation blaze with a bright light in the spiritual heaven; they contain the divinely inspired solution to the fundamental problem of angelology. The Seer describes a vision of the new heaven and the new earth, of the great city, holy Jerusalem descending from heaven from God and possessing the Glory of God (Revelation 21:10-11). It has twelve gates and on them twelve angels, and on the gates are written the names of the twelve tribes of the sons of Israel (21:12). "And he measured its wall one hundred forty-four cubits by human measurement, which is also the angel's measurement" (21:17). BY HUMAN MEASUREMENT WHICH IS ALSO THE ANGEL'S MEASUREMENT — these words express the ontological correlation of both worlds.[18]

The angels' co-humanity is the fundamental condition of their angelic service. This interior correlation is revealed in the appearances of angels to humans which are accomplished in human form, only with certain attributes, namely, wings (and even this feature is not universal).[19] Of

18. On the contrary, "the number of the beast is the human number" (Revelation 13:18). And in actual fact the theomachy of the earthly animal element, although inspired by Satan, belongs entirely to this world. As if not having its own foundations in genuine being, and on the contrary being entirely connected with the assault of sin, it does not have any basis in "heaven," in the angelic world, and is limited to the human world.

19. In the visions of the prophet Daniel in which with particular clarity the co-humanity of angels is shown, the appearance of the archangel Gabriel occurs simply in the form of a man. "And when I Daniel had seen this vision and was searching after its meaning, behold there stood before me one in the likeness of a man. And I heard by the Ulai a human voice which called out and said, 'Gabriel, explain this vision to him'" (Dan-

course, one may say that angels appeared in human form so that they would be visible to humans. But such a consideration would transgress by its naïve and excessively rational anthropomorphism. The form is not a mask which the appearing creature assumes arbitrarily without any interior foundation, because for such an appearance other means could also be chosen: fire, light, thunder, etc. The one or other form is assumed only insofar as there is an ontological foundation for it in natural correlations.[20] The Lord Jesus Christ appeared in the form of a human for he took human nature, and became human. But he did not assume the form of an angel because he did not assume angelic nature. That angels appear to humans in human form does not mean of course that they are humans, all the more so because in other circumstances the form of their appearance differs from a human form, but their conformity with humankind, or their co-humanity, is attested by this. The appearance of angels in the form of animals does not contradict this and even confirms it — Ezekiel's vision of the four animals about one of which it is said that "his visage was like that of a human" (Ezekiel 1:5), and the similar vision of the four animals by the Seer, which have a human face among the four faces, as in Ezekiel (Revelation 4:6-8) — correlative with this are the representations of the four evangelists. The general meaning and the basis of such representations is that the human being is a pan-animal (as well as a pan-plant); it includes in itself and generalizes by itself; it exhausts the whole animal world. On this basis as if in some analytical decomposition, the co-humanity of angels can also be portrayed as pan-animality (although it is not exhausted by this animality alone, as is directly indicated in the vi-

---

iel 8:15-16). "While I was continuing my prayer the man Gabriel whom I had seen before in the vision came in swift flight around the time of the evening sacrifice" (9:21). And his appearance is described by the following texts: "and I raised my eyes and saw: behold, one man, dressed in linen clothing and his loins were girt with gold from Uphaz. His body was like topaz, his face like lightning, his eyes like burning torches, his arms and legs had the look of sparkling copper and the sound of his words like the sound of a multitude of people" (10:5-6). Cf. also 12:5-7 (the vision of two men). Angels are described at the resurrection of Christ likewise as youths in linen clothing.

20. Bishop Ignatii Brianchaninov draws together the form of the angel and of the human soul freed from the body on the basis of his general considerations about the corporeality of angels and on the basis of diverse visions (from the *Prologue* and the *Paterikon*). In this drawing together he sees the difference between the human and angelic world only in the incarnate condition of the human being. "What is a human being? The same sort of created spirit as the angels but clothed in a body. Other created spirits differ from a human being in that they do not have its body, its flesh" (volume 3, p. 236).

sions of Ezekiel and John the Theologian). Separate features of the human or animal form are appropriated by angels: their having many eyes and being six-winged, etc. Paganism knew this pan-animality of the human in vague premonitions, e.g., Egyptian zoolatry and its corresponding iconography refer to this, as does to a certain extent even totemism. As keepers of the whole creaturely world, angels are correlative to that world, in particular to the plant and animal world.[21]

This co-humanity of the angels, as such, is inherent in the entire angelic world *as a whole,* in the totality of all its hierarchies. Coming to light in the guarding of all creation, it is immediately revealed in their relations to the human world, in particular in the existence of guardian angels. Guardian angels are our heavenly co-humans (or as one sometimes expresses this idea, the human is an angel who took fleshly being). This co-humanity of angels and humankind's corresponding co-angelicity, which is rooted in the image of God as the common foundation of the creation of humans and angels, is a fundamental dogmatic fact and one must explain it equally in all its significance for both angelology and anthropology (and further for Christology, Soteriology, and Eschatology).

---

21. In the *Shepherd of Hermas* one of the visions (Vision IV, II, 4) relates that the angel of animals *(ton epi ton therion)* named Thegre received the injunction not to harm him. Athenagoras teaches that spirits exist that are obliged to follow the correct movement of the heaven, the earth, and all the elements. Origen says that angels exist who are occupied with the birth of animals and the growth of plants, etc. St. Epiphanius, in harmony with pseudo-Enoch, knows angels of thunder, lightning, cold, heat, and many other things. St. Basil the Great, St. Gregory the Theologian, and blessed Jerome oppose this view but it appears once again in St. John Chrysostom and blessed Augustine.

CHAPTER 2

The Guardian Angel

Take care that you not despise one of the least of these: for I say to you that their angels in heaven continually see the face of My heavenly Father (Matthew 18:10). With these words the Lord indisputably testifies that *not one of these least ones* is deprived of its guardian angel. The literal sense of this text is that *all have* their own guardian angels, and no limitations are introduced into this idea. True, the partisans of a restrictive interpretation, by referring the supplementary definition of verse 6 to verse 10, which says *of these least ones who believe in Me,* understand here those who belong to the Church, that is, the baptized. However, in the text cited these words have a much more general form, which in any case permits a more extended interpretation. Besides, this is said before the saving passion and *before* Pentecost and the institution of baptism (with the present form *blepousin* [they see] having a pan-temporal, metaphysical meaning). The existence of guardian angels even for Old Testament humanity (consequently likewise before the redemption and before baptism) can be corroborated by sacred texts.[1] So too the presence of the angel of God near the Gentile Cornelius (Acts 10:3) attests that it is extended to Gentiles as well, at least *on the eve* of bap-

---

1. Genesis 24:7, 40, treats the marriage of Isaac for which Abraham sends his servant. The Lord "will send His angel ahead of you and you will take a wife for my son." Genesis 48:16 — the blessing of Joseph by Jacob — reads, "May the angel, who delivers me from every evil, bless these offspring." Psalm 33:8 (34:7), "The angel of the Lord will be encamped around those who fear Him and he will deliver them." Psalm 34/35:5-6, "Let them be like dust before the face of the wind and let the Lord's angel drive them away. Let their path be difficult and slippery and let the angel of the Lord pursue them." Psalm 90/91:11, "He will command with His angels on your account — to protect you on all your paths." The story of Tobit (book of Tobit) is referred to here.

tism.[2] Without a doubt every baptized person receives a guardian angel, as it says in the prayer: "O holy angel . . . given to me for the preservation of my soul and sinful body *through holy baptism.*" The opinion of the holy fathers concerning this question goes in two directions. Some (such as St. Basil the Great and others) straightforwardly affirm that a guardian angel is given at baptism and consequently only to the faithful, i.e., first and foremost, to members of the Orthodox Church, and further to those baptized outside Orthodoxy. Others (like Tertullian,[3] Origen, etc.) consider that guardian angels are given to each human being at birth. The church has not made a final determination about this question and thus both opinions maintain a relative force. But it is entirely possible to reconcile and unite them. To be sure, through holy baptism, which erases original sin and thereby removes the partition between humankind and God, the fruits of redemption are appropriated by a human being, and through this a new, more direct and immediate relationship with the guardian angel is established as well. Through the fall humankind was alienated not only from God but also from the angelic world. Its accessibility for humans was diminished, even though not at all discontinued, and this barrier is done away with by holy baptism. Here is manifested one of the consequences of the divine incarnation in the alteration of relations between angels and humans (see below). And in this sense one can and must say, of course, that a guardian angel *is given* to us in a new way, becomes close and perceptible in holy baptism. But this doctrine does not at all exclude the possibility that a positive ontological correlation exists between the angel who receives access to a human being to whom he is given in holy baptism and that same human *prior to* baptism. Does a given angel belong to a given human already from birth and before baptism or is he chosen anew for service, in keeping with God's will, at holy baptism? In the Word of God it is said definitively time and again: "the angel who delivers me from evil" (Genesis 48:16), "they said, this is his angel" (Acts 12:15), "their angels" *(hoi aggeloi auton)* (Matthew 18:10). The existence of the guardian angel for the chosen leaders of Old Testament humanity as a whole and as individ-

2. The presence of guardian angels among pagan peoples is attested by the prophet Daniel ("prince of Persia," "prince of Greece"). Ought one not extend it to individual members of these peoples?

3. The power of the divine will modulates, no doubt through some intermediary, every preparatory stage of the begetting, arranging, and fashioning of the human being. *Omnem hominis in utero serendi, struendi, fingendi paraturam aliqua utique potestas divinae voluntatis ministra modulatur* (Tertullian, *De anima* c. XXXVII, PL 2, c. 756). Bulgakov's citation has been corrected and translated. Translator's note.

uals is not subject to doubt. But with respect to baptism are they not in the same situation as pagans? Before the redemptive sacrifice of Christ and Pentecost there were no graced gifts of baptism in the world, but after Pentecost Jews and pagans were immediately baptized, with Judaism as a whole rejecting Christ while pagans primarily accepted the preaching of Christianity. In this way we must come to the conclusion that the presence of a guardian angel in the midst of Old Testament humanity removes the indissolubility of its connection with baptism. It can exist even independently of baptism. This connection arises in a different way, but how precisely?

Obviously the relation between a guardian angel and a human being, which is based on personal love and election, is pre-established and rooted in the general correlation of heaven and earth. That each human (let us even assume only each baptized human) has *its own* guardian angel, its own heavenly friend, already presumes such *an affinity* and such friendship. And this in turn presumes their well-known affinity or identity, even as they maintain their otherness. Otherness refers first and foremost to the general distinction of human and angelic nature and likewise to the difference of their hypostases, whereas identity or affinity refers to the unity of ontological theme or idea. A guardian angel has an affinity of individual character with a human. Inasmuch as individuality in general exists, it only consists in a particular *how*, in a form of perception for everyone's sake of one and the same world — the Wisdom of God which is revealed in it. This distinction does not introduce a difference in the sense of *fullness* of possession, and thus does not abrogate the unity of human nature, its oneness in being, just as in the Prototype of humankind, in God, the triplicity of hypostases does not destroy their oneness in being, their equal dignity and equal divinity. Distinction is introduced only in hypostatic being which, as if repeating itself in a multitude of different I's, is individualized by them at the same time. One can say that there exists a *likeness* between the hypostasis of a guardian angel and that of a human: it is one and the same individuality living in two worlds, in heaven and on earth. One must, of course, understand this likeness by taking into account all the distinctions in the disclosure of individuality there and here. That which in angelic being is given in the form of the personal that comes to light and is spiritually achieved, that lives in the fullness and blessedness of divine knowledge, is in the human only a grain producing a sprout, the plant itself undergoing all the dangers and failings of the world and hence able to fail entirely to open up and blossom. In addition, the form of being remains distinct in the spiritual and human world, in

41

heaven and on earth. Here one should not speak about identity but only about correspondence or likeness.[4] Sometimes this idea is expressed in the straightforward convergence of an angel and a human soul which after its liberation from the body assumes a certain luminous shell similar to an angel's (Bishop Ignatii Brianchaninov). Sometimes this idea is cloaked in the form of a poetic myth about an angel "conductor of souls" bringing its own soul into the world (the prophetic insight of Lermontov's *Angel* where something authentic is made known).[5]

Each human being has its roots in the empyrean world; it finds there its likeness, its friend, in whom it regards and loves its own self without self-love. Therefore, by inquiring whether or not every human has a guardian angel one is essentially asking whether or not every human is a human, has a human soul, and contains its own idea of human personality. The earth is created together with heaven and on the foundation of heaven.[6] This in no way means that the human world is *a repetition* of the angelic world which, like every repetition, is boring and pointless. It would not correspond to divine might and the inexhaustibility of God's creative thought. But the unity of the ontological idea which is realized in two different worlds signifies not repetition but plenitude, unity in diversity. The angelic and human worlds do not simply exist one alongside of the other but they are mutually permeated by the ontological rays of the Sophianicity of their being. They are one in Sophia because the Wisdom of God, the Beginning of the world, is one, but they are distinguished in the form of their being, with purity and clarity inhering in the bodiless world, fullness and complexity in the incarnate world. But this duality does not destroy the unity of creation. The world is *one* although it consists of earth and heaven. This *and* namely includes the idea of identity without repetition and affinity without confusion. Everything in the world exists as the other for its own self, in two worlds, and being ontologically one, it doubles or "becomes other" in its own being.

And so, the guardian angel, "the faithful mentor, guardian of soul

4. Likeness is not equality inasmuch as similar figures can be distinguished between themselves by magnitude; it is not in a literal sense identity. And yet identity of form or idea which is disclosed in each of similar figures is included in likeness.

5. Bulgakov refers to the famous poem by Mikhail Lermontov (1814-1841). Translator's note.

6. The Canon of the Bodiless Powers, tone 8, ode 1, tr. 2: "O maker of angels, you placed a bodiless creature as the principal of creatures." "Principal of creatures" can equally signify an indication about the time of the creation of angels before the human world and the ontological foundation of creation, established in "heaven" for earth.

and body," is not simply *a servant* but is our heavenly I — the Sophianic foundation in the heavens of our being on earth. We would not be if he was not, and he would not be if we were not. Here exists the full ontological coupling, the unity of the ontological root in both worlds. From this coupling flows the co-humanity of the angels which couples into one the fates of the human and angelic world although the boundary between them is impassable. In the same sense one can of course speak about angelic nature, or more precisely, about the co-angelicity of the human being as this is implied perhaps by the possibility for people to take the angelic rank.[7] The genius of language gives evidence of the many diverse uses of the word "angel" as applied to humans.

Guardian angels, entering into the hierarchies of the angelic world and in many diverse ways uniting with them, immediately reunite the angelic and human world. They are exactly that foundation of Jacob's ladder by which it is firmly established on earth. One should not think that this direct bond of the two worlds is of concern only to the guardian angels, to each of them separately irrespective of the others. First of all the unity of the human *race* speaks against the admissibility of that supposition; owing to that unity each guardian angel in the person of the human under his protection comes into contact with the life *of the whole* human race in its entire history. Likewise the holy angels, although they do not form *a race* but only *a choir or rank,* nevertheless are not estranged one from another in their love and service (this is attested to externally by the fact that angels appear to humans not only alone but in a multitude). Further it is known that besides individual angels there exist guardian angels and protectors of human communities, natural and spiritual — peoples, cities, locales, realms, churches. In each of these communities the fates of separate persons and, consequently, of their angels are intertwined. And the very existence of particular angels for these communities is evidence that the correlation of the angelic world with the human world is not limited to the preservation of separate persons by guardian angels, but goes deeper and broader, along paths unknown to us, but *analogously* to human multiunity. This bond stretches not only in breadth and depth but also *in height* insofar as the lower ministering hierarchies receive enlightenment and consequently help from the higher ones. All bodiless powers without exception are called *angels,* i.e., they are determined for service to the human race. In this extended sense one can say that *all* angels are guardian angels

7. Here Bulgakov is thinking of monks, whose habit and way of life are often referred to as angelic. Translator's note.

of the human race, some directly and immediately, others intermediately and hierarchically. The general *co-humanity* of the whole angelic world is once more confirmed from this fact. All those places in the Word of God which speak about angelic hosts in general without reference to a specific person are oblique evidence of this: thus, at the birth of Christ "there appeared with the angel *(toi aggeloi)* a multitude *(plethos)* of the heavenly host . . . the angels *(hoi aggeloi)* went away to heaven" (Luke 2:13, 15). In a similar way it is said in the parable about the harvest of the world which will be carried out by angels: "The Son of Man will send His angels *(tous aggelos autou)*" (Matthew 13:39, 41). The same is said concerning the joy among the angels of God *(enopion ton aggelon tou theou)* over one repentant sinner (Luke 15:10) — here there is direct evidence that angels (without restriction) take a very vital part in the fates of separate sinners and to that extent co-participate in the effort and care of their guardian angels. Finally concerning the end of the world it is said: "for the Son of Man will come in the glory of His Father with His angels *(meta ton aggelon autou)*" (Matthew 16:27), or in another place it is specified: "*all* angels *(pantes hoi aggeloi)* with Him" (Matthew 25:31). This appearance *of all* angels at the Last Judgment *of all* humans, when in their turn "humans will judge the angels" (1 Corinthians 6:3), clearly testifies to the correlation *of the whole* angelic world with *the whole* of the human race. Therefore the particular question whether guardian angels are chosen from all the hierarchies or only from the lowest levels loses its primary significance, because all angels co-participate in the efforts and cares of the guardian angels. This is obliquely confirmed by the prayer of the Church addressed to all bodiless powers.[8]

Here in passing one can touch on certain particular questions concerning separate angels and the first question to be posed concerns the relation of the archangel Gabriel. He stands before God in the highest ranks of the cherubim and nonetheless is sent to the Virgin Mary, according to the prologue of the Gospel of Luke. He is sent beforehand as well to Zechariah to announce the conception of the Forerunner. On the basis of this latter mission, however, no conclusion can be reached about the relation of the archangel Gabriel to Zechariah or the Forerunner, all the more so

---

8. The holy Church testifies: "The archangelic powers, O Christ, who stand before Your throne, pray for the human race" (Service for Archangels and Angels, verse on "O Lord I have cried," tone 6). The troparion runs the same way: "with your prayers surround us with the veil of wings of your immaterial glory, preserving us." Likewise the prayer "to all the angels": "to you as to defenders and guardians of my life I, accursed one, fall down and pray" etc. (*Priest's Prayer Book*, p. 169).

because this very episode in its context happens in connection with the Annunciation as an extraordinary preparation for the Nativity of Christ. The archangel is sent personally and immediately to the Virgin Mary (which is why he remains forever joined with her in the icon of the Annunciation which crowns the Royal Gates).

According to the liturgical texts Gabriel appeared to the Most Pure Virgin while she dwelled in the temple, bringing her the bread of angels and conversing with her.[9] Therefore the Most Pure was not surprised at his appearance at the Annunciation and he was not required to call himself by name as was the case when he appeared to Zechariah. The angel who appeared in a dream to Joseph (Matthew 1:20) and communicated to him in brief words the same news of the Annunciation, is he not the same Gabriel? In accordance with church tradition, he announced to her the approach of her honourable Dormition and he stood at the head of her funeral procession.[10] His hierarchical pre-eminence before the throne of God makes him worthy to be the intended angel of the Virgin Mary. If the distinctions of the hypostases of the Trinity make an imprint on the angelic ranks, it is then natural to think that Gabriel, who announced to the Virgin Mary, "The Holy Spirit will come upon you" (and the very descent of the Holy Spirit happened when these words were uttered), finds himself in a special personal relation with the Third hypostasis. Mary, as the Spirit-Bearer, the elect vessel of the Holy Spirit, has the archangel Gabriel who serves the mystery of the incarnation likewise intentionally from the Holy Spirit. Does it not result from this mission of the archangel Gabriel that he is so to say the proper guardian angel of the Most Pure?[11] His hierarchic stature would only correspond to the exclusiveness of this service.

9. Service of the Presentation in the Temple, verse on the "O Lord I have cried," the glory: "then was Gabriel sent to you, all immaculate one, bringing you food." The verse on the verse . . . "and you are being fed by the angel's hand, all-immaculate one. . . ."

10. "Rejoice, you who received the good news about your transitus to the celestial kingdom, rejoice, you who received from Gabriel, the herald of good news, the prize of joyful paradise" (Akathist of the Dormition of the Most Holy Theotokos, ikos 4). "Let us cry out, faithful ones, who have Gabriel as the captain of the rank" (Service of the Dormition).

11. A similar opinion has already been expressed. "In the opinion of the church the Virgin Mary was the particular object of the archangel Gabriel's ministry. To his heavenly safe-guarding were entrusted both the first and last years of her earthly life and when the time for her departure from earthly life arrived, the same archangel announced this to the Theotokos" (Archpriest G. S. Debol'skii, *Days of the Liturgy of the Orthodox Catholic Church*, 7th ed. [St. Petersburg, 1882], vol. 1, p. 274).

It seems that this assumption contains no abasement for the Theotokos. Although in her glorification she exceeds all creation, "more honorable than the cherubim and more glorious beyond compare than the seraphim," in her earthly life the Theotokos remains a human all the same for whom nothing human is foreign (except personal sin). As a human, by uniting with the whole human race, the Most Pure through her humanity unites also with the whole angelic world in the person of the highest archangel chosen pre-eternally for this. But here a substantial limitation must be made. The holy angels as heavenly ranks exceed by their holiness every human being. But in the given case the relation is the reverse, for the Theotokos exceeds by her holiness every creature — the angelic assembly as well as the human race. In her glory the Most Pure proves to be holier than her own guardian angel, whose humility bows down before the humility of the Lord's Servant. Nevertheless the gracious ascent of the Most Pure begins from her naturally human condition. She is the ladder along which ascend and descend the angels of God, but this ladder is firmly planted on earth, and it would be a diminishment of her humanity to deny for her what is inherent in humankind — to have for oneself a fulcrum in the angelic world too, a guardian angel. However, while he is the guardian angel of the Virgin Mary in the sense *of service* to her in her earthly life, the archangel Gabriel is not her heavenly prototype, which she, the Spirit-Bearer, on the whole does not have in the angelic world since she is more glorious *beyond compare* than the seraphim. If in humankind the image of God is realized through the instrument of an angelic prototype, *a direct* immediate divine likeness is proper to the Virgin Mary (and is it not in this sense that she is called Daughter of God — *theopais* — and Bride of Christ?). We see indirect evidence for this in that although the archangel Gabriel announced her departure from the world to her, the Lord Jesus Christ Himself appeared in order to receive her honorable soul, as this is portrayed on icons of the Dormition and in the service for the feast.[12] Gabriel merely preceded the "heaven-bound" ascent with "the victory wreath of paradise" in his hands.

12. At the Lity, the sticheron of John, "The all-immaculate Bride and Mother of the Father's favor, who is pre-betrothed to God to be for Him the abode of the unconfused union, today hands over to the Creator and God her most pure soul which the bodiless powers raise up in splendor." Of Anatolios, "She who is higher than the heavens and more glorious than the cherubim and more honorable than all creation . . . today hands over her soul into her son's hand." (Cf. the following verse, also in the Akathist.) "The Bridegroom summons you, bride of God, into the divine palace; O Bride of God, rejoice always, pleasing to God" (Praises, stasis I, Service for the burial of the Mother of God).

On the basis of what has been said one can conclude that although the archangel Gabriel, the minister of the mystery of the divine incarnation, is *the personal servant* of the Virgin Mary and remains in a special union with her by virtue of the Annunciation, he cannot be considered the guardian angel of her human person, for on the whole she does not have such an angel by virtue of her proximity to God. Her personal form as Spirit-Bearer is foreordained not in the angelic heavens but in the very heaven of heavens where she rests at the right hand of her Son.

Naturally another question arises: What is the relation of the archangel Gabriel to the Forerunner, whose birth he was likewise sent to announce? This mission has a general basis in the connection of the service of the Forerunner and the Mother of God (as is attested in the Deesis).[13] But except for the announcement of the nativity of the Forerunner, there are no indications of a further personal link between the archangel Gabriel and the Forerunner. In general did the Forerunner, himself "an angel," have a *personal* guardian angel or did this not correspond to his particular nature as one personally called to reunite in himself the human and angelic worlds? In the latter case, although his life in this world was safeguarded by angels, and in their number first of all by the archangel Gabriel, still he did not have in the angelic world a *personal* prototype or friend inasmuch as he already belonged to it in his predestination. Still one consideration suggests itself. The Forerunner is an angel, as the one who heads the whole angelic and human world together with the Theotokos in his station before the Lord (the Deesis), and in the opinion of some he took the place of the fallen first angel (Lucifer). In that case this place in the heavens was empty after Lucifer's fall, and concern for the Forerunner on earth naturally was the business of the whole angelic world, as this is shown in the example of the archangel Gabriel. Although he took part in the direction of his destiny in keeping with the direct command of God, Gabriel was not his guardian angel in his later life. In any case there are no indications whatsoever. This corresponds to the exalted position of the Forerunner both in the midst of the human world as "the greatest of those born of woman" and in the midst of the angelic world as the angel-human who stands at its head. It is natural for the *whole* angelic world to safeguard its future head in his earthly existence, the friend of the Bridegroom, the angel-witness of the divine incarnation before humans.

This is connected with a more general question: could not the devas-

---

13. See my work, *Friend of the Bridegroom,* trans. Boris Jakim (Grand Rapids, MI: Wm. B. Eerdmans Publishing Company, 2003).

tation in the heavens which was produced by the fall of the angels be reflected in the destinies of the earthly world which in the fallen angels lost its guardian angels and received in their stead hostile hordes of demons? An answer to this question is sometimes given in patristic literature in the sense that humankind was created as it were to replenish the void that was formed after the angels' fall (which is why the number of humans, evidently, must correspond to the number of fallen angels, perhaps deducting those who do not participate in this replenishment because they are predestined to the eternal fire prepared for the devil and his angels from the foundation of the world). The creation of humankind is considered here to be the result of the angels' fall and is consequently in and of itself an ontological accident, the outcome of the shadow which fell on all creation after the angels' fall. If we talk this thought out to the very end it will turn out that there would be no humans if the angels had not fallen. Of course, such a strange and barren concept would not correspond either to the sense of the biblical narrative in Genesis 1–2 or to the general fundaments of Christian anthropology and angelology. Although between *heaven and earth* a positive congruence exists, there remains at the same time an opposition; hence, the *replacement* of a part of one world by a part of the other world is generally an ontological misunderstanding. Therefore the question stands in all its force: Does the fact that a part of the angels is lost by heaven, namely the fallen ones, have any significance for the earthly world? Was not the world left incomplete or unprotected because of this?

In order to pose the question fully, it is necessary to take into consideration that for the angelic host the necessity of continual struggle with the demons arose, at first in the heavens and then after the fall of Satan "like lightning" in the aerial sublunary region and on earth for the defense and safeguarding of the world and humankind. "And war broke out in heaven. Michael and his angels fought against the dragon, and the dragon and his angels fought against them. But they did not stand, and no place was found for them in heaven" (Revelation 12:7-8). "They defeated him by the blood of the Lamb and by the word of their testimony and they did not love their soul even unto death" (v. 11). Here that power is named which made it possible for the angels effectively to defeat the dragon and his angels, i.e., to replenish the void generated after the fall; this is the blood of the Lamb, the power of divine incarnation, the help of the Godhuman. But the angels too displayed self-renunciation "even unto death" in this struggle. Consequently the angels who remained faithful took upon themselves the labor and tasks of the fallen ones and were as-

48

sisted by the power of Christ. It is obviously necessary to extend this to the guardian angels. The human race itself did not replenish the diminished number of angels but those angels who withstood and were confirmed in the struggle took it upon themselves to replenish the missing number of guardian angels, if such a shortage took place. Of course we cannot know if among the fallen angels there were any who were to become guardian angels. But such a devolvement or combination of services requires from the angels the broadening and replenishment of their powers so that this new and so to say extraordinary service would find a sufficient ontological basis. The Lord in His providence when He created the spiritual world was able to endow it with this capacity for delegated replenishing, of course, on the basis of sacrificial love.[14] Thus Divine Wisdom did not leave the human world deprived of the fullness of protection owing to the fall of the demons.[15]

There still arises a final, ultimate question in the doctrine of guardian angels: did the Godhuman in keeping with His human nature have a

14. "They did not love their souls even unto death" (Revelation 12:11). Does not the "death" of the angels here signify precisely this voluntary self-surrender for a new service, which is accompanied by the sacrifice of original proper nature, as it were? The angels defeated and drove the fallen angels out of heaven by occupying their ontological place in heaven, and themselves became what they were before their fall, depriving them in the same way of a fulcrum in the heavens, in the celestial pleroma.

15. Another question: Are not the souls of those who will be sent into eternal fire "prepared for the devil and his angels" (Matthew 25:41) at the Last Judgment found in a personal relation with the demons, having an affinity with them analogous to that which exists between humans and guardian angels? Of course those people in their earthly life were not deprived of the guardianship of the angel appointed to them whom they rejected by their sins and fell into the hands of demons, their proper, authentic doubles. In such a case the heavenly division into angels and demons corresponds in a certain degree to the division of the human race into "sheep" and "goats."

In ecclesiastical literature one can sometimes encounter the opinion that each human has not only a guardian angel but also its own demon-tempter, and is protected in a twofold manner: on the right and on the left. This idea cannot be supported in so general a form: a guardian angel is given by God, whereas a demon draws near on the basis of the sins of a given human in conformity with its sinful weakness. The presence of a demon near each human does not have that positive ontological basis which the attendance of a guardian angel possesses. But is there not here a distinction between the dark souls marked by personal proximity to the demonic world and who receive as their domain eternal fire "prepared for the devil and his angels" and other people who although accessible to the approach of demons thanks to their sinful weakness are nonetheless not subject to them? The black shadow of the fall in the heavens shrouds a certain portion of the human world but without being in a position to pervert the whole of it.

guardian angel? In orthodox theology a *negative* answer was already at one time given to this question (Bulgaris) and that answer is convincing above all because the hypostasis of the Logos is also His human hypostasis. It therefore cannot have for itself any likeness or prototype in the creaturely, even if angelic, world. The possibility *of a personal* guardian angel is here evidently excluded. But this does not at all exclude the angels' service to His human nature (besides their continual worship of His Divinity), with the whole angelic assembly taking part in this service of course (without any possibility of exception because no angelic rank is so lofty that it would prove to be too high for such service.)[16] Thus at the Nativity of Christ a multitude of the heavenly host suddenly appeared (Luke 2:13) praising God. In the wilderness after the temptation "angels served Him" (Mark 1:13; Matthew 4:11). The word of the Lord to Nathanael also refers to this: "from now on you will see the heaven open and the angels of God ascending and descending on the Son of Man" (John 1:51). But apart from these pieces of evidence about the holy angels' ministrations, there are generally in the Gospel indications concerning the service to Christ of separate angels, sometimes speaking about *one* angel, sometimes about *two.*

Let us investigate in order the appearances of *one* angel. First of all there is one such appearance in the Gospel of Matthew concerning the Nativity of Christ: "behold an angel of the Lord appeared to Joseph in a dream" with news of the Annunciation (Matthew 1:20-24), and similarly with a warning about the wickedness being prepared by Herod and about the necessity of flight into Egypt (2:12, 19). Is it not more natural to see in this angel, who in essence repeats to Joseph the news of the Annunciation, the same archangel Gabriel, the herald of good news? To him too is entrusted the further protection of the Child and His Mother. A second case of an appearance of *one* angel we find in the garden of Gethsemane when "an angel from heaven appeared to Him" *(aggelos ap' ouranou),* and strengthened Him (Luke 22:43). This angel is not directly named and only conjectures about him are possible. Is he not the same Chief Commander of the heavenly host Michael who was at the head of the host of heaven which defeated Satan "by the blood of the Lamb and the word of their testimony" (Revelation 12:11) — the guardian angel of the Hebrews from whom the Savior originated according to the flesh?[17] He is also the in-

---

16. In this one can see indirect proof that *the whole* angelic rank takes part in the service and protection of *the whole* humanity in the humanity of Christ, although not all angels are guardian angels in the immediate sense.

17. As prince of the Hebrews the archangel Michael is found in a special relation

tended servant of the One Who was the Glory of His people Israel.[18] In general if it is possible to bring Gabriel into a special bond with the Third Hypostasis according to the character of his service, then Michael finds himself in a similar bond with respect to the Second hypostasis as the prince of the Hebrews and the guardian angel of the human nature of the Lord.[19] In the Gospel account of Christ's Resurrection we find parallel pieces of evidence about the appearance of one and two angels. In the evangelists Matthew and Mark namely we find mention of *one* angel; in Luke and John, of *two*. According to the Gospel of Matthew "the angel of the Lord, after coming down from heaven, set about rolling away the stone from the door of the tomb and he sat on it" and informed the women about the Resurrection (Matthew 28:2-3, 5-7); in Mark 16:5-7 we find "a youth dressed in white clothing." On the other hand, in the Gospel of Luke we read: "suddenly two men in brilliant clothing stood before them" and announced to the women the Resurrection (Luke 24:4). Likewise in the Gospel of John we read, "and [Mary Magdalene] saw two angels in white [clothing] seated one at the head and the other at the foot where Jesus' body lay" (John 20:12). Is it not natural to see in one of these angels the archangel Gabriel, the messenger of the Holy Spirit by virtue of whom both Christ's conception and His resurrection were accomplished (Romans 8:11) and in the second Michael the chief commander? Is it not all the more natural to see the latter in the *one* angel who rolled away the stone from the tomb, spoken about by both Matthew and Mark? The angel who strengthened Him in the garden of Gethsemane naturally was the

---

with Moses as well, its leader and prophet. This is confirmed in the mysterious indication in Judith 9: "Michael the archangel when he was speaking with the devil while arguing over Moses' body did not dare to pronounce a reproachful sentence but said 'May the Lord prevent you!'" (Cf. 2 Peter 2:11). This indication (in which one generally sees a connection with the apocryphal *Assumptio Moysis*) is interpreted by ecclesiastical hymnography in the following manner: "Michael, the captain of the heavens and guardian of your body, appeared to you, O Moses, who led the Jewish tribe of old" (Service for the prophet Moses, 4 September, canon ode 7, tr. 3).

18. An opinion holds that the archangel Michael was likewise the one who came down to stir the water in Bethesda (John 5:4).

19. As Israel entered the Promised Land, which was as it were the historic cradle of the Savior (according to His human nature), "the leader of the host of the Lord" (Joshua 5:14-15), i.e., the archangel Michael, appeared to Joshua son of Nun and at first commanded him to remove the footgear from his feet "for the place where you are standing is holy" (as God also said to Moses on Mount Horeb) and then he spoke directly to him as Lord (6:2), i.e., in the person of the Lord. The archangel Michael is here the herald of the Word.

servant of the Resurrection. It also speaks about *two* angels in the Acts of the Apostles concerning the Ascension of Christ: "suddenly two men in white clothes stood before them" (1:10). Ought one not to see in the angels of the Ascension the same angels of the Resurrection? And so, Christ did not have and could not have had a personal guardian angel, because it would not correspond to the pre-eternal nature of the Logos, *through whom all things came to be* (John 1:12). But according to His human nature He too was being guarded and was receiving ministration from the angels (Mark 1:13), in the whole host together, and separately from one and from both of the pair of supreme archangels.[20]

The Christological facts lead us once more to a question that we have already examined, namely, do all the angelic ranks take part in the safeguarding of the human race or only the three lowest hierarchies (as Pseudo-Dionysios, Pope Gregory the Great, and others teach)? It must be resolved in this sense, that no hierarchy can be considered excluded from this service, if not directly then obliquely, because *all* bodiless powers in general are called *angels*. Not without foundation is this general idea connected with a text from the apostle Paul, Hebrews 1:14: "are not they all (i.e., angels) ministering spirits *(pneumata leitourgika)* sent for service *(eis diakonian)* for those who are to inherit salvation?" With this are associated separate facts (besides those indicated above) concerning the ministerial participation of even the most exalted spirits in human affairs: the seraphim in Isaiah 6:6 who burns Isaiah's lips with coal, Gabriel who appears to the prophet Daniel (Daniel 16:9, 21), the cherubim with the flaming sword at the gates of paradise (Genesis 3:24), and the chief commander who appears to Joshua son of Nun (Joshua 5:3-15).

20. The holy Church appeals to the holy archangels Michael and Gabriel: "O pair who have precedence now over the archangelic assembly" (Canon of the Bodiless Powers, tone 6, ode 4, tr. 2). Who would not naturally see this pair in the pair of angels of the Resurrection and Ascension of Christ?

CHAPTER 3

Angels in the Life of the World

Among many other mysteries, the Revelation of St. John the Theologian shows that human history, which has of course the history of the Church as its spiritual focus, is accomplished under the constant and active interaction of the angelic and human worlds. Angels and humans make human history and the form of this activity extends across the whole length of this prophetic book. Let us stop briefly at some particular visions. The first vision refers to the seven churches, including perhaps a general typology of church life. The Son of Man holds in his hand seven stars and seven golden lamps, "the seven stars being angels of the seven churches and the seven lamps, seven churches" (Revelation 1:20). With this a direct correspondence is already established between the human and angelic church,[1] with Christ later on addressing the churches in the person of their angels: "to the Angel of the church in Ephesus write" (2:1), and "to the Angel of the church in Smyrna write" (2:6), further to those in Pergamum (2:12), Thyatira (2:18), Sardis (3:1), Philadelphia (3:7), and Laodicea (3:14). Then follows the vision of chapter 4: the one seated on the throne and the twenty-four elders. They portray the plenitude of the human world: the twelve Old Testament forefathers of the tribes of Israel together with the twelve apostles, the forefathers of the new Israel.[2] With them are united before the throne of the Lamb the

---

1. True, sometimes one sees in the angels of churches the churches' bishops. But even if one were to allow such a conception, one should not accept it in a restrictive sense; if bishops can be called the earthly angels of churches this is only by virtue of the existence of their heavenly guardian angels and therefore one interpretation does not only not exclude but even presupposes the other.

2. This variant has been encountered since ancient times in the interpretation of

four living creatures who represent the angelic world (these four angelic living creatures are deliberately co-human, for they are the symbolic companions of the four evangelists, who wonderfully created an impression of Christ fourfold). Further "the mighty angel" (5:2) forewarns of the opening of the book of the consummation of the destinies of the world and the removal of its seals, thereby testifying to the power of the divine incarnation. "No one, *in heaven or on earth or under the earth,* could open and read this book" (5:3). "And when He took the book, the four living creatures and the twenty-four elders (i.e., the highest representatives of the angelic and human world, heaven and earth) fell before the Lamb . . . and they sang a new song, saying 'Worthy are You to take the book and remove the seal from it: for You *were slain and with Your blood purchased us for God out of every tribe and race and people; and You made us kings and priests for our God, and we shall reign on earth.'* And I saw and heard the voice *of many angels* around the throne and of the living creatures and elders, and their number was myriads of myriads and thousands of thousands" (5:8-11). "And I heard *every creature that is in heaven and on earth and under the earth, in the sea and all that is in them,* say: 'Blessing and glory and honor and power to the one seated on the throne and to the Lamb for ever.' And the four living creatures said: 'Amen'" (5:13-14). The Seer gives here a comprehensive expression of *the unity* of the angelic and human worlds, of heaven and earth, in the worship of the Lamb.

---

the image of the twenty-four elders (in Andrew bishop of Caesarea) but it is not the only one. Some, e.g. Zahn, object by alluding to the fact that the Seer, himself a chief apostle, could not have addressed one of the elders with such deference, calling him *kurie* (Lord) (Revelation 7:13-14) and receive elucidation from him, since he himself, as an apostle, is one of their number. This is a weighty objection but not indisputable because in Revelation events generally unfold not so much in temporal sequentiality as in interior connection. It is therefore not impossible for the Seer who remains within human limitations on earth to receive instructions from one of the patriarchs or apostles in their supercelestial glorified state. It is likewise difficult to make the conception of the elders as angels agree with their song to the Lamb that "You *have purchased* us for God from every tribe and race and nation and people" (Revelation 5:9). Nevertheless to the point is another interpretation which sees in the elders angels who find themselves in a particularly close relation with the twenty-four priestly rotations — angels who are especially human, if it can be so expressed. In such an interpretation the angel-animals correspondingly express the natural elements (the four cardinal points, the four signs of the Zodiac, arranged along perpendicular diameters, the totality of the vital forces of nature). And then we have in the angelic world the fullness of the earthly world both human and natural. And all angels and "every creature" are joined in their praises. The angelological and anthropological, or more precisely, the angelo-anthropological sense of this scene in the different interpretations of details remains in general one and the same.

First the elders and living creatures are named, then innumerable angels are named apart and finally every creature "in heaven and on earth and under the earth and in the sea and all that is in them" are joined in praising and the *Amen* of the angels confirms it. But this prayerful unity expresses of course *a vital* unity too, the unity of fate and common cause. The animal-angels and the human elders sing *together*: "You *purchased* us for God out of every tribe and tongue and people and race and made us kings and priests for our God and we shall reign on earth." *Angels together with humans speak of their redemption through the blood of the Lamb and of their co-reigning on earth.* These mysterious and full meanings of the words bear witness with majestic brevity to the unity and community of destinies of the angelic and human worlds, which in any case presupposes the unity of their whole life. This is as it were an epigrammatic expression of the relation of heaven and earth, a divinely inspired formula that expresses the connection of angelology and anthropology in all their inseparability.

With the removal of the first four seals (chapter 6) each of the four living creatures forewarns of the appearance of four horsemen with the words: "come and see." After the removal of the sixth seal, the Seer sees four angels standing on the four corners of the earth and restraining the four winds of the earth (7:1). But "another angel ascending from the rising of the sun and having the seal of the living God" (7:2) stops their harmful activity "until we mark the seal on the foreheads of the servants of our God" (7:3) and it was impressed on 144,000, on 12,000 from each of the tribes of Israel. After this there is again a vision in the heavens: "a great multitude of people which no one was able to count, out of all tribes and nations and peoples" stood before the throne and the Lamb in white clothes and with palm branches in their hands . . . and "all angels *(pantes hoi aggeloi)* stood around the throne and the elders and the four living creatures," worshipping and praising the Lord. Again all saved humanity and all angels are united here before God's throne (as it says in the letter to the Hebrews: "You have drawn near to Mount Zion and the city of the living God, to the heavenly Jerusalem, and myriads of angels and the triumphant assembly, and to the church of the firstborn who are written in the heavens, and to God the Judge of all and to the souls of the righteous who attained perfection and to Jesus the intercessor of the new covenant" (Hebrews 12:22-24).

After this follows the removal of the seventh seal and the vision of the seven angels to whom were given seven trumpets. The offering of incense by another angel precedes them, and he throws fire from the censer on the earth out of which "come voices and groans and lightning and earthquake" (8:5). Next comes a depiction of the calamities that are the result of the angels' sounding their trumpets (8:6ff.). At the sixth trumpet (9:13f.) are released four angels who were bound at the great river Euphrates and "had been prepared for the hour and day and month and year to kill a third part of the people" (9:15). Next, after the appearance of the angel wrapped in a cloud and announcing the accomplishment of the mysteries of God (chapter 10), at the seventh angel's trumpet in heaven echo the voices about the arrival of the kingdom of Christ with the new worship of twenty-four elders.

Chapter 12 speaks about the archangel Michael's and his angels' war in heaven against the dragon, about his overthrow, and about the dragon's activities on earth *after* his overthrow; these are disclosed in chapter 13. In chapter 14 we see "an angel flying in the middle of heaven who had an eternal Gospel to proclaim to the dwellers on earth and to every race and tribe and people and nation" (14:6-7). The angel appears as *the herald* of a new Gospel to all humanity and he speaks about the approaching judgment of the world. This text invites comparison with Matthew 24:14: "And behold the gospel of the kingdom shall be proclaimed throughout the universe as a testimony to all nations." From this comparison it follows that the ultimate proclamation of the eternal Gospel is the affair of this angel too, although of course it will be accomplished as well by the succession of the apostles. After this angel comes another angel with news about the destruction of Babylon, and a third with threats against "those who bow down before the beast and his image." The book of Revelation does not say how and through what means these angelic reproofs have an effect on the souls of people; it is only important that they reach them and in their own way guide their will. Characteristic is the end of chapter 14 which portrays an angel who finally appeals to the One sitting on the clouds and holding a sharp sickle: "take Your sickle and reap, because the time of harvest has come; for the harvest on earth is fully ripe" (14:15). In answer to this the One sitting throws His sickle down on earth. (In this case, by the way, the character of angels' participation in human history is elucidated: they are not only passive envoys for the execution of definite commands, as instruments, but also active and responsible agents who appeal to Christ Himself for timely and effective intervention in the destinies of the world.) Then after one angel with a sharp sickle *came out of the temple found in heaven,* another angel who had authority over fire came out from the altar and appealed to him. With a mighty shout he cried out to the one holding the sharp sickle to let loose his sickle and cut off the clusters of grapes, which he does (14:18-19). (Here we have a new example of the active quality of angelic service: one angel summons and prompts another to responsible and timely action in the world.)

Further, (chapters 15 and 16) seven angels receive seven chalices of God's wrath given them by one of the four living creatures, i.e., by the highest angel (a new manifestation of the active spontaneous action of the angelic world). One of these seven angels leads the Seer and shows him a woman sitting on a crimson beast, and he explains the vision (chapter 17). Although it is not said that this angel was sent deliberately by God to give this explanation, he does so as if on his own initiative. The following angel announces the fall of Babylon (chapter 18) and another angel casts down a millstone into the sea as an indication of Babylon's fall. Chapter 19 contains an episode about John falling at the feet of an angel who proclaimed to him the blessedness of those invited to the supper of the Lamb. John intended to worship him but the angel did not allow this, saying: "I am your fellow servant (*sundoulos,* co-slave) and the fellow servant of your brothers who have borne witness to Jesus; worship God" (19:10). With a loud voice an angel standing in the sun summons birds to the great supper of God to devour the corpses of the kings. Whatever the significance of these birds might be, in any case it is clear that here too the action of the angel is expressed in the leadership and direction of some spiritual and likewise earthly hosts.

In chapter 20 an angel binds Satan and the indirect result turns out to be the arrival of the thousand-year reign of Christ on earth (however it is to be understood) and "the first resurrection." In chapter 21 one of the seven angels holding the seven chalices with the seven last plagues shows the Seer vast Jerusalem, having the glory of God (vv. 10-11). "It had a great high wall and twelve gates *and on them twelve angels and names inscribed which are the twelve tribes of Israel*" (v. 12). This text must be compared (in addition of course with Ezekiel 48:31) with the text from Deuteronomy 32:8: "When the most high divided the tribes, dispersing the sons of Adam, he established the limits of the peoples according to the number of the angels of God" (in the LXX: *kata arithmon aggelon theou;* on the contrary, in the Hebrew text, the Vulgate, and in the Russian translation: "according to the number of the tribes of Israel"). The general idea of both texts consists in the establishment of a direct and positive bond between angels and humanity having spiritual roots in the twelve tribes of Israel. But in addition to this particular idea, the text itself contains an even more general idea about the unity and internal correspondence of the angelic and human worlds, about the *angelo-humanness* of creation. And this idea receives definitive and generalizing expression in verse 17 already known to us: "the one speaking with me [one of the angels] measured its wall [of the city] to be 144 cubits by human measure, which is also the measure of an angel."

In a manner of speaking, these mysterious words represent the grand total of the revelation about angels and humans which is contained in the Apocalypse; for they affirm the commensurability, the correlativity based on a kind of *identity* between an angel and a human in their common "measure." It likewise merits attention that one and the same angel shows the Seer the holy city descending from heaven with all its details, the river of life in it and the tree of life too. In this manner the cherub is removed who once barred the entrance into paradise and to the tree of life with his sword flaming and turning (Genesis 3:24). And when John fell once more at the angel's feet to worship him, he said again: "You must not do that, for I am your fellow servant. . . . Worship God" (Rev. 22:9). And in the final chapter of Revelation the very words of the Lord Jesus Christ are spoken by that angel in the first person, as if he were merging with the Lord Himself.[3]

Individual features of the texts cited from the Apocalypse demand a corresponding interpretation which with difficulty they sometimes yield. But one fundamental fact is attested in it with thunderous power and final certainty: the history of the world and humanity is *the common work* of angels and humans; it is not only human but angelo-human. The active participation which the angelic world takes in human life is laid bare for all to see in Revelation, although of course still not in its full extent. This would not correspond to the purpose of that prophetic book which is dedicated to the portrayal of the church's history in its fundamental moments and in the last times, in particular.

With respect to what interests us here, the eschatology of Revelation ought to be compared with the eschatology of the Gospels. The scene of the angels' harvest in the parable of the wheat and the tares is especially pertinent. "The harvest is the end of the age and the harvesters are angels. . . . The Son of Man will send His angels and they will gather out of His kingdom all temptations and those who commit transgressions" (Matthew 13:39, 41). A similar thing appears in the parable about the seine: "So shall it be at the end of the age: the angels will come out

---

3. A different understanding of Rev. 22:6 is possible in this respect. It is possible to consider that the angel's speech changes into the words of Christ himself beginning with verse 12 or at least with verse 16. In any case this cannot be said about verse 7, which is close to it in meaning, and it can be called into question with respect to verses 12-15.

and separate the wicked from the midst of the righteous and cast them into a fiery furnace" (13:49-50). To this corresponds the place of the holy angels at the second coming of the Lord: "the Son of Man will come in the Glory of His Father with His angels" (Matthew 16:27; Mark 8:38), "the Son of Man will come in His Glory and all the holy angels with Him" (Matthew 25:31), "in the appearance of the Lord Jesus from heaven, with the angels of His power" (2 Thessalonians 1:7), "at the voice of the archangel" (1 Thessalonians 4:16). The curtain separating both worlds will finally fall, the *unity* of both worlds will become evident, and the angelic world will become visible to humans. But this appearance of the end, of course, only completes the whole historical angelo-human process and springs from it, so to say.

The participation of angels in human destinies is likewise attested in the Old Testament, but much more fortuitously and fragmentarily. First of all it is manifested as the service of the express executors of God's commands, *instruments* of God's will, particularly God's wrath. As living instruments they mediate between God and the world. Such in particular are the following cases: 2 Samuel 24:16ff.: the angel of the Lord is a destroyer who strikes the people on account of David's sin; 1 Kings 13:18, 1 Chronicles 21:12: an angel who speaks to the Jewish nation the words of the Lord; 1 Kings 19:5 and 2 Kings 1:3: the angel who appears to the prophet Elijah; 2 Kings 19:35, cf. 2 Chronicles 32:21 and Isaiah 37:36: the angel who exterminates 185,000 Assyrians. (In its meaning Exodus 11–13, the tale about the extermination of the firstborn of Egypt, also handles this. But here although it is natural to expect the participation of an angel, it says "the Lord[4] struck all the firstborn in the land of Egypt" (12:29). The same point is dealt with in the appearance of the angel to Daniel in the lions' den (Daniel 6) and in the fiery furnace (Daniel 3), likewise the appearance of the archangel Gabriel to him (Daniel 8f.).

Appearances of angels in whom the Lord himself speaks occupy a special place and they will be spoken of on their own.

Texts which treat the service of angels as invisible guardians and guides of the earthly life of both individual persons and whole nations have, of course, an enormous, fundamental significance in the Old Testament. Relevant here, first of all, are Jacob's dying words before his sons when he is blessing Ephraim and Manasseh: "May the angel who delivers me from every evil bless these children: let my name and the name of my

---

4. Here we have a case, the reverse of the usual, when God himself speaks in the appearance of angels.

fathers Abraham and Isaac be pronounced on them and let them grow in great number in the midst of the earth" (Genesis 48:16). These words, first of all, can be related immediately to the guardian angel but they have a more general meaning since the mention of "my name and the name of my fathers" occurs in connection with the angel's blessing. This compels one to see in "the angel who delivers from every evil" not only a personal guardian angel but also a generic one, belonging to the whole generation of Hebrew patriarchs and in them to the whole Hebrew nation. (Is it the archangel Michael?) The passage from the book of the prophet Daniel "about the prince" of the Hebrew nation (Michael) ought to be compared with this. Here it speaks both about "the prince of the Persian kingdom" (10:13, 21; 12:1) and about "the prince of Greece" (10:20). It is difficult to believe that this enumeration had a comprehensive character, i.e., that from all the pagan nations only these two were singled out as having their own "princes." Rather, it is natural to understand this indication to have exemplary character. If the Lord "judges the nations justly and rules the tribes on earth" (Psalm 66:5) it is natural to think that all these nations and tribes have among God's servants their own guardian angels. This idea is suggested by a comparison with the fact that in the prophetic books there are prophecies about many pagan nations; one can say that they *are made worthy* of prophecy. Their sovereigns evidently find themselves under the special observation of God and consequently have their own heavenly protectors: not only Cyrus, "my shepherd" (Isaiah 44:28) and "my anointed" (45:1), but also Nebuchadnezzar, "the king of kings to whom the God of Heaven granted the kingdom, authority, power and glory" (Daniel 2:37-38; 5:18-19), and even Balthazar, about whose demise an especially mysterious sign is given by God in the guise of a hand tracing the letters "mene mene tekel parsin" (Daniel 5). Therefore a corresponding doctrine is usually expounded by the Church meaning that all nations in general have guardian angels.

The tale in the prologue of the book of Job has a similar meaning: "And one day the sons of God came and stood before the Lord, and among them Satan also came" (Job 1:6; 2:1). Although only the Lord's conversation with Satan is related, the object of this conversation about life on earth can on good grounds not be referred only personally to Satan. At the very least the Lord's questions to him in and of themselves are not solely intended for him but can be addressed to any of the sons of God as well, "who came" together with him. The vision of the prophet Micaiah has a similar sense (1 Kings 22:19f., 2 Chronicles 18:18f.). "And Micaiah said, 'Hear the word of the Lord: I saw the Lord sitting on His throne and all the heavenly host was standing before Him, on the right and left hand. And the Lord said: "Who will persuade Ahab that he should go and fall at Ramoth-gilead?" And one said one thing, another said something else. And one spirit stepped forward and stood before the Lord and said, "I will persuade him""" etc. (cf. Zechariah 3). This is again a vivid picture of the participation of angels in the direction of history.

Finally one ought to remember the book of the prophet Zechariah in whose six chapters one can see an Old Testament semblance of the visions of the Apocalypse explained to the prophet by angels. The first vision of a man on a chestnut horse accompanied by chestnut, piebald, and white horses is explained by the angel through the lips of the man himself: "These are they whom the Lord sent to go round the earth. And they answered the angel of the Lord and said: we have gone round the earth and behold the whole earth is inhabited and peaceful. And the angel of the Lord answered and said: Lord, Almighty One! How long will You withhold mercy from Jerusalem and on the cities of Judah with whom You have been angry for a hundred years already? Then in answer to the angel who was speaking with me the Lord uttered words of blessing, comforting words" (1:10-13) which he communicated to the prophet. In chapters 2-6 an angel explains to Zechariah different visions which concern the history of the Jewish nation and the whole world. But in addition to these prophetic visions and testimonies, the angels' participation in human history is disclosed in the Old Testament through all the instances of angels' appearances and actions which we have already noted in another connection, beginning with the cherub with a fiery sword barring the way into paradise. Perhaps having the most symbolic significance is the appearance "of the captain of the heavenly host" with a drawn sword to Joshua son of Nun near Jericho (Joshua 5:13-15) in that critical hour of the history of God's chosen people when its earthly hosts were preparing to conquer the land promised them by God and destined to become the place of the Son of God's birth.

*   *   *

According to the above cited testimonies of the Word of God, the holy angels actively participate in the life of the human world, and *together with* us they make its history. Of course, they realize their own share of participation, so to say, from above or from outside; they preserve their angelic nature and are not confused with humanity, performing *a common work* with it. A series of conclusions of exceptional, paramount importance manifestly springs from this fundamental fact which is established on the basis of Revelation. It is necessary to turn away completely from an understanding of angels as passive executors who display no creative work of their own. Such a reduction of the bodiless spirits to the role of simple instruments is incompatible with their dignity and their nature equally. Even in human terms an authentic executor or envoy is not a slave or merely an instrument, but makes the goal of the mission one's own purpose and realizes it creatively. All the more ought one to think this about the spiritual world, and the service of angels.

Of course, angels are ministering spirits, *leitourgika pneumata eis diakonian apestalmena*. But this ministering predetermination of theirs only attests that the purpose and goal of their activity is not found in themselves but in the human world with which therefore their existence is united by indissoluble bonds. But this connection in no way signifies that angels were less active even than humans and were less responsible in their service. Of course, in cases of exceptional importance angels *are sent* directly by God for a definite commission. The most important case when direct sending takes place is the Annunciation. The archangel Gabriel was *sent* initially to Zechariah and then to the Virgin Mary. But it is impossible even here to think that he was merely a simple instrument for the transmission of God's will, with no deliberate, *personal* relation to it. For the omnipotence of God every means of announcing his will is open. But if for this supreme sending precisely the archangel Gabriel was chosen, then this election corresponded to his personal qualities and his particular vocation. And the very fulfillment of his sending, the Annunciation, presupposes from his side the particular effort of creative exertion and inspiration.[5] Surely this mission, which is in general the summit of angelic service, constituted his goal and purpose already from the hour of God's judgment on the fallen primogenitors when the paradise evangel of "the Seed of the Woman" was announced? True, the Word of God bears witness that the mysteries of the divine incarnation and redemption were not revealed even to the angels (1 Peter 1:2; Ephesians 3:10). But this in no way excludes the possibility of their foreknowing and penetrating God's future ways, although only on the basis of Old Testament prophecies given

5. The holy church indirectly confirms this by developing the brief words of the Gospel of the Annunciation into an entire conversation of Mary with the archangel, in the canon and stichera of the feast (Service of the Annunciation). (See *Festal Menaion*, translated by Mother Mary and Archimandrite Kallistos Ware [Faber and Faber, 1969], pp. 448-60. Translator's note.)

to people and known, of course, to angels. And the greatest knowledge and penetration is natural in an archangel, who burns with desire to serve this mystery from the very beginning of the history of the human race, and it could not remain passive. It was expressed of necessity in the archangel's participation in human affairs, in his influence on their destinies, as the Word of God partly opened this to glimpses. The archangel Gabriel appears to the prophet Daniel in order to announce to him the fortunes of the Hebrew nation in connection with the history of the pagan kingdoms, generally speaking in the context of universal history. With his lips he outlines the plan of universal history, leading to Bethlehem as to its focus (Daniel 8–12), he pronounces the saying about the seven weeks which must be fulfilled before the coming of the Messiah, i.e., before the Annunciation (chapter 9), and finally he utters to Daniel the prophecies concerning the dread last times, the appearance of antichrist (8:11, 36) and the last judgment (chapter 12). On the whole the angel of the Annunciation is the Old Testament interpreter of universal history; his gaze penetrates into the future and already beholds in it that work which the Lord will give him to complete: the Annunciation. The relation of the archangel Gabriel to human history is not merely passive contemplation of what has been announced by him but active participation in it, in accordance with his own testimony.[6] Therefore one can say that in the person of the archangel Gabriel the form of the relation of the angelic world to the human world is disclosed, namely, the sending of angels, which must be understood not only as the fulfillment of God's command but also as inspiration proper and creative work, both of which accord with it.

This is particularly underlined in Revelation when it speaks about the struggle of the archangel Michael and his angels with the dragon (Revelation 12:7, 11) that ends with the casting down of the latter out of heaven. In spite of this in the given case where it is a question of an event

---

6. The archangel Gabriel speaks about himself to Daniel: "Now I return to fight with the prince of Persia and when I come out then see, the prince of Greece will arrive. I am informing you what is inscribed in the true scripture and there is no one who would support me in this except Michael your prince. Since the first year of Darius the Mede I became for him a support and reinforcement" (Daniel 10:20-21; 11:4). It is necessary to read these verses with open eyes. Some recent commentators (Charles, Lomeyer) see in "the strong angel" (Revelation 10:1) (*ischuros;* Hebrew *gvr*) the archangel Gabriel. If this conjecture is true, it only supports our observation with respect to the text of the prophet Daniel. This angel who placed one foot on land and the other in the sea announces the final mystery, that "time will be no more," and gives a mysterious little book to the Seer to eat.

that occurred *within* the angelic world itself, in the heavens, there is no mention of angelic service as a sending. But here it is directed especially to the self-renunciation of the angels "who did not love their own souls even unto death" (Revelation 12:11) in this struggle. And the power of angelic service to the world is not only obedience to the will of God out of love for God but also their own love for the world. The words of the Lord about what "joy there is among the angels of God over one repentant sinner" (Luke 15:10) bear witness to this love of the angels for humankind.[7] Angelic ministry is the angels' sacrificial love for humans but in virtue of this it is also their own creative self-disclosure. Similar to this the angels who were confirmed in the good with the archangel Michael at the head found new powers of sacrificial love through the struggle with the dragon and his host, and through this they were disclosed for themselves in a new way. The degree and form of their participation in the history of the world has for them on the whole an analogous significance where they likewise grow and find a new self-disclosure. Although angels are already finally determined in the good this does not exclude even for them the possibility of subsequent growth and self-disclosure, for as creaturely beings they are not absolute and they possess the capability for growth, above all in eternal life in God but further in creation together with the world and humankind.

Creative work does not exist without *freedom;* the latter is realized for a limited creation as the choice of one definite possibility from a whole series. Thus, for angelic service as well as for any creative work, the law retains its force that because it does not have absolute perfection, which is proper only to the creative work of God, it tolerates different possibilities and fluctuations in its realization. According to a natural interpretation the mysterious text of 1 Corinthians 6:3 has precisely this sense: *do you not know that we will judge* (krinoumen) *the angels?* The historical destinies of the world and humans depend not only on themselves but also on angels and consequently on the degree of their zeal and the higher expediency of their activity.[8] Angels are not all-knowing and almighty. They did not

---

7. Other words of the Lord hold a similar meaning: "Any who confess Me before people the Son of Man confesses before the angels of God; and whoever rejects Me before people will be rejected before the angels of God" (Luke 12:8-9). Confession before the angels of God excludes, of course, their passive-indifferent relation to the world; on the contrary it presupposes their deep participation in its destinies. (Characteristic in this sense is a variant of this text in Matthew 10:32, "and I will confess *before my Heavenly Father,*" by Supreme Love.)

8. Perhaps in order to develop this general idea it was said before that "the saints will

know fully the mystery of divine incarnation, and only learned about it through the church (Ephesians 3:10); consequently they did not thoroughly comprehend the hidden meaning of universal history and in particular, of Old Testament history which is wholly understood only by way of the divine incarnation. According to the Church's testimony in her sacred hymnody they *were astonished* at the Theotokos's entrance into the temple and her honorable Dormition, as well as at the ascension from earth into heaven.[9] But inasmuch as their knowledge is limited, so too is their action. Of course, their wisdom and knowledge, in conformity with the nature of the bodiless spirits and their sanctity, immeasurably exceeds human powers (although one must not forget that their knowledge of our world occurs as it were from the outside and in that respect it characteristically proves to be limited in comparison even with human knowledge). True, the face-to-face vision of God and the effusion of divine grace make angels into beings who are filled with divine illumination as "second stars," even though they are created. Nonetheless angels remain limited as creaturely beings and in virtue of this limitedness they are also relative or, what is the same thing, not unerring. Thus they are also changeable, i.e., they grow. In other words the history of the world exists not only for humans but also for angels although differently as a result of the distinction of their nature. Above all it is for them the domain of angelic service and consequently of creative work which continually sets its own tasks.

Angels do not have God's omniscience and their comprehension of what unfolds in a worldly process remains creaturely-limited. But this knowledge is essentially other than human knowledge. Angels are not born and they do not spring up in their being in an earthly process. According to prevailing church doctrine, all angels are created simultaneously at the beginning of the world. Here there is no begetting, no multiplying, nothing similar to marriage, for angels "do not take a spouse or marry." Therefore angels contemplate the course of world life from the heights of supernal being. But this contemplation does not remain idle or passive. Angels took part as servants of God in the good ordering of this world in all its parts and principles. Through this service angels compre-

---

judge the world" (1 Corinthians 6:2), where the concept of "world" is creation in general; then comes a more particular disclosure: to judge angels (and already of course, humans).

9. Of course *astonishment* here means not only amazement before the unknown but also admiration for God's destinies as they are being accomplished and a new, deeper comprehension of them. (Such is the philosophical meaning of *thaumazein* which is *the beginning* of philosophizing.)

hend the ways of God but at the same time they determine their own correlation with this world. For as "the heaven" *in its entirety* is reflected in the universe, so does each angel in his own domain form a certain creaturely prototype of the earthly world. Each angel finds himself in the universe and has in it his own domain and task. (This is not changed by the fact that not all angelic ranks immediately have an earthly ministry, even if this is actually the case. By reason of the unity of the angelic world and the community of its "assembly," the highest ranks of angels take *their* part, though indirectly, in the common cause of the world.) The angelic world in its entirety, as does every angel separately, realizes its own proper task, and has its own vocation in this world (even if it was not yet disclosed to this world). It is difficult for us to distinguish these *separate* services which are shown to us in the massive and magnificent images of Revelation and other sacred books. Our comprehension of the guardian angels comes all the more easily: having been assigned to each human from conception and brought near through baptism they "always see the face of the Heavenly Father" (Matthew 18:10). These angels have a direct and immediate task — to watch over their *friend,* their earthly relative, their image and likeness.[10]

According to St. John of Damascus and other fathers, an angel possesses the image of God as does a human. The image of God is imprinted *in two ways:* in the world of angels and in the human world. This doubling has as its basis that one and the same idea or prototype of a given person exists in the angelic world as an angel and in the human world as a human, and this unity of Sophianic theme forms the basis for the correlation of a guardian angel and a human. But this pre-eternal design for creation in God is supertemporal, existing from all eternity, and is realized in the angelic world in time, but before the birth of a given human as well as the appearance of all humanity. Though not as yet born on earth, a human pre-exists not only pre-eternally in the creative design of God but also in the creaturely world, not, however in the earthly, but in the heavenly world, because in creation that one's angel already exists. One can say that through the creation "of heaven," i.e., of the angelic world "in the beginning" the Sophianic seeds of the whole earthly, human world are already created. This world is not a repetition of the angelic world, which re-

---

10. Nothing prevents from seeing in the so-called anticipatory grace *(gratia praeveniens)* the activity of the guardian angel who is the medium of gracious influence. In general the place of the angels' influence ought to be introduced in theological teaching about grace, which thus far has not happened.

mains different in nature from it, but it is one with it in a Sophianic manner on the basis of the unity of the Wisdom of God. The heavenly world is the ideal anticipation of the earthly, and the earthly is the real fulfillment of the heavenly, and in the aggregate both comprise a single creation "in the beginning," i.e., in the Wisdom of God, "heaven and earth." In precisely this sense one can also say that a guardian angel is *pre-created* for the human under his protection who is to come into the world. He loves his likeness beforehand, his friend; he wills and expects his arrival in the world. Through him he has his own fulcrum in the world, and he himself becomes a participant in the universe. But this expectation cannot be understood as passive and inactive. If in the history of humanity everyone has so to say their own place, being linked by the unity and continuity of a pragmatic bond, by the solidarity of all humanity in the common work of history, we must accept the same concerning the angelic world in no less a degree. For angels, as far as they abide in service to humankind, this common work holds good. A guardian angel is connected with the human entrusted to him not as with a solitary entity but as with a member of the common human family by the most intimate means, as with a son of his own time, nation, family, and finally, with a successor and son, a father and forebear. In a human family no one member can be singled out or isolated. Therefore in serving his proper purpose, a guardian angel unavoidably extends it to the limits of pan-humanity.

A guardian angel *makes ready* the realization of his own Sophianic idea in the world, the coming of a human into the world with whom he stands in *a personal* relation as with his own other. In this sense he is the servant of God in the work of creating that human. In the angelic world the idea of a human precedes one's birth and is preserved, of course, even *after* one's departure from this world, after the death of a human, because one's angel from the angelic world continues and corrects one's work, unfinished or spoiled. How? We do not know now, but God's work cannot remain in the world unfinished. The image of the harvest in which angels *separate* the darnel from the wheat and *burn* the darnel speaks precisely about this activity of the angels who gather and thereby fulfill and correct the works of the children of humankind.

Angels make history together with humankind but along their own paths; and in particular, the life of each individual human is made ready before birth and directed by one's angel in such a manner that we are not now able to see. This labor of a guardian angel is the creative effort of his love, active love. This love craves to be poured out on its friend, to give him the fullness of its gifts and, at the same time, to be united with him in a certain blessed syzygy, although this union of angelic and human worlds concerns only the future age. This reunion is necessary not only for humans but also for angels for the fullness of their life and blessedness to which they were called in their creation.

The *personal* character of a guardian angel's relation with his human likeness is unbreakable for it has its ontological foundation in the unity of their Sophianic root. An angel is created as a guardian and friend, as the other, of precisely a given human person; here is his proper place in the world. But there can exist a disparity between him and the human person similar to what can exist between the image and likeness of God in the human. Having the image of God as its inalienable ontological foundation, as the original givenness, the human is called with its freedom to realize in itself the likeness of God, as its project, and to show in a creaturely manner and in this sense to repeat in itself, as it were, the image of God. But being given for its realization to human freedom which already conceals different possibilities in itself, the likeness can also not be realized. Then "his work will burn" so that he "himself will be saved but as if by fire" (1 Corinthians 3:15) and "being clothed he will prove to be naked" (2 Corinthians 5:3). It is possible for a human not to succeed, not in its divine foundation which remains inviolable in the capacity of a proto-garment, but in its creaturely free realization — the image is not united with but separated from its likeness. And the result of this human failure in a certain sense extends to the guardian angel inasmuch as he is still in need of the human fulfillment of this likeness, even though in and of himself he has his own divine image that is realized in an angelic likeness.

After the fall of Satan and his angels, the angels, according to the teaching of the Church, were firmly established in the good to such a degree that they lost their ease of creaturely changeability. They *exceeded* their creaturely freedom in the sense that they overcame the different possibilities included in it, having retained a single one — full obedience to the Creator. They worthily realized it and in this way proved to be higher, on the other side of freedom. In spite of this, the guardian angels of fallen humanity remain without their personal human likeness. Nonetheless, angelic labor is not futile nor is their love. They have its fruit in all saved humanity which will acquire the force of *all* humanity similar to how the good angels acquired the whole fullness of the angelic world and compensated by themselves for the devastation in heaven caused by the fall of Satan and his angels. Here is disclosed the power of the mysterious words of the parable: "Take from him the talent and give it to the one who has ten talents, for to everyone who has it will be given and increased and from the one who has not, even that which he has will be taken away" (Matthew 25:28–29; Luke 19:26). "For to the one who has it will be given and increased; and from the one who has not, even that which he has will be taken away" (Matthew 13:12; Mark 4:25; Luke 8:18). This is said about the last metaphysical removal and increase both in the angelic and in the human world. But this possibility of removal and increase, being realized by the creative act of God's judgment, is the guarantee that no angelic labor, and no human labor, will remain fruitless, that it cannot be smothered in the sands of non-being, but bears its fruit directly or indirectly.[11] The whole harvest will be gathered into the Lord's granary and he will burn it up, and only that which already belongs to non-being will be cast down into non-being. Divine infallibility and immanent expediency serve as the guarantee of this, despite the confusion, complication, and direct destruction which are introduced into it by badly directed creaturely freedom. But that by which all are able to find personal salvation from fire and not be deprived of their talent is of course the most favorable possibility for the creature. The guardian angel immediately cares for this very thing in the continuation of the earthly life of a human. But this labor *begins* long before the human's arrival in the world. It is more accurate to say that this work begins with the very creation of the world and of the human in the world, and it is impossible to indicate a time when an angel's loving concern for his human likeness would have left an angel of God. The emergence of the world *before* humankind is already the preparation of a place for human life. The creation of Adam is already the beginning of life for *each* of his descendants, and this means that in him is foreseen the task for each guardian angel too. We do not know in what this particular work of each guardian angel in the world consists. But we can confidently indicate one of the forms of this assistance of the angels, prayer before the throne of God. Prior to our earthly birth, throughout our life, after our death and at Christ's Dread Judgment our guardian angel prays for us before the Lord and is our faithful friend. Does not the presence of the angels of God at the Dread Judgment, so expressively indicated by the Lord himself (Matthew 16:27; 25:31; 2 Corinthians 1:7) attest that the holy angels as servants of God for the making of the world's history, as fellow

---

11. This metaphysical moment of removal and increase, indicated beforehand in its ontological necessity by the Word of God, does not exhaust the whole of eschatology. The latter contains further mysteries (if only of "the salvation as through fire" indicated by the apostle Paul, in which the final disclosure of the non-futility of angels' labor even on behalf of sinners is completed).

participants in human destinies, are naturally called to bear witness about humans, and to what measure they have approximated their heavenly prototypes? Does not the saying of the Lord speak about this too — "Whoever confesses Me before people the Son of Man will confess *before the angels of God*" (Luke 12:8)? Angels will be not only natural and summoned witnesses, but the final division will occur through them: "It will be thus at the end of the world: the angels will come out and separate the wicked from the midst of the righteous" (Matthew 13:49).[12]

Our ignorance of God's ways in human destinies hinders our uncovering the guardian angel's concern for us prior to our birth. We only know that through our own birth we are empirically given and defined, being attached to a certain point of space and time. We are born from specific parents and we receive our homeland in a specific place; we belong to a specific nation and historical epoch. We live in a specific milieu, cosmic, geographic, historical, and sociological. We trace the threads of our bonds and the roots of our provenance as long as our eyes last. The biography of every human being begins in this sense before one's birth in the world in a given definite point of space and time and the time and place of one's birth in the world is of course not accidental. One belongs ontologically to that place and time and Goethe's utterance that the ones who live for their own time lived for all times contains of course a self-evident truth (as the contrary, vain regrets that we were not born in other better times bear witness only to an insensitivity for our own self). All points in the world's space and time are equally worthy and valid. Empirically we have an infinitesimal grasp of this interior necessity of our biography and genealogy. But it is shown to us by the Word of God in the genealogy of Christ, the central line of history. We must in any case postulate this necessity. It will be disclosed for us before our eyes only when the history of the world is displayed for us from the beginning to the end in its plan and connection. But knowledge that the guardian angel was standing at the head of our cradle when it was still empty, that he carried our soul in his arms after receiving it from God at the hour of our birth is for us a postulate of faith, arising from our love and respect for our guardian angel.[13] In

---

12. St. Basil the Great notes apropos of this that "thus the apostle, knowing that the angels are appointed to people as pedagogues and tutors, summons them as witnesses" (*On the Holy Spirit,* chapter 13).

13. This does not touch upon the origin of the human soul (the hypotheses of creationism or traducianism). In any case our soul has in itself a divine principle which is implanted in the human being (which constitutes his birth). The mediating ministering participation of the guardian angel takes place with this implanting.

a word he remains and watches over us even before the cradle; without him, without his assistance and participation our birth would not have happened and we are obligated to him for our entrance into this world.[14] Of course, he is only the executor of God's creative command, but this execution already contains in itself the participation of the executor.

The guardian angel's love for us beyond the limits of this life is so unknowable for us and at the same time so knowable. According to the doctrine of the Church, the guardian angel stands before our death bed and receives our soul;[15] he accompanies it through the toll gates and guides its life in the new world. He becomes visible and accessible to us after its separation from the body. When the body's curtain falls, "an opening of the senses," a broadening of experience occurs. The soul finds itself in a world of spiritual, bodiless entities and first of all comes to know its own guardian angel. This contact is one of the first enrichments of our spiritual life which the state of bodily death gives. And this contact with our guardian angel, provided its possibility is not removed by grave sins, constitutes a school in which our soul grows and is strengthened for eternity, and comes to know its very self through its heavenly friend. On the whole little has been revealed by the Church about the soul's sojourn beyond the grave and its life which of course cannot come to a standstill or cease. But what is revealed is sufficient in order not to doubt in the continuation of the guardian angel's loving care for us. The prayers of the earthly church are effective for the dead; those who live on earth can help the deceased. We turn to the Mother of God and to all the saints with prayers for help at the hour of death, as well as after death and at the Dread Judgment. This same possibility of help, of course, is not taken away from the guardian angel which the Church portrays as not abandoning us on the verge of death and beyond its threshold and even in the resurrection, at the Dread Judgment.[16] And if his closeness to us beyond the

14. Therefore malicious suicides, which in general are a rebellion against life, are blasphemy against the life-giving Holy Spirit and an especially grave sin against the guardian angel, a rejection of his love and concern.

15. In a general parable form this is shown in the parable about the rich man and Lazarus: "a poor man died and he was brought by angels to Abraham's bosom" (Luke 16:22). It is remarkable that this truth was known to the pagan world. In Plato we read: "they say that each person's demon *(daimon)* leads the deceased, who was given to him in life, and he guides him to a certain place from which those who are assembled must be directed to Hades after instruction" (*Phaidon*, 130).

16. "When my Judge and God will judge and condemn me who am condemned by my conscience before that judgment, do not forget your servant, O my guide" (Canon of

border of this life can be explicit, is he not then our tutor in eternal life, does he not open to us the mysteries of the world and of our own destiny that we do not know but only sense? Does he not liberate us from that childish ignorance out of which we must come to the fullness of knowledge, do not his lessons fill in that fragmentariness and transitoriness of our life, which is the cause of our ignorance? For he is free from this limitedness, he lives for all time with the world. And if this earthly life is only a birth for the future age, is he not the tender mother who watches us, by giving the first lessons to a maturing infant (as this is depicted in icons in the image of an angel taking in hand our infant soul)? Is not our whole life from the time of our emergence from non-being until our birth into the life of the future age filled with contact with our guardian angel and through him with the angelic world? And will this blessed bond of love and friendship cease even beyond the border of this world under a new heaven and a new earth?

But here the human word breaks down. . . .

---

the Guardian Angel, ode 7, tr. 2). "When thrones are set up and the books opened, and the ancient of days is seated and humans are judged and angels stand before, and the earth shakes and everything shudders and trembles, then show me your philanthropy and deliver me from Gehenna, by imploring Christ" (Ode 8, tr. 2). "When the trumpet's dread sound shall raise me from the earth for judgment, then stand near me quietly and joyous, and with the hope of salvation take away my fear" (Ode 8, glory).

CHAPTER 4

The Nature of Angels

The whole angelic world is immediately turned towards humanity through the company of guardian angels. In them, by them, and through them the *co-humanness* of the whole angelic world is established. If its division into hierarchies removes the highest ranks from direct service to the human world, all the same, *the whole* angelic assembly takes part in the safeguarding of our world, owing to its spiritual unity and the unity of its common work, and is its *collective* guardian. And since on earth the world is essentially human, has its focus in humankind, and is humankind, the angelic host serving this world is co-human, and must be understood in keeping with its bond with humankind.[1] But this bond in its turn can be understood only in their proper life. The holy angels are the creaturely glory of God, "second lights," the creaturely mirror of God's powers and perfections. Their continual glorification is the effective reflection of this contemplation in their own spirit: the Glory seen by them, the Wisdom of God, glorifies itself in them and through them, and they are the creaturely glory of uncreated Glory. Glory in glory begets the glory of Glory — glorification. Angels are continually immersed in the abyss of divine life and are nourished by it. It is their proper life by participation, but not by nature. Scholastic theology in the west endeavors to differentiate what belongs to angels by nature and what is given them by grace. But this distinction (as in anthropology) cannot be sustained to the end. For angels are created as "second lights" already *according to their nature.* Just as fish live in water and birds in the air by nature, so too is it proper to an-

---

1. In the apocryphal *Ascensio Moysis* we meet the characteristic expression *ho aggelos tes anthropotetos,* the angel of humanity.

gelic nature that angels live not for themselves, not in their own nature which, in this sense, one can say, does not even exist, but by divine life. Of course, against this one can object by alluding to Satan and the fallen angels: having been torn away from God they continue their life, as it were, in their own nature. But their life is not the proper life of ontologically self-legitimate beings; on the contrary, it remains parasitical — around humankind and its world as the self-named "prince of this world" and his minions. Outside this parasitism when the prince of this world will be driven forth, no nature or proper life will remain in the demons but only an empty hypostatic mask, lacking independent nature, with its one thirst (hellish fire, second death, fiery lake, unsleeping worm — all these images speak of a burning without combustion, a thirst without slaking).

Hypostasis is proper to angels and it is in a literal sense *hupostasis* or *substantia,* the support or receiver of divine life which is of course for them supernatural, graced. Their nature is to live by grace, like a mirror, like second lights. They can be called gods according to grace, by communicating in divine life before and more immediately than humankind. Does not the psalmist say about them "God has taken his place in the council of gods, in the midst of gods he makes judgment" (Psalm 81/82:1)?[2] Perhaps someone will point out that the same must be said about humankind which is predetermined for divinization, for the reception of grace. But a difference remains between an angel and a human: a human has its own world and its own nature which *is preserved* even in the reception of grace, hence the Chalcedonian dogma of the indivisible but unmixed union of *both* natures in Christ, divine and human. Humanity lives its own proper life and in its own proper world even when God will be all in all. Angels do not have in this sense their own proper nature and their own world. Because their nature is perfectly transparent for God, theophanies can also occur as angelophanies. For this reason the Son of God was not able to assume an angelic nature — as Hebrews 2:16 underscores this point — His becoming an angel would signify only His assuming His own proper nature and in this sense repeating Himself. Therefore the apostle deliberately attests that "[Christ] does not take upon Himself angels, but the seed of Abraham" (Hebrews 2:16). Therefore for angels

---

2. More clearly in Psalm 96/97:7 in the Russian translation (consequently according to the Hebrew text): "bow down before Him, all you gods," whereas in the LXX and the Church Slavonic translation, "*all His angels* bow down to Him" (likewise in Hebrews 1:7).

both their nature and their life are a direct reception of grace, a communion in divine life.

The image of God in angels about which the holy fathers bear witness is realized for them in hypostatic existence, personal self-consciousness. It unites of course with *the possibility* of independent life, characteristic of spiritual beings. But *the content* of this life is determined not by the proper nature of the angelic world but directly and immediately by the nature of Divinity. Thus, if humans are called *gods* in the Word of God and ecclesiastical literature, in an even more direct and immediate sense this is applicable to angels who are rays of Divinity, creaturely hypostatized. Sophia, the Wisdom of God, realized herself as a creature in hypostatic choirs, heavenly hierarchies which know her and live by her. This is the creation of the angelic world. And already in connection with this creation and on its foundation she again realized herself as a creature in the human world, in the fullness of the image of God, i.e., in the unity of hypostasis with its *proper* nature. She integrally and chastely became the creaturely nature of humanity, multi-hypostatic but of one essence. One cannot speak about the angels' oneness of essence or about angelic nature in the same sense as one speaks about human oneness of essence, following the example of the tri-hypostatic Trinity, one in essence and indivisible.

From the absence of a proper nature in the angelic rank arises an important consequence with respect to the individuality of angels in comparison with humans. Strictly speaking, humankind does not have individuality, so far as this relates to its nature. It has a hypostasis which however is not individuality in this sense, so far as the human race is of one essence, of one nature. Each human exists hypostatically *for its own sake* solely and personally, but at the same time, naturally. Each is *one and the same* in all hypostases, a single Adam-Christ, who includes in His human nature the whole fullness of humanity and in it, in His Body, contains all human possibilities. Each human has the fullness of the image of God. But this means not only that because each one has a hypostasis, each human can be combined collectively with other hypostases in a multi-unity in the manner of the tri-hypostatic God but also that each human possesses the fullness of nature, as God possesses His Wisdom, Divine Sophia, Ideas, the Uncreated World. Humankind is Sophianic in its nature and this does not make room for a *natural* distinction in humankind which supposes the principle of individualization through limitation, according to the principle *omnis individuatio est negatio*. Of course, in the order of historical, temporal emergence each human is limited and consequently individual, fastened to some one point of being. It is deprived of that universalism, Sophianic universality, which is concealed in it and will be revealed in the fullness of time. This is connected with the state of the whole sinful world's becoming dark and heavy as a result of Adam's fall. But each human already has *everything* potentially in its nature and is this everything, which belongs to each one from birth. In virtue of this humankind is a *generic,* single though multi-hypostatic being, which comes to be by the path of *birth,* i.e., by repeating itself in multiple hypostases. A new creative act for the creation of each human being is superfluous,[3] for humankind is *one* in nature. Hypostases are modes of this single being, which are distinguished as different centers of the self-consciousness of a single essence, but utterly similar among themselves.

An angel, on the contrary, really is individual not only by means of his hypostatic choir that in virtue of this hypostaseity is single and unrepeatable, but also by his *nature,* so far as the latter is a single ray of Divine Sophia in creaturely-hypostatic consciousness, but not the whole Sophia in her integrity. Of course the concepts of partialness and divisibility as they exist in the natural world are not applicable here. Sophia is one and indivisible, but she admits plurality, multi-centrism in her creaturely revelation, a dynamic (and not a mechanical) plurality. Each ontic ray, isolated out of her all-unity, without ceasing to dwell in it, lays the foundation for an individual, particular being. The being of each angel is thus a ray or radius, descending from a single sun. It exists together with other rays, is inseparable from them, and they all compose "an assembly," the fullness of the noetic heaven. But angels could not arise through simple reproduction, i.e., self-repetition, as humans did, but are created simultaneously, each by a special creative act, according to the doctrine of the Church. Therefore the ontological individuality of being is inherent in them; each of them is not only a hypostatic form of being, but also its natural mode. According to the principle, *omnis individuatio est negatio,* such individualization would be detrimental to their being and limit it if each angel had this innate nature for themselves and in themselves. But this cannot be the case (except for the fallen angels who perverted their angelic being by their self-affirmation). Angels have their nature not in themselves, but in God; they live by means of communion in the divine life — or as it could also be expressed, not by means of their own life but of a foreign life (if the

---

3. Deserving of attention is that in this respect a human is put on the same footing as the representatives of the pre-human-animal world. God equally says to the creeping water creatures, fish, and birds formed on the fifth day: "be fruitful and multiply" (Genesis 1:22) as he says to humankind (Genesis 1:28).

life of Divinity can ever be called foreign for any sort of creature). By being immersed in the deepest reaches of divine life, they destroy their soul; by communing in the Divine Pleroma, they lose their individuality as *limitation*. But this is possible on condition that these individualities of the angels even in their creaturely interrelations, as hypostatized rays of Glory, also remain in union among themselves. Not being natural this union can only be hypostatic, i.e., *a collectivity,* full concord in the mutual love of angelic hypostases. The Church therefore names it *the angelic assembly* which is distinct from *the human race.*

The collectivity of the angelic world is based not on oneness of being as is human collectivity, in which is realized only human nature, one in essence and multi-hypostatic. Rather, it overcomes the ontological individualization of angelic nature by love. Therefore it is constructed *not on multiformity* (multi-hypostaseity) *in unity* (like the human collectivity), but on the union of plurality which is preserved but not absorbed by it. Such a union in which difference is preserved can only be *hierarchical,* and we know that the angelic world consists of hierarchies in nine ranks. The doctrine concerning them, already incompletely outlined in the letters of the apostle Paul (Romans 8:38; Ephesians 1:21, 3:10; Colossians 1:16, etc.) is taken by the Church from the work of the mysterious Pseudo-Dionysius the Areopagite, *On the heavenly hierarchies.* According to him nine ranks of angels exist, which are distinguished by their proximity to God and which hand down divine enlightenment and initiation into the divine mysteries from the highest to the lowest rank: cherubim, seraphim, thrones, principalities, dominions, powers, authorities, archangels and angels.[4] An intimate comprehension of the hierarchic structure of the angelic world is inaccessible to humankind in the present age, but will be revealed in the

---

4. Interestingly, Bulgakov does not follow Pseudo-Dionysius here. The usual order places Seraphim first, but here Bulgakov echoes the ranking found in Augustine's *Confessions,* XII:22; it is likely, however, that he was influenced by the liturgical text establishing the Mother of God as "more honorable than the cherubim, more glorious beyond compare than the seraphim. . . ." What is more puzzling, however, is the disruption of the ranking after "thrones." Pseudo-Dionysius lists the hierarchies as follows: 1. Seraphim, 2. Cherubim, 3. Thrones, 4. Dominions, 5. Powers (Virtues), 6. Authorities (Powers), 7. Principalities, 8. Archangels, 9. Angels; Bulgakov's list runs: 2. Cherubim, 1. Seraphim, 3. Thrones, 7. Principalities, 4. Dominions, 5. Powers (Virtues), 6. Authorities (Powers), 8. Archangels, 9. Angels. The Western tradition from Gregory the Great (found already in Augustine with the exception of ranking of 1 and 2) has 1. Seraphim, 2. Cherubim, 3. Thrones, 4. Dominions, 7. Principalities, 6. Powers, 5. Virtues, 8. Archangels, 9. Angels. Translator's note.

future "to the children of the resurrection," who will be "equal to the angels," according to the Lord's word (Luke 20:36). But the general foundations of this hierarchic structure can be grasped even now on the basis of the whole doctrine about angels which is revealed by the Church. This distinguishing can of course find for itself a subjective foundation in the different spiritual capacity and ardor of the angels, in general in their creaturely freedom, in virtue of which, and all else being equal, distinctions in *the degree* of spiritual achievement can take place.

But is it appropriate to transfer the qualities of human freedom with its discursiveness to the angelic nature, which after the trial in freedom, the result of which was the fall of the evil angels, was irrevocably confirmed in the good and attained the ultimate perfection that was within reach of all angels in general and of each angel separately? Is it not more natural, on the contrary, to admit that each of the holy angels realizes the whole fullness of sanctity accessible to them? And if so, then it is erroneous to begin looking for the grounds for distinguishing the hierarchies in a subjective moment, in a different degree of the perfection attainable by each of the angels in their own rank. It is better to consider that subjectively all angels are equally holy, as they realize the perfection within reach of each one. Therefore the foundation of hierarchic distinctions must be seen rather in an objectively ontological principle, namely in the individualization of angels, in the distinction of their Sophianic ideas, in their real dissimilarity one to the other, their non-oneness of being.

The uncreated world, Divine Sophia, the Divine All, Chastity and Wholeness, contains the spiritual organism of the ideas, of the prototypes of creation in general and of the angelic world in particular. These ideas, which in their spiritual articulation form a divine unity, when disclosed in a creaturely fashion are *a hierarchical* whole, a cosmos in which every creative idea, the seed of being, has a definite place, indispensable and irreplaceable for the whole, and in this sense they are equally worthy and yet special, hierarchically determined. In other words the hierarchy of angels is defined not by their subjective condition or achievement (as are human hierarchies, for there are no ontological distinctions among people), but by their original creation. In the earthly, visible world everything forms by itself a single being and this is the human, the microcosm and macrocosm. But the whole distinction of its parts remains in force: minerals from plants, plants from animals, animals from humankind (of course in the limits of each section of the universe). In this sense a cosmic hierarchy exists which is defined by the proximity and relation to that which constitutes the center and meaning of the life of the world, to humankind. One can say that theoretically everything in the world is equally indispensable for this supreme and single goal, for humankind; everything is humankind and yet the distinctions in humanity or the hominization of the elements of the cosmos remain as the foundation for the cosmic hierarchies. It is of course difficult to establish such a parallel, yet it must be said that the hierarchical structure of the angelic world, similar to this, is rooted in the distinctions in the spiritual world, in the Sophianic ideas which in their entirety form the divine cosmos, Heavenly Humanity. It is to be understood that we can go no further than this *general* foundation; no concrete distinction in the angelic world is accessible for us. Perhaps it only remains to remember what is known to us from revelation about the different services of the angels — about angels of the elements of the world, of fire, waters, winds, etc., about the guardian angels of different people, nations, kingdoms, and the like. Here already are outlined the possibilities of hierarchical distinctions.

Another question follows concerning the hierarchy of angels: is the triunity of persons of the Holy Trinity reflected in its structure? In other words, do the individual angelic ranks all bear equally the seal of the Holy Trinity, or do they do so with the predominance of the individual hypostases of the Trinity? Although there is evidence in the church's hymnody about their creation by the Holy Trinity[5] and their reception of the three-sunned light,[6] it does not speak about the angelic ranks relating *uniformly* to the individual divine hypostases. Angels are created in the image of God which necessarily includes the tri-hypostaseity of Divinity so far as its reflection can be accommodated in creation. Does this reflection leave a trace in each of the angelic hypostases indivisibly (and how) or do different angelic ranks reflect in their hypostatic being primarily one of the divine hypostases, with the fullness of the image of the divine Triunity only leaving a trace in the angelic assembly as a whole? There is no *direct* reply to this in church doctrine. But the doctrine of the 9 or 3 x 3 ranks of angelic hierarchies with its twofold triadic character hints precisely at the

5. "The Father, who is God above all, and the only Word and Spirit, brought the powers of celestial minds, formless and immaterial singers, of his three-sunned glory" (Service for Archangels and Angels, tone 6, verse on "Lord I have cried"). "O Lord, by Your hypostatic Word, you fashioned the angelic nature, and having sanctified it with the Holy Spirit, you instructed it to praise the Trinity, O God, for ever" (Canon, ode 7, tr. 3). "The angelic ranks, mirrors of divine-original light, as far as this is conceivable, receive the radiance of the three-sunned torches" (tone 1, ode 1, tr. 1).

6. "Archangels, enlighten with the enlightening dawns of the Trinity those who sing you with faith" (ibid.).

latter idea. In such a case one ought to make out the triple structure of the assembly of angels as those who stand before the whole Holy Trinity but serve primarily one of Its hypostases.

Divine Sophia is the life and self-revelation not of only one hypostasis (of the Second, as is sometimes thought), but of all three divine hypostases. Similarly the angelic world, the bodiless creation in Divine Sophia, is not defined by the one hypostasis of the Word, through whom all things were made, but neither can it accommodate the image of the entire Holy Trinity in an individual mono-hypostatic spirit. The latter is therefore fully disclosed not in individual angels but in the whole angelic assembly. On this condition it is unavoidable that one divine hypostasis especially should leave a mark on individual angels (and perhaps on entire ranks), and hereby the distinction of angels who stand before the holy and undivided Trinity but are marked by the image of only one of Its hypostases appears. What that hypostatic marking might be is a mystery of the angelic world, out of bounds for humans; however, it can be brought closer to us on the basis of what has been revealed about the distinction of the divine hypostases. Therefore in the threefold triple hierarchy of the angelic ranks one can distinguish not only a triplicity of degrees according to their proximity to God, but also a triplicity of modes of their standing before the three persons of the Holy Trinity. This is confirmed by the appearance of God to Abraham in the guise of three angels (Genesis 18), in which the Church perceives a revelation of the Holy Trinity with each of the three angels representing a separate Trinitarian hypostasis, each imprinted with it.

Such a comprehension of this appearance by the Church is expressed most clearly of all in iconography. Indeed, the depiction of the three angels at table by the oak of Mamre has become for us the icon of the Holy Trinity, of Pentecost. This tradition, absent in western iconography, appears in the Russian Church at the end of the fifteenth century with the famous icon of the Holy Trinity of venerable Andrei Rublev, located in the temple of the most Holy Trinity of Sergiev Lavra. (It was painted by the iconographer in obedience to Nikon, a pupil of Sergius, and it is possible that the pupil here carried out the behest of the confidante of the most Holy Trinity, venerable Sergius himself.) So too the icon of the Synaxis of the Archangels, according to its accepted recension, contains the dyad Michael and Gabriel as the two central figures, shown as angels of the Second and Third hypostases, holding a medallion depiction of the Savior Emmanuel; but in their midst (and somewhat higher) there is yet a third archangel, usually unnamed (sometimes Raphael), and in front of him is the depiction of Christ referred to. Does not this archangel who finds for himself no direct interpretation and yet is *silently received* in iconographic tradition correspond to the First hypostasis? In such a case the icon acquires the sense of an obvious symbolism of the whole angelic world in the triplicity of its hierarchies which correspond to the trinitarity of Divinity, with the three supreme angels surrounded by the whole countless heavenly host. Is it not fitting to connect on the basis of their content both of these icons of the Holy Trinity — that of the three angels' appearing to Abraham and the Synaxis of Archangels with the three archangels at the head? The two *named* in the "assembly" of angels, Michael and Gabriel, can also be found in the appearance to Abraham (which is quite natural), the third nameless angel is the one who in the biblical narrative is especially singled out and called "Lord" (Genesis 18:13, 14, 17, 20, 22, 23) in contrast to the two "angels" who come to Lot. The first angel of the manifestation of the Holy Trinity is pre-eminent, though remaining nameless. But the angelic assembly is turned towards the world through the Second and Third hypostases. Therefore their angels, Michael and Gabriel, are the "pre-eminent dyad" of the angelic rank for humans,[7] while the third and prime angel is left on his own as though unknown.

The *Father's* hypostasis which eternally reveals Itself in the Son and the Holy Spirit, is Divine Silence, begetting the Word, and Divine Darkness, exuding the Holy Spirit. The supreme angelic spirits, "covering their faces," are immersed in this ocean of divine Mystery; in sacred terror they stand before the Father's throne. They form as it were the divine foundation of the whole angelic world. They are supercelestial, supernal and not-for-the-world spirits. They are entirely turned towards God and are the mediators of the revelation of divine mysteries to the angelic world. This is the world before its manifested creation, in the entrails of God, unexpressed and unrealized. This is the beginning of creation. If, according to the opinion of the Church's teachers, there are angel ranks which do not serve the world or humans, for their life consists entirely in standing before God, it is all the more appropriate to think this about the angels of the Father's hypostasis, about those hypostatic movements of the Father's Will, which is Goodness, about these substances of Love, who are mute in superabundance, wonderstruck over the fullness, growing faint in the blessedness of God's Love! They are supermundane, but with the

---

7. "O dyad, you who now have precedence over the angelic assembly, save from all harm those who fly to your protection" (Service for Archangels, tone 6, canon, ode 4, tr. 2).

world and for the sake of the world, they are the eve of creative day, the darkness in which light begins to burn, the night in which creation is born, non-being *(me on)* in which all being arises.[8] It is an analogy in the angelic world of the primordial "earth" of our world, in which everything is already created and contained beforehand, although it appears "invisible and empty." It is the apophatic aspect in the angelic world, coupled with the kataphatic being of angels. It is "the heaven of heavens," the heaven of heaven itself spoken of in Solomon's prayer at the consecration of the temple: "heaven and the heaven of heavens do not contain You" (1 Kings 8:27; 2 Chronicles 6:18). It is the eyes that always gaze on the Lord, the circles of wings and eyes in iconography.

Angels are *minds* who represent the radiance of the Logos. They are the very creaturely hypostatic Idea of the world. They possess a multiunity of creative ideas which the world-creating Word embraces. In them is realized beforehand the ideation of the world. They are the ideal form of the world, the world in idea, its ideal content, the *all* which *"was"* through the Word ("all was through him" [John 1:3]). Here everything exists in an ideal prototype, in fullness, like a creaturely form of the world, its ideational and logical foundation. (This is encompassed by the concept of the Logos which contains ideational diversity, the content of the cosmos as well as its necessary conformity to laws, the unity of connection, the logic of things.) The earthly world sees in the noetic heaven its prototype and it is reflected in it like a blue sky in watery depths: this is the contemplated (theoretical) verity of the world, the world in its own truth. This is the meaning of the earthly world, outlined in the heavens before its creation. There is nothing really existing (and not illusory halfbeing arising out of the shadow of non-being, out of the play of light and shadows) which would not be in the angelic world, in the minds, multieyed in contemplation and six-winged in the execution. Noetic powers are creaturely Sophia in heavenly form, as the prototype of the earthly form, Sophia, as the word of things, the ideal *all*. It is the starry sky surrounding the earth, containing earth's destiny through the things written in its constellations, beholding and piercing with myriads of eyes the life of the world.

Angels, servants of the Word, were contemplating His works in the

---

8. Let us recall here that meonal non-being is not nothing *(ouk on)* out of which the world is created by divine omnipotence (it is said about it that the world is created out of nothing). The *me on* is already creation; *nothing*, containing in itself every *what*, it is *something*.

creation of the world when new forms were summoned to being by the creative Word, when ideas and forms received their realization, "when the morning stars exulted together, when all the sons of God shouted for joy" (Job 38:7; Slavonic text, "when the stars were created all my angels praised me with a mighty voice"). These are the noetic powers of cosmourgic service corresponding to the cosmourgic character of the Second hypostasis. They press themselves close to the world and penetrate it, as its ideal foundation, ideas and forms. Their interior hierarchy is the hierarchy of world ideas, the ideal structure of the world, or more correctly the contrary: the world in its constitution carries the form of the hierarchy of the angels of the Word. The Logos of the world as its ideal content and inner regularity is inscribed in heaven in these hierarchies, and everything really existing in worldly being has a correspondence for itself in an angelic rank. Here once more it is incumbent to remember Plato's percipient doctrine of ideas. The error of Platonism, which it has in common with the whole pagan world, is that it does not distinguish the Sophianicity of being from Divinity itself, and imagines that it is expounding a doctrine about God when in reality it is teaching about Divine Sophia.[9] This is why it falls into polytheism (as this was clearly stated in Neo-Platonism, with its attempt at a philosophical restoration of paganism, with its promotion of Magism against Christianity). Platonic ideas are in reality angels of the Word, and Plato's sagacity, which compels us to recognize him as "a Christian before Christ" (according to ecclesiastical literature) is that he recognized the necessity of grounding the earthly world in the heavenly, becoming in being, things in ideas. And with this he transferred to the language of philosophy the revelation of paganism: *panta plere theon,* all is full of gods. Paganism, in its elemental clairvoyance, knew the heavenly foundation of the universe, but in its blindness it equated the angelic hierarchies with gods, or more precisely, the gods, "sons of God" (Job 1:6; 2:1), with the very God. The Christian sense and truth of Platonism is disclosed only in angelology as the doctrine *about heaven and earth* in their interrelations. Platonic ideas encompass everything themselves, and this is the ontology of the world. But these ideas exist not as logical abstractions and schemes of things, but as hypostatic essences, as angels of the Word.[10]

9. I have pointed out the Sophiological but not the theological meaning of Platonic idealism in *Unfading Light.*

10. In theosophical (and anthroposophical) doctrines the hierarchies are assigned a significant place and it is impossible to deny these perspectives a certain value. But they are cheapened by the general context in which they are provided, or more precisely, by the

The blessed spirit-souls form the hierarchy of the Third hypostasis, the Life-creating Spirit who fashions everything as "a living soul,"[11] the Bestower of Life who fills and completes all things, the Comforter, who comforts all things by clothing them with Beauty. "The Lord has ascended His throne, He is robed in elegance"; the enthronement of the Lord is His enrobing in elegance, in beauty, by the operation of the Holy Spirit. The power of reality, which gives being to ideal form, the *let there be fiat* as the one thing said to *all* subjects on the sixth day of creation, beauty as a living manifestation of truth — this is the domain of the Holy Spirit. To this domain belong the angels of the Holy Spirit, the blessed spirit-souls.[12] Inherent to them are a particular vision of reality and a ministry of life as such. Everything in the world has not only its inner word, an ideal meaning, an idea, but also being, mysterious and inseparably intertwined with the word-sense. This intertwining is also reality, the force of life, the *let there be.* But this intertwining contains in itself not only the inner word as the truth and sense of a thing, its idea, but also its ontic perceptible (in this sense one can say sensible) shape, the form that envelops this idea. This realization of the idea, by which it becomes completely transparent in being, is a supreme artistic work, a perfect image, adequate to the idea. This transparency of the image that is adequate to the idea is Beauty.

Truth is manifested in Beauty and Beauty manifests Truth, as the vital force of Truth. The angels of the Holy Spirit are servants of Beauty, which lives in them prior to its appearance on earth. The world is clothed

---

theosophical theology in which there is no Creator God, but there is an evolving world of spiritual essences. From this comes pluralistic pantheism, the world as a system of evolving hierarchies, a peculiar polytheism which joins with atheism, a type of religion of the angels without God. This is the very thing, evidently, against which the apostle Paul warned in a rather dark text from his letter to the Colossians, 2:18, "Let no one seduce you with wilful self-abasement and *service (latreia) of angels,* intruding on what he did not see, irrationally becoming puffed up with his fleshly mind."

11. This expression is applied in the Bible equally to all living things: about the crawling creatures of the fifth day it says "a living soul" (Genesis 1:20), about animals of the sixth day, "a living soul according to its type" (1:24), and about humankind, "and the human became a living soul" (2:7).

12. By designating the angels of the Third hypostasis with such a name we do not wish to diminish their spiritual nature in comparison with the pure souls and minds, the angels of the First and Second hypostases, but we wish to designate their property impressed on them by the Third hypostasis. It differs from both the inaccessibility of the first ones and the noetic power of the second.

in Beauty. Beauty in nature nourishes the soul by its contemplation and fills it with amazement even for those who do not wish to see heaven and who search for the key to the cosmos in humankind. Humans, they say, know and love beauty, for they fashion it according to their image and likeness. Granted, but where is this beauty of the world from, the beauty in the great and the small, wherever the human gaze penetrates, in astronomical worlds and in microscopically small entities, in the primordial thick of the forests and in the ocean depths, in the plant and animal worlds? From where, for whom, and for what purpose is the beauty of the innumerable meadow flowers that are more beautiful than what King Solomon wore, and yet are not known by anyone and are unknowable by anyone or anything, and are so to say, non-hominized? There are no words and no imagination will suffice to exhaust this bottomless ocean of beauty with which God's world is robed. Beauty is human but not in the sense that it was created by humankind or that it constituted only its subjective perception, but it is *perceived* by humankind as a microcosm, containing the threads of the entire macrocosm in itself. And those who have grasped the objectivity and so to say autonomy of beauty in nature prove to be compelled to acknowledge the special aesthetic power poured out in nature (Haeckel),[13] without noticing the contradiction into which they fall by simultaneously interpreting nature as a mechanism of material or strong atoms and at the same time ascribing to it an ideal and completely spiritual capacity for the creative work of beauty. But "the heavens tell the glory of God and the firmament proclaims the work of His hands" (Psalm 18:2/19:1), and "the invisible things of God, His eternal power and Divinity, from the foundation of the world are visible through examining his works" (Romans 1:20). The beauty of the world is a similar (and for many souls the most and even the only irresistible) witness about God, the creator of the world.

God is Beauty, for He is Truth and Life, Word and Life-creating Spirit. The beauty of the world is the beauty of the noetic heaven, and it shines in it as the blue sky is reflected in the depths of the waters. The world is enrobed by beauty, in which the noetic heaven presses against the world, and the beauty of nature is the reflection of this heaven. The whole beauty of the world pre-exists in the angelic world in the spirit-souls of the Third hypostasis. As the executor of Its commands, as the guardians

13. Ernst Haeckel (1834-1919), a German zoologist and promoter of Darwinism who made important though often discredited contributions to biology and zoology. Translator's note.

of creation, they envelop it in beauty. The beauty of the world is brought by the angels of creation, who perform their labor upon her and by loving her, robe her with beauty. Is it not by angelic power implanted in them in keeping with the will of God that flowers blossom? Is it not by their guardians that all forms of beauty, from the lowliest animal to the human body, are robed with beauty? We pray: "for an angel of peace, a faithful guide, a guardian *of our souls and bodies* let us ask the Lord." This is said not only for the preservation of our bodies from external troubles and diseases but also for the preservation of the body in the whole perfection of its forms, which we still only remotely imagine. The whole beauty of the world is nothing other than a ray of light in heaven, the transparency of the angelic world for our sake. We involuntarily speak about "angelic form, angelic beauty, angelic singing," etc. — this genius of language bears witness to our percipience of the angelic world.

The idea that the beauty of the world is the work of the angels protecting it must not be distorted in meaning, as if beauty were foreign and not inherent to the world itself and humankind, that it was only light cast from another world. On the contrary, in the same measure that meaning and reality belong to the world, so does beauty belong to it. One can say even more: beauty is its only genuine reality, ugliness or deformity is semi-being or non-being, their chiaroscuros. But this reality has a basis and prototype in the heavens, in the angelic world. The azure of the waters and air does not cease to be real just because it is a reflection of heaven, does not exist alone, not for itself, but together with and on the basis of heaven. And in the real beauty of the earthly world the ideal beauty of the angelic rank is reflected which by God's command safeguards it in its "very good."

What has been said makes possible an explanation for the general idea about the Sophianicity of beauty in the world.[14] Beauty is Sophianic; it is the obvious, tangible revelation of Divine Sophia as the pre-eternal foundation of the world. But without further explanation such an idea conceals in itself the possibility of an inclination to pantheistic world-divinization (right up to the most recent hylozoism of Haeckel). Beauty is inseparably connected with the flesh of the world, which she clothes with herself. Therefore an immediate convergence of God as pure absolute spirit with the earthly world runs up against philosophical difficulties and religious ones even more so. For, creation is completely transparent for the Creator, but the Creator in Himself remains transcendent to cre-

---

14. See *Unfading Light*, the chapter on the Sophianicity of the world.

ation, although He reveals Himself to it, inasmuch as He becomes immanent. But this immanence to the world is not realized immediately, but through the mediation of a being, which though creaturely is spiritual all the same, and has a support in the divine nature. The world is Sophianic on the basis of Divine Sophia, but it is Sophianic through creaturely Sophia which is hypostatized in the angelic world. Therefore the beauty of the world is Sophianic through the operation of angels; it is the tangible presence and operation of the angels in the world. Our heart is opened by the power of beauty, and our spirit is borne on high to the angelic world. The world is an artistic work, coming from the hands of the Great Master, and He is the Creator. But the accomplishers of His creative design are the holy angels, the servants of God in the world. And therefore one can say that if the world is a work of art, it is the art of angels, the immediate servants of Beauty, the angels of the Holy Spirit.

*   *   *

Does a distinction exist in the angelic world corresponding to the male and female principles in humankind and conditioning *the fullness* of the image of God in humankind ("in the image of God He created him; male and female He created them," Genesis 1:27)? It goes without saying that it is impious and absurd to imagine for the angelic world distinctions of *sex* connected with marital relations, inasmuch as these distinctions are connected with the physical being of humankind, moreover in its fallen sinful state, and with the mode of multiplying the human race that was established by God at its creation (Genesis 1:28). Angels, differently than humans, were created by a simultaneous creative act. Being an *assembly* and not a *genus* they do not know reproduction and they have no body; consequently, sex, as a *bodily* distinction, here falls completely by the wayside. But the distinction of the male and female principle is not only bodily but also spiritual. It is rooted in the different form of the spirit, in its "personal quality" which is determined in the first case by the logical principle, by the primacy of reason, of thought, over the sense of beauty and the activity of the heart, and in the second case, by the primacy of the aesthetic sense and the heart over mind. The primacy of Truth and the primacy of Beauty, equally subordinated to the primacy of the Good, constitute the basis of the distinction between the male and female principle in the human spirit. Both principles are present in it inseparably, but with the definite predominance of one of them, and both show themselves mutually supplying one another.

The fullness of the image of God in the male-female or female-male spirit of a human has a foundation in the Divine Triunity where the image of Truth, the Logos, is the personal determination of the Second hypostasis and the image of Beauty, of inspiration, is inherent in the Third hypostasis, both of Them equally having one "principle" from the good Father, the source of the Good ("no one is good except God alone"). Conforming to this the Word and Son of God assumed the male nature when He became human, whereas the Holy Spirit chose the Most Pure Virgin Mary, the female nature, for the sake of His indwelling; the fullness of the human image in the heavens is Jesus-Mary.[15] Likewise the human image is elevated by the apostle (Ephesians 5:32) to the prototype "of Christ and the Church," which is headed by the Virgin Mary, the Unwed Bride of the Divine Bridegroom. In this way, by the bi-unity of the androgyne principle in the human spirit the fullness of the image of God is imprinted in it. But in humankind this bi-unity exists only as *twoness* which makes each human individual not self-sufficient but looking for its completion, not only for its *other*, or its *friend*, but also as it were for its own half. Therefore *sex* is spiritual incompleteness, halfness.[16] In the life of grace this halfness is supplied for and overcome by union with Christ in whom "there is neither male nor female" (Galatians 3:28) and by reception of the gift of the Holy Spirit.

Every soul, without the distinction of human gender, is related to Christ the way the Church, the Bride of Christ, is related to the Divine Bridegroom. And every soul in the Church is shadowed over by the Holy Spirit, is inspired by Him and has in Him its Comforter. With this, the natural incompleteness of the human creature *graciously* wanes. But remaining in their proper human sphere, humans in their spiritual nature look for completion, in keeping with the word of the Lord, "It is not good for the human to be alone, let us create for him a helpmate, similar to him" (Genesis 2:18). The fullness of the image of God, of the Holy Trinity, in humankind cannot be realized in a separate human person, a single hypostasis, but only in the whole human race united in the Church. This fullness is not contained in the male or female creature in their fragmentedness but presupposes their reunion. In the earthly life of humans, the institution of marriage "in the image of Christ and the Church" is such a reunion; its purpose in the life of the body is to reproduce the

---

15. On this see *The Burning Bush.*

16. The translator's attempt to render the difficult term *polovinchatost'* meaning "the quality/condition of half."

human race, and in the spiritual life, to overcome the fragmentedness of the human spirit in an androgyne unity (which is "the meaning of love," the spiritual-syzygic union perceptively pointed out by Vladimir Solovyov).[17] Can this spiritual distinction of male and female be transferred to the angelic world *by analogy* with human nature? This analogy has a foundation in that general co-humanity of the angels which we already dealt with and will do so again. According to the doctrine of the Church guardian angels belong to the human creature, male and female, without distinction. Does this human distinction correspond to anything at all in angelic nature? If guardian angels are generally correlative with the individual principle in humankind, to be understood in the broadest sense (which is why not only individual protector angels can exist but also collective angels for separate nations and kingdoms, localities and cities, churches and communities, etc.), is the distinction between the male and female principle excluded because of this individual characterization? And if it is not excluded then a new question necessarily arises: how can this correspondence with angelic nature proper be expressed, inasmuch as the correlation of a guardian angel and the human entrusted to him is based on a certain ontological kinship?

On the other hand this same question is directly posed in the Gospel in the words of the Lord himself whom the Sadducees tested by asking to whom the woman will belong in the resurrection who belonged to seven brothers. All three synoptic Gospels have this story. Let us begin with the Gospel of Luke (20:34-36): "The Lord said to them in reply, the children of this age marry and are given in marriage. But those who are made worthy of attaining that age and the resurrection from the dead neither marry nor are given in marriage, and they cannot die for they are *equal to the angels* and are children of God, being children of the resurrection."[18] This testimony about the children of the resurrection enjoying a certain *equality* with angels is applied, of course, first of all to marital life, which was the point of the question, and not to the impossibility of their death, which was not directly asked. The latter is obviously connected with the former as its result. In Matthew 22:23-30 it is said that "you are deceived,

17. See Vladimir Solovyov, *The Meaning of Love,* ed. and trans. Thomas R. Byer, Jr. (Lindisfarne Press, 1985). Translator's note.

18. The foregoing words "they are equal to the angels" are even strengthened by the words "they are children of God," understood in the light of comparison with Job 1:6, 2:1, where angels standing before the face of God are called "children of God," for they once more confirm the equality with angels of humankind.

not knowing the Scripture or the power of God, for in the resurrection they neither marry nor are given in marriage, but *they are like the angels in the heavens*" (vv. 29-30). In this way St. Luke's expression, "equal to the angels," is here replaced by an expression equivalent in meaning, "they are like the angels in the heavens."

And so, first of all, what is said and what is not said in the Lord's words? Here the state of earthly marriage, to which is attached only a temporary importance for earthly life, is rejected for the sake of the future age. Marriage has as its immediate earthly goal the birth of children, and this in its turn is connected with the dying out and changing of generations in which alone the human race exists in its unity. This (fleshly) means of reproducing humankind is connected with the condition of the fall and the incarnating of humankind. Death is connected with it. (We do not know how the birth of a sinless and hence immortal human would occur). In the resurrection there will be no place for either birth or death. All those who have to be born in order to pass then through the gates of death are already born and resurrected. They form the integral human race that cannot be torn asunder by death and the change of generations, and that already possesses immortality. And in this the human race resembles the angels who, being created by a single act, always exist as "an angel assembly," which includes the sum totality *of all* angels (except the fallen ones). Together with the cessation of reproduction and the removal of death, marriage also loses its importance inasmuch as it is connected with reproduction.

But the change of our body from carnal to "psychic" or "spiritual" (1 Corinthians 15:44) will lead to the extinction of carnal desire, of that "attraction to her husband" (Genesis 3:16) of the wife and the reverse attraction of the husband to his wife, which were the result of the fall and the clothing in leather garments: in the future age "they do not marry" and "are not given in marriage"; sexual life dies away together with death. Human sex in its corporeality, as carnal necessity, "bonding," falls by the wayside, and in this is the new feature of existence equal to angels, for angels, as bodiless entities, of course, are free from sex, inasmuch as it is connected with the body. The words of the Savior, "they do not marry and are not given in marriage," contain yet another idea — concerning freedom not only from the bodily captivity of gender, but also from psychospiritual captivity, from the thirst of love for spiritual completion, which the fragmented, dependent creature seeks (like the severed halves of an erstwhile double-sexed integral creature according to Plato's myth in *The Banquet*). The "meaning of love" in the earthly state of humankind consists in the extinction of this fragmentedness. In the future age a human becomes a self-sufficing, complete creature, not losing its inherent capacity for love but being satisfied in it. And this constitutes the new feature of its state of equality with angels.

But equality in the sense of likening does not mean identification, and if humans are said to be "equal to the angels," or "as angels," this in no way means that they become angels by ceasing to be human and losing their human nature. And of course it is incorrect to go that far in the exegesis of this text. But this happens when on the basis of the Savior's words one affirms what is not said in the texts and what is even tacitly repudiated, namely that the distinction of the male and female principle in humankind should utterly cease in the future age. From the beginning prior to the fall humans are created by God as man and woman; consequently both of them are destined for immortality. That the creation of humankind as man and woman is primordially so is expressly indicated by the Lord Jesus as if in His own name when He said in response to the Pharisees testing him with the question about divorce (Matthew 19:4): "Have you not read that the Creator made them man and woman in the beginning?" (Genesis 1:27). If the male and female in humankind, as spiritual principles, have their highest foundation in the personal properties of the Second and Third hypostases, and are correlative to them, then they cannot be subject to annihilation in the resurrection. For they are not connected only with the fleshly, sinful life of the present-day, corpulent body and its concupiscence; on the contrary, they are subject to the fullest manifestation, enlightenment, and perpetuation. For both the Lord Jesus Christ, sitting at the right hand of the Father, and His Most Pure Mother and Ever-Virgin Mary sitting at His right in the heavens, preserve their humanity which is proper to them in the form of male and female nature. Precisely Virginity, as an inalienable ontological quality, or *Ever-Virginity, liberates* the male and female principles from sex, which as attraction to the other sex and dependence on it, contains the principle of captivity and limitation. Virginity is freedom from sex, but male and female natures are preserved. It is impossible to allow that the children of the resurrection in their new immortal life should appear depersonalized, having ceased being their own selves, for resurrection is the restoration and perpetuation precisely of the primordial condition of humankind, liberated from the perversion of sin and the depletion of existence in the flesh. But the male and female principles are not reduced to a corporeal, sexual distinction, no, they are extended to the spiritual essence of humankind too and qualify it. Not in vain does the Church perpetuate the memory of male and female saints in their proper forms, not depriving them of that human distinction which they had in earthly life, just as Adam and Eve were led out of Hades by the Lord in the male and female nature proper to them. Thus, it is impossible to regard the state of resurrection as a complete abolition of the male and female principle with its replacement by some sort of middle, undifferentiated condition, which would be tantamount to the impoverishment and simplification of human nature.[19]

If a human resurrects in the body, each one in a bodily form proper to them, it is necessary to conclude from this that the distinction of male and female nature in humankind, which existed already in the paradisiacal state before the fall, is preserved and perpetuated in the resurrection body. Of course it is freed from what is bound with the life of bodily sex (as some of the fathers, e.g., St. Gregory of Nyssa, point out). But humankind exists both spiritually and bodily in two forms. Likewise Pre-Eternal Humanity in God, the Wisdom of God, is the self-revelation of the Father not only in the Son, the Heavenly Human, the New Adam, but also in the Holy Spirit who rests on Him and is inseparable from Him, and who descended upon the Virgin Mary. This bi-unity in the human is expressed in the twoness of its essence, which is coupled into oneness. In earthly life this coupling is connected with the life of sex and childbirth, "the children of this age marry and are given in marriage," and this form of union is established by God and sanctified in the sacrament of marriage.

But if in the future age humankind is freed from sex, and reproduction becomes superfluous, is anything left of the mutual relations of the male and female nature? The Sadducees' provocative question, "of which of the seven will she be the wife, for they all had her" (Matthew 22:28), refers precisely to this. No one will "have" her physically because in the future age the very possibility and need of such possession falls by the wayside. But with the exception of this possessing, does any sort of possibility remain for mutual relations of the male and female principles in humanity? Without a doubt it remains and this possibility is *love*, which binds together and reciprocally completes male and female nature after the image of Christ and the Church. Humanity in its multi-unity and oneness of be-

---

19. Some mystical thinkers abolish the male and female sex through mixing them in each essence, like an androgyne. By doing so, they do not take into account the significance of the divine incarnation and divine motherhood, the presence of the Human in the form of Jesus and Mary in the heavens.

ing even now does not represent a herd composed of mutually indifferent individuals but a family or clan, whose members are connected among themselves by diverse guises of *concrete* love-friendship (i.e., of life in the other and by the other) with the whole gamut of nuances of the male and female principles (not only mother and wife, but also father and mother, son and daughter, brother and sister). In this manner even now the male and female principles contain the basis for the diverse unity of humanity in love-friendship, beyond sexual love and marriage. But marriage too has in itself different possibilities for relations, namely not only husband and wife who generate children and enter through this into the life of the clan, but also friendship and purely personal love. Life "in one flesh," although sacred and natural, and established in paradise (Genesis 2:23-24; cf. Matthew 19:5-6), is still very much an Old Testament law which does not have force in the life of the future age. But then the fullness of personal love comes into effect as mutual fulfillment or *friendship* in the proper sense, comprising the "meaning of love."

This friendship, in different forms, both male-female love and love in the limits of one and the same principle, is known already to this age, but it becomes the possession of the future age in all its force in virtue of the liberation from sex and the overcoming of captivity by it. One should not allow that in that life there could be forfeited anything of the relations of love between people already existing in this life; everything worthy of perpetuation is shown in all its force. New and endlessly developing possibilities of love and friendship are revealed, however, for only in the age of the resurrection will the human race exist in all its wholeness, not in generations that give place to one another; the whole human race will become one family and concord in God. "The saved nations will walk [in the New Jerusalem] in the light of the Lamb, and the kings of the earth will bring to it their glory and honor . . . and they will bring to it the glory and honor of the nations" (Revelation 21:24, 26).

Each human being will preserve what constitutes the glory and honor of their life — love — and it will be increased. But in his answer to the Sadducees the Savior points precisely to such liberation from the chains of the limitation of earthly, carnal love. According to the sense of their question, the difficulty of the situation lies first in the matter of which of the seven brothers will have the woman carnally, "for they all had her" (a negative answer is given to this: "they neither marry nor are given in marriage"), and second, who will have her in love-friendship? The latter question, although not directly uttered by the interlocutors, is understood, for it is answered in the Savior's words, who does not simply give a negative explanation relating to physical possession,[20] but adds, "you are mistaken, not knowing Scripture or God's power" (Matthew 22:29; Mark 12:24). The manifestation of this power of God, revealed in Scripture, consists in the fact that the children of the resurrection in the future age "sojourn like the angels of God in the heavens" (Matthew 22:30; Mark 12:25), are "equal to the angels" (Luke 20:36). What is understood here by "the sojourning of the angels" in the heavens and the human state of equality with angels? If it is impossible to conceive this as a general abolition of the distinction between human and angelic nature, one ought to understand these words as applied to that very feature which is outlined in the question posed. It is a question of the relations of mutuality and possession between man and woman and more broadly of *love* in general (of "the meaning of love"): the nature of the relations of human love, after divesting it of the leather garments of sex, is determined in conformity with angelic love and is as-similated to it (therefore the equating refers not at all to angelic and hu-man *nature*, which remain different, but to love). What content can be brought to light in this answer?

The angelic assembly is united in a polyhypostatic multitude, after the image of the Holy Trinity, not through the unity of its nature, which is absent for lack of this very nature, but exclusively through love, above all for God, and then reciprocal love one for another. The angelic assembly is united in the fusion of personal reciprocal love in which the angelic hypostasis seemingly dies for itself in order to resurrect and live in *the as-sembly*, in a multi-one, collective, pan-angelic I. This assembly of pan-angelic love will become the form of pan-human love after all humanity stops being an abstract intelligible concept, but it will be an immediate re-ality when people stop being born and dying, "being children of the resur-rection" (Luke 20:36). This is the form of *ecclesial* union in which "the an-gelic assembly" and "the human race" are united constituting the one Church ("one church completed by angels and humans").[21] This univer-sality of love which in any case remains personal and concrete, presup-poses not a herd instinct but the individuality of personal relations out of which is woven as in the nervous system the general sensory apparatus of

---

20. This aspect of the answer is expressed more briefly in the exposition in Mat-thew 22:30 and Mark 12:25, and more extensively through juxtaposition in Luke 20:34-35, "the children of this age marry and are given in marriage (take a husband) but those fit-ted to attain that age and the resurrection from the dead do not marry and do not take a husband."

21. Canon of Archangels, tone 8, ode 9, tr. 1.

love. This personal love is based on particular choices and attractions, *Wahlverwandschaften*,[22] having their foundation in individual attributes.

For a full understanding of this thought it is necessary to comprehend the mysterious words of the Lord in all their force, *"they are like the angels of God in the heavens"* (Matthew 22:30), not only in a negative sense, with respect to carnal sex and marital relations resulting from it, but also in a positive sense, as an indication concerning the mutual love of the angels which binds them into one *assembly*. In its fullness, this is a mystery of the future age. The Lord, however, touches on this in His answer, alluding to Scripture and with this bears witness that now it is not entirely concealed from understanding. The assembly of angels, having love for God and life in God as its foundation, is fastened together by their mutual personal love, which is nourished by reciprocal loving contemplation of individuals, of the personal properties of each angel. In the collectivity of the angelic world, in angelic love, creaturely Sophia lives in the angelic polyhypostaseity of her rays, combined into plenitude by love. The heavenly world is created by love; it is a hymn of love and its flame. In the diversity of this love no ontological property, no ray of the pleroma of the angelic world is left unnoticed and unloved — all-seeing love gazes on and loves everything. To be sure, this concrete plenitude and, if one can express it thus, this exhaustive multitude of motifs and the diversity of this love are out of reach for us now; because it is abstract, only an empty schema remains for us.

If the angelic world is characterized by a triple form after the image of the three divine hypostases, then the particular form of its reciprocal love is supposed by this distinction. The distinction of the angels of the Second and Third hypostases corresponds to that distinction of the male and female principle *in the spirit*, which we know in our human nature. Does not this distinction contain the foundations for the particular mutual attraction of reciprocating love, of syzygy-like communion between the angel choirs of the Second and Third hypostases each bearing individually the identical Sophianic idea, which is manifested in a different way as Mind and Feeling, Truth and Beauty? Is not the Sophianicity of creation laid bare in general in a certain primordial syzygy-like twoness which is united in rings of personal love from which it forms the golden chain of the universe? A direct analogy with the human world leads to this idea. The analogy not only cannot be entirely discarded, but must rather be adopted at least in those cases when a positive correlation is estab-

22. Elective affinity. Translator's note.

lished between angels and humans, as occurs in the words of the Lord that are being examined. They inquire of him, for which of the seven men will the woman be a wife? He replies that she will be the wife of none of them for in the future age they do not marry at all; consequently, the bearer of the male principle is not a man in the sexual sense, and the possessor of the female principle is not a wife and woman in the sexual sense either. They stop being for each other buck and doe, so that the animal principle of sex in humankind completely dies away.

But by this it is certainly not said that husband and wife cease to be themselves, or that they pass over to some neuter state which is supposedly in *this* sense "equality with angels." Furthermore it is *nowhere* said, and especially not here, that the image of angelic being is determined by this neuter indifference, by a spiritual non-characterization. Unless it is darkened and distorted, the male and female principle in the spirit is in no way at all reduced to sex. Male and female, created as such from the beginning, remain themselves forever, although they are freed from their garments of skin. Their spiritual correlation, the rings of their love, are liberated only now; it is precisely in this liberation, and not in the passage to the lack of characterization of the neuter state that their equality with angels[23] is expressed. Spiritual love does not have those boundaries which are proper to corporeal possession. Therefore the veiled answer of the Lord to the question, *to whom* namely will the wife of seven men belong in the future age, can be understood in this way: to the one of them who is close to her in spirit, who is found in spiritual syzygy with her (if there is such a thing), and consequently, *to all of them,* inasmuch as spiritual love is not exclusive, but complex and multiform. In the explanation of this spiritual communion (which can be called spiritual wedlock) the Lord points to the structure of the angelic world, which is the prototype of the human world. Human existence reverts to a norm, to an angelic prototype.

But in this prototype there is not only a distinction of forms of possessing its own content, in conformity with the male and female principles in humankind, in the angels of the Second and Third hypostases, but also an image of the First hypostasis, of fatherhood above qualification and yet being qualified in the images of the Second and Third hypostases. This finds an analogy in human love which has its basis in fatherhood

---

23. Monastics who receive the angelic habit and renounce sex still preserve their male and female nature, which are never assimilated by the Church. For example, the boundary which separates woman from the ministry of priesthood remains in force.

and motherhood, in parenthood generally, and generally in the production of offspring, as sons and daughters. As the life of the angels of the Second and Third hypostases finds its principle and source of continually flowing light in the angels of the First hypostasis, so too the chain of human life, consisting of rings of reciprocating love, rises up to that principle in universal sonship and fatherhood, which is named after the image of the heavenly Father (Ephesians 3:15).

Another question arises related to the foregoing discussion. Does a particular spiritual correlation exist between a male or female human being and their guardian angel? Based on the general analogy between "heaven and earth" and the personal character of angelic ministry, we must conclude that such a positive correlation exists and therefore angels of a corresponding form are predestined for each half of the human race. This thought is particularly persuasive if we recall that the existence of one's guardian angel precedes human birth, which the angel prepares, as we have stated above. The immediate disclosure of this correlation remains inaccessible for us, and we are able to express here only personal conjectures. At first glance it can seem that the angels of the Second and Third hypostases stand in direct correlation with the male and female principles as their heavenly prototypes. But one ought to take into account that the hypostatic individuation of angels does not separate them from the plenitude of angelic life. Similarly, a human being, whether male or female, possesses the plenitude of human nature identically and equally. Therefore there is no necessity in the direct correspondence of modality between a guardian angel and a human, of their direct repetition as it were. An angel's service in "guarding" humans consists in assisting them to become themselves, to rise to the plenitude of those creative tasks which they are called to accomplish in their self-creativity. But for this very task does not reciprocal suppletion serve better than self-repetition? The male spirit seeks to find himself creatively, by being immersed in his element, in a revelation in the other tangible for him. And the female spirit from the depths of her sensing being seeks to ascend towards the creative light, which would illumine her and would be her reason. Each soul seeks itself, its manifestation in the other, in the friend. And this friend, this heavenly friend, "safeguards," by helping the human not with what it already has as a given, but what it seeks as something proposed, cherishes as a dream and loves in advance as the slaking of the thirst of being, as consolation. Does not the masculine spirit, which is already marked with the seal of the Logos, and carries it within as the power of his being, have all the more need of a heavenly guardian of the image of the Third hypostasis who inspires and gives joy and comfort? And on the contrary: the feminine spirit, already imprinted with the seal of the Spirit Comforter and through Him provided with the force of life and beauty, requires the heavenly guardian of the image of the Logos which the trembling feeling element seeks and gazes upon spiritually?[24]

If it is so,[25] then still another facet of the idea comes to light con-

---

24. Is it not a contradiction to what we have expounded that the archangel Gabriel, the angel of the Virgin Mary, can be regarded as belonging not to the Second but to the Third hypostasis, when on the basis of what is said in the text it would appear that it ought to be the contrary? No, and for this reason: in the archangel Gabriel's service to the Virgin Mary we have an entirely exceptional relation, not repeated in the relations between a guardian angel and a human. As Mother and Bride of the Logos, the Virgin Mary has no personal guardian angel who would be her heavenly prototype, completion, and friend. As more honorable than all creation and higher than the whole angelic rank, the Virgin Mary is creaturely Sophia herself, the heart of the world, the personal head and incarnation of the Church, encompassing the angelic and human worlds. The Virgin Mary does not have her own guardian among the angels because her Son Himself is her Guardian. This is confirmed by the fact that He Himself, and not Gabriel, receives her honorable soul at her Dormition. The archangel Gabriel is her intended servant in the mystery of the incarnation, but this service essentially has a temporary and limited character, for he does not ascend together with the Virgin into the Heaven of heavens, although he heads the service of the whole angelic rank for the human race. The divine incarnation is the work primarily of the Holy Spirit, who came down upon the Virgin Mary and therefore the service of this mystery is the work of the angel of the Third hypostasis. Thus the annunciation of the nativity of the Forerunner of Christ is entrusted to this angel although he likewise does not appear to him as a personal guardian angel. The Forerunner, like the Theotokos, does not have such an angel for he unites in himself angelic with human being. But it is natural to conclude that the archangel who in keeping with his special mission from God announced the nativity of the Forerunner will remain with him in a special protective relationship throughout his earthly life (although direct indications of this are absent). And in this sense the relation of the archangel Gabriel to the Forerunner is analogous to his relation to the Most Holy Virgin (already directly attested in tradition), with all the difference respecting the importance of both ministries. The Prologue of the Gospel of Luke deliberately unites both missions of the archangel Gabriel as his ministry to the work of incarnation. (See *Friend of the Bridegroom.*)

25. Indirect confirmation of this idea can be seen in the story in Genesis about the birth of giants in antediluvian humanity: "then the sons of God saw the human daughters and that they were beautiful, and they took them to themselves as wives, whichever one they chose" (6:2, cf. 6:4). The interpretation of this passage about "the sons of God" is generally disputed, but the opinion exists that sees in them angels (in the book of Job 1:2 angels are without a doubt called "sons of God") and perceives in the carnal desire the reason for the fall of the angels. This latter opinion is usually rejected in theology. But without seeing here a story about the cause of the fall of angels, it is nevertheless possible

cerning life equal to the angels in the future age. Communion with one's guardian angel, which is the possession "of the children of the resurrection" in the future age, will give to each human being the absolute quenching of the thirst for spiritual love. That feeling of dissatisfaction and loneliness is hereby completely eliminated which is the scourge of contemporary human existence. The human is not alone; there are two of them, each having its own inseparable friend — a heavenly friend, a guardian angel. Each recognizes that their earthly yearning was for this friend. And liberated from sensual desire the human is liberated from spiritual desire too: "they do not marry nor are they given in marriage." The human becomes self-sufficing, all the while preserving its male or female nature. And through its guardian angel, in a revelation of love, it enters into communion with the angelic world.

To be sure, this angelic love does not close but rather opens the paths of human love in all those bonds of personal love which are given humankind in its earthly life and then beyond its bounds. Limitedness and egoism are the law of our sinful nature even in love; therefore the stern commandment is fitting that enjoins hatred for those one loves, i.e., liberation from this limitedness of love: "If anyone comes to Me and does not hate his father, mother, wife, children, brothers and sisters, indeed his own life, he cannot be My disciple" (Luke 14:26). This concerns expanding one's heart from a limited, personal love to a universal love. The heart of a human being, created in the image of God, conceals in itself unlimited possibilities of love, universal and at the same time concrete, in which the personal relation and personal character of any love are not forfeited. Is not this liberation from limitation in love connected with the overcoming of that spiritual incompleteness, that halfness ("of sex"), which is inher-

---

to refer it to already fallen souls, who perverted their own being right up to desiring sexual intercourse with "the daughters of men," in their striving for intimacy with the human world as close as possible for the sake of ruling over it ("they saw that they were beautiful"). Of course, for bodiless spirits such intercourse is impossible and it only remains to surmise their influence on fitting people. This story in any case presupposes in its basis some sort of distinction between the *sons* of God and the *daughters* of men, as a possibility of a sinful union, based, however, on some sort of election ("whichever one they chose"). Whether this is a primordial election that is now distorted in its application or something that happened ad hoc is unclear from the text.

Ought one not see an echo of Talmudic thought about such a possibility in the words of I Corinthians 10:11, "a wife must have on her head [a sign] of the authority [over her] *because of the angels*"? By the way, the opposite understanding of this obscure passage is equally possible — namely for the expression of respect for the angels.

ent in humankind now, when *personal* love becomes exclusive through the power of things, spurning other possibilities of love?

Universal love is love of all for all and for each in Christ through the Holy Spirit, for all are united in the body of Christ. But this universal love of humans, this universal spiritual marriage of male and female nature in humankind, in the image of Christ and the Church, already exists, outlined beforehand in the angelic world. And in this way is disclosed the ultimate meaning of the Lord's words that the children of the resurrection live like angels or are equal to the angels. This does not signify a simplification and metaphysical impoverishment of their being, but the opening of that power which gathers "the angelic assembly" into one, the power of universal love. Clear too is the source of this power of *chastity*, which is universality: it is the participation in Divine Sophia, who is the wisdom of wholeness and its efficacy — chastity, perfect Virginity. Not only the Virgin Mary, who heads human nature in Her Sophianic glory, together with the Forerunner, has perpetual Virginity, i.e., the perfect integrity of her being and the positive overcoming of sex, of the fragmentedness, the halfness of being, but also "the children of the resurrection," who no longer "marry or are given in marriage," participate in this essential Virginity in their glory and in this they likewise become "like the angels of God." It follows that angelic being, participant in Glory, necessarily participates in this perpetual Virginity which constitutes the authentic Sophianic form of creation. That which is accessible to humankind is accessible beforehand to the angelic world which although essentially differing from the human world is none the poorer in spiritual gifts; on the contrary, in respect of them it prefigures human attainments. And if angels differ from humankind by the absence of sex, this in no way signifies that they do not participate in the power of Virginity.[26] On the contrary, this power is the single source of universal love, uniting both angels and humans in their existence equal-to-the-angels, and this ever-virginal ecclesiastical assembly is headed by the one who is more honorable than the cherubim and more glorious beyond compare than the seraphim, *the Ever-Virgin.*

---

26. It is clear that Virginity does not have an exclusive relation only to young women, as bearers of female nature. Virginity is the image of integral being, which is identically inherent in both male and female nature, which has been liberated from sex and given communion in universal life.

CHAPTER 5

The Life of Angels

Angels are perfectly holy, each realizing in himself the measure of perfection implanted in them at their creation. They are in all fullness their very selves and in this sense they are Sophianic. Only the Lord God is holy by His own nature, whereas the holiness of every creature arises from its participation in the holiness of God. Therefore the realization of creaturely holiness depends not only on the measure given but also on the measure and manner by which it is received; in other words, it depends not only on the degree of proximity to God and the heights of creation corresponding to this, which it cannot surpass by its own powers, but also on the creaturely freedom by which the degree of holiness accessible to it is entrusted not as a ready-made gift but as its own achievement or act.

The holy angels in keeping with their creation occupy the highest place for it is impossible to be closer to God *by nature* than "the second stars," "the mirrors of Divine light."[1] They do not even have their own nature; their life is participation in the nature of Divinity itself, and they are creaturely gods. God's nature belongs to the Holy Trinity, to the three divine hypostases, to each one separately and to all in their triunity. But over and above this, divine nature is the source of life for the *creaturely* angelic hypostases, in keeping with the graced communion of their life in this nature.[2] Therefore the form of divinization proper to the holy angels is dif-

---

1. "Bodiless angels, who stand before the throne of God and are made bright with the luster of that place, eternally radiate brilliant beams, and are second lights" (Service for the Bodiless Powers, tone 1, sticheron).

2. It is an axiom of patristic theology, expressed particularly by St. John of Damascus (*A Brief Exposition of the Orthodox Faith,* book 3, chapter 9-11 passim) that no innate nature ex-

ferent from that which is graciously granted to humans, who are thus named gods *by grace*.[3] *By nature* angels are sons of God although *by hypostasis* they are created. And if only that which is above nature *(supra-naturale)* is called grace in the exact sense, then for them innate nature and graced gift merge into one. Their life is gracious only in the sense that participation in divine life is proffered here *to creaturely* hypostases which received being through the will *(thelema)* of God, and not through a generation that surpasses every sort of will.[4] But since the exact sense of the concept grace signifies precisely supernaturality, it is incorrect to distinguish and contrast in the life of angels their natural condition and their graced being[5] (as Catholic theology does, and in its wake sometimes Orthodox as well). They do not have a nature distinct from divine nature. Al-

---

ists unhypostatized *(anupostatos)*; on the contrary, every spiritual being is hypostatized *(enupostatos)*. But he adds that it is not necessary for each nature to have its own hypostasis: it can be hypostatized through a hypostasis that already has its own nature. Such is the divine incarnation in which the human nature of Christ is hypostatized through the divine hypostasis of the Logos. Developing this thought we can state that human nature which is hypostatized through human hypostases in the first Adam is hypostatized for a second time in the second Adam, Christ. Similar to this, divine nature which belongs to the divine hypostases is hypostatized in creaturely angelic hypostases, mirrors of divine hypostases — second lights. This communion in divine nature is for them a natural-supernatural, natural-graced condition. The problem of the correlation of hypostasis and nature on the whole is far from being definitively explained in theology.

3. A characteristic distinction in word usage: angels are called (Job 1:6; 2:1; 38:7) "sons of God" (of course in the plural number, in contrast to the only begotten Son of God) simply, as such. On the contrary, for humankind a new graced birth is required for this: "he gave authority to become children of God, who are born not from blood or from desire of the flesh or from desire of a man, but from God" (John 1:12-13).

4. In the Arian controversies what the Arianizers ascribed to the Son of God, namely, generation from the Father out of his own nature but only by the will, refers in reality only to the angels and not to the Son of God who "became so much the more excellent than the angels as the name he inherited is more glorious than theirs" (Hebrews 1:4). Generally a whole series of arguments relating to the necessity of mediation between God and the world to which Arius attributed a Christological character (and in this he was completely repudiated by St. Athanasius the Great) could be referred in reality only to the angels.

5. True, in Orthodox liturgics one can sometimes encounter similar expressions. "O Christ, You have established singers for Your greatness who are rational in essence, incorrupt by Your grace, having fashioned Your angels according to the image, inaccessible" (Canon of the Bodiless Powers, ode 6, tr. 2). But in the given context it speaks in general about the creation of angels and the expression "by Your grace" only points to their creatureliness.

though it is *given* to them as to creatures, nonetheless because it is given it already constitutes their very essence.

Whence it follows that the natural proximity of angels to Divinity or their *natural* divinization, can no longer be increased, and even the divine incarnation in this sense has no influence on their essence. As its ontological precondition the divine incarnation has *the presence and difference* of both natures, divine and human. The latter has its own albeit creaturely uniqueness and only on this basis is it possible for the natures in Christ to be "indivisible and unconfused," which is attested by the Chalcedonian dogma. The communication of divine life to humankind, their divinization and adoption as children of God by grace, is the result of the divine incarnation. For the angelic world this precondition is absent, for angels do not have a proper nature other than the divine (and therefore the assumption by God of angelic nature as indicated above would signify only the taking upon himself of His proper nature, a self-repetition, which is an ontological nonsense.) On the other hand the goal of such a new divinization of angels is absent because they have received it in full measure at their creation.[6]

Out of the properties of angelic nature arises their personal *immortality*. Immortality in humankind at the beginning, before the fall, is only a possibility *(posse non mori,* not *non posse mori),* which had to become reality through human effort, assisted by grace, whereas after the fall by which death entered, it could be given only through the divine incarnation by virtue of the resurrection of Christ.[7] Humankind does not have the power of immortality naturally, although it was able to overcome the possibility of death, owing to *that same uniqueness* of its nature and the creaturely *complexity* connected with it, which is the cause of the instability of the union of body and soul. This complexity is absent in angelic nature, as is uniqueness. The angels are already created immortal not in possibility but in reality; such is their nature. "Having a nature hostile to

6. This contrasting is obliquely contained in the letter to the Hebrews: "Since the children share flesh and blood, He also took them upon Himself, so that through death He might deprive the power of the one who has authority over death, that is, the devil . . . for He does not take upon Himself the angels, but rather He takes upon Himself the seed of Abraham. Therefore He had to become like His brothers in everything" (Hebrews 2:14, 16-17).

7. An independent question is whether or not the divine incarnation is necessary for the positive power of immortality even of prelapsarian humanity. This leads to an even more general question which already sprang up in theology long ago: is the purpose of divine incarnation reduced to redemption or does it have a more general and independent meaning, does it lie on the paths of the world's creation and apart from the fall?

corruption, the most divine minds stand around Your honorable throne."[8] Even Satan is not punished with death after his fall, but remains just as immortal as before it.[9] The fall is for him, of course, a type of spiritual dying, as a state of life, but in him there is nothing to die in the sense of a cessation or interruption of life, in consequence of the dissolution of his very essence. Death in humankind is just such a dissolution of the soul and body which *in their union* form human nature. A soul does not die even after death, but a soul without a body and outside a body is not a human being; it is deprived of the fullness of its nature. True, one still speaks about the death of the soul, as a sinful estrangement from God, but this refers to the state of life and not to death as the destruction (temporary or final) of nature itself, which represents some ontological catastrophe. There is no place for such a catastrophe in angelic nature. Hypostatic spirit is immortal as such (without distinction, be it in the angelic or the human essence); it has in itself the power of supra-temporality and the stamp of eternity, the prototype of the divine hypostasis is pellucid in it.[10] Therefore a hypostasis in itself cannot die. The possibility of death lies in the hypostasis' connection with bodily nature and in that nature.

But angels, as has been explained above, do not have their own nature for they share the life of Divinity and are nourished by eternity. Therefore they are eternal, although *by means of a creaturely* eternity, i.e., although they are not without beginning and are not their own principle, they possess the endlessness of life, or immortality. This power of life is derived by them from their *divine participation,* for creaturely entities do not have in themselves the source of life, but in the Word of God and the Life-giving Spirit. Between their life and this source no mediating medium exists which can prove to be a hindrance — such as nature and in particular corporeality are for humankind. The life of angels consists in perpetual divine participation and vision. "Around the throne of the king of all are forever exulting all the angel ranks," "with the illuminating dawns of the Trinity,"[11] "the chief commanders standing around God,"[12] "with tri-luminous dawns richly adorning the angels, incomprehensibly they receive Your lu-

8. Service for the Archangels, tone 6, canon, ode 4, tr. 1.

9. Even if one applied the phrase "the second death" (Revelation 20:14) to him, this does not at all signify a loss of immortality but even presupposes it.

10. See "Chapters on Trinitarity (Glavy o Troichnosti)," *Pravoslavnaia Mysl'*, I, 1928. This has now been published in S. N. Bulgakov, *Trudy o Troichnosti,* ed. Anna Reznichenko (Moscow: OGI, 2001), pp. 54-180. Translator's note.

11. Service for the Archangels, tone 6, stichera.

12. Canon, ode 5, tr. 3.

minous revelation everlastingly,"[13] "O angel of God standing immediately before the Holy Trinity,"[14] "as lights you have shown, O wise one, the immaterial essence of your angels, filled with ineffable light."[15] Immortality constitutes the natural property of such entities.[16]

As creaturely entities who are already immortal in keeping with their creation, they have the power of life not in themselves but in the Godhead, thanks to their divine participation. Although they do not need the physical food which is necessary for humankind, spiritual entities still require spiritual food. "The bread of angels," about which one sometimes speaks, is this spiritual communion, the spiritual Divine Eucharist in which the Lamb of God, through whom all things came to be, is slain pre-eternally for love of the creation. The Church bears witness to this active participation that the heavenly powers have in our earthly Eucharist: "now the heavenly powers serve invisibly with us." But the Eucharist of the divine incarnation and Golgotha's sacrifice is the fulfillment of the pre-eternal Heavenly Eucharist, of the sacrificial love of the Son in obedience to the Father and in reception by the Holy Spirit. And the holy angels who stand before the throne of the Holy Trinity gaze on this Supernal Eucharist and serve it in its earthly celebration: "For the King of kings and Lord of lords comes to be slaughtered and given as real food; *angel choirs go before him*," and this going before unites the heavenly mystery of the Holy Trinity with its earthly manifestation. One should not believe that the holy angels co-share in the Divine Eucharist only as ministers; they are co-participants, although they receive and administer spiritual communion.[17] And this communion of the angels, by which they advance from strength to strength, is the food of angels, "the bread of angels," with which they are fed. (In the Word of God it is deliberately emphasized that when angels appear to humankind either they take none of the food set before them, as in the appearance to Gideon, Judges 6:20-21, in the appearance to Manoah, Judges 13:15, 20, and in the story of Tobit, Tobit 12:19, or

13. Ode 6, tr. 3.

14. Ode 7, tr. 2.

15. Tone 1, canon, ode 7, tr. 1.

16. "Having an essence hostile to corruption, the most divine minds stand around Your honorable throne, having inherited the source of immortality, O lover of humankind" (Ode, tone 6, 4, tr. 1).

17. In the Prologue one can encounter an indication that an angel gave communion to hermits in their solitude. It is more natural to relate this precisely to the spiritual, angelic communion of the Divine Lamb "destined before the foundation of the world" (1 Peter 1:20).

they partake only for show, as the three angels did who appeared to Abraham, or Raphael on the journey with Tobit, Tobit 12:19.) A real eating of earthly bread is impossible for them, for it does not correspond to angelic nature,[18] and angels, as immortal, do not require food in the earthly sense and do not know bread. For this reason the witness of tradition, preserved in our liturgical books, that the archangel Gabriel fed the Virgin Mary during her stay in the temple with the bread of angels which he brought, cannot be understood literally — as if in addition to earthly bread there should exist the bread of angels, heavenly manna. The feeding with heavenly bread can be understood only spiritually: the archangel Gabriel in personal contact communicates that heavenly power which he himself receives as he stands before the throne of God. Divine participation is also the food of angels. Therefore the immediacy of communing with an angel is indicated here, and through it the favor which was given to the Ever-Virgin Mary in Her childhood.[19] As immortal and bodiless entities angels do not know material bread and they do not require it. But as creaturely entities who do not have the power of their immortality from themselves, they are in need of food, but this is spiritual food, the bread of God which gives life to the world (John 6:33), "the bread of life" (John 6:35), Who having come in the flesh gives Himself to be eaten to both angels and humans, bestowing on them the power of immortality.

18. In a similar sense, the marital relations of "the sons of God" with "the daughters of men" before the flood were sinful, for apart from all else, they were unnatural.

19. The text of Psalm 77/78:24-25 presents some exegetical difficulty: "and he rained manna on them as food and *he gave them heavenly bread. Humans ate the bread of angels.* He sent them food to satiety." "You fed your people with the food of angels and sent them bread from heaven without their toiling, ready bread having every delight according to the taste of each" (Wisdom of Solomon 16:20). Manna is called here heavenly and even the bread of angels or, by the apostle Paul, "spiritual food" (1 Corinthians 10:3). But manna was food sent miraculously by God, having all the properties of ordinary bread: taste, color, weight, and even the capacity to spoil and to cloy (Exodus 16:14-26; Numbers 11:7-9). And by contrasting manna with the true bread that comes down from heaven, the Lord straightforwardly says, "Your fathers ate manna in the desert and died. The bread which comes down from heaven is such that whoever eats it will not die" (John 6:31-51). It follows from this that the naming of manna as "heavenly bread," "bread of angels," must be understood in the sense of its miraculous provenance and not of its qualities, by which it did not differ from earthly food. And of course this cannot mean that the angels were fed with manna, for angels in general do not know material food, only spiritual. Blessed Theodoretos (in his 69th question on Exodus) asks, "Why did the prophet call manna the bread of angels?" And he replied, "Because angels served in offering it. A bodiless nature itself has no need of food."

Angels are holy according to their nature, which is divine. A depletion of divine life in angels is against nature or not natural for them because it deprives them of the nature inherent to them. But, it is possible, for it corresponds to *freedom*, which is proper to all creaturely spiritual entities, to both angels and humans. The holiness of angels is proper to them in a twofold sense: according to their nature and in their freedom — as a primordial given and as a possibility which they *freely* realize (or do not realize). The Lord does not create His creation as a thing that has in itself the law of its own being, but as free entities realizing themselves by virtue of their freedom, who assume for themselves their own law. The freedom of creaturely entities is simultaneously the stamp of the image of God by which God pays homage to His creation, and the stamp of creaturely non-being out of which God called creation to existence.

In the first sense freedom is the basic property of self-moving and independent spirits in their similarity to the self-existent God (their *aseitas*); in the second sense creaturely freedom is the shadow of that nothingness out of which creatures were called to existence. It is erroneous to think that creaturely nothingness in its freedom contains in itself any new sources whatsoever of life and creativity apart from God which contain something completely new that would enrich God Himself. Such an illusion is a self-deception: emptiness which seems to be depth, bottomlessness which seems to be inexhaustibility, bad infinity which seems to be eternity. In reality creaturely *nothingness* contains nothing in itself[20] (and in this sense it is the opposite of *Divine Nothingness* in the entrails of which all is concealed). One thing is accomplished by it: the potentialization of being, the reception of reality as possibility, the conversion of *on* into *me on*, meonization. Deceiving through its unformed and amorphous state, meonality as the condition of an as yet undefined definiteness, of an unaccomplished possibility, seems richer and deeper than itself. The theme of a being, its divine idea and task, is given in the general Sophianicity of creation, but it is afforded to creaturely freedom to have the theme not as a given but as a *possibility*, which is realized by creaturely freedom. Therefore creaturely creative activity is not creation out of nothing; the very idea of such an absolute creation is godless and anti-Sophianic (this is the posture of Lucifer which deceives and attracts others). Creaturely creative activity has its own theme which becomes its own only inasmuch as it is appropriated, and not rejected for the sake of the non-existent, in the emptiness of rebellious nothingness. But this does not prevent such the-

---

20. Cf. *Unfading Light,* the section on creation: Creaturely Nothingness.

matic creative work from being not only unlimited but also infinite, for this theme is divine, and thus contains in itself unlimited possibilities of realization. "Be perfect as your heavenly Father" (Matthew 5:48).

And so, freedom is the realizable but not yet realized possibility to become oneself. This freedom for spiritual entities is revealed in two ways: in the pre-temporal moment, on the verge of their entrance into life, between non-being and being, in the act of creation, and in time, throughout the course of life. The first self-definition of freedom, lying behind or above our creaturely being, and at the same time at its base, is connected with the fact that God creates us as free entities, not apart from us, not without our consent to our very selves, not without our acceptance of creation, though in a creaturely manner. Our I, summoned to existence by God, as His image or self-repetition, is pronounced by our own lips, by our own selves, for this cannot be done for us or without us. This union of God's creation with human self-creation is a mystery of God's creative work, which is already found and realized beforehand in our consciousness, but remains inaccessible to further disclosure. Our temporal memory retains no remembrance of our creation, but our ontological memory, our self-consciousness, keeps it, and testifies to us that it is so and cannot be otherwise. In the act of creation we ourselves received ourselves, consented to ourselves, and became ourselves in our own thematic plan and task. But with this the act of primordial freedom exhausts itself, it becomes some kind of metaphysical reality in which freedom and necessity are completely balanced and cancelled in the self-existence of the person, in its personal characterization, in the impossibility of self-negation or metaphysical suicide and death. This is the act of freedom in creation: exhausted for already created entities, it remains metaphysically behind.[21]

On the contrary, the second aspect of freedom — in time, as becoming — is hence only beginning; it consists in assimilating what is its own, in self-realization. In it possibility is overcome by actuality, potentiality by reality. The possibility of life as self-creative work is revealed to the creaturely spirit. This self-creative work is a going out of meonality toward the ideational crystal of reality, and the idea passes into becoming, *genesis* (in Plato). The presence of this freedom, as the self-existence of the spirit, as the godlike self-initiation of life, as the will to exist, is an inalienable feature of a spiritual entity, the stamp of God's image. But freedom as potentiality, which is expressed in the presence of different possibilities — being as well as non-being or half-being, partial being — is subject to a

21. Cf. *The Burning Bush*, the doctrine of original sin.

surmounting, is a kind of creaturely preliminary state, a spiritual *immaturity*, in consequence of which a vacillating choice between different forms of realization of one's self becomes possible. But when that realization is already completed, having become the sole possible and real one, it stops being free in the sense of spiritual immaturity and indeterminateness; rather it becomes a nature, the life of which is simultaneously free, as the life of a spiritual, autogenous and autonomous entity, and necessary, as the already sole possible life for it. It stands thus *on the other side* of freedom and necessity. And the surmounting of creaturely freedom, as non-actualized potentiality, unaccomplished self-determination, comprises the goal and limit of the development of each creaturely entity; from being changeable and mutable *(treptos)* in keeping with its creaturely infirmity, it becomes unchangeable *(atreptos)*, and attains stability in itself.[22] But, obviously, this immutability can be reached only on a positive path and in the good, and not on a negative path, in evil, for evil, which does not have the positive power of being and is its parasite, does not contain in itself its own depth, which would correspond to eternal life. God did not create evil, which came into the world out of creaturely *nothingness*, out of creaturely limitedness, and is only fed by it.[23] Therefore only in recovering the divine seeds of its own being, "in salvation" through the soul's participation in divine life, in holiness, do the surmounting of creaturely freedom with its bad infinity and the self-creative work for eternal life consist. "Be holy because I am holy" (Leviticus 19:2).

Let us now apply these general considerations about freedom to the angelic world. Angels, by nature created holy, in keeping with their divine nature were meant to reveal in themselves and in personal freedom that holiness given them, and through it to realize in themselves all their possibilities — their very selves. Already in their creation angels were determined each for their own service in their hierarchical position, and in the act of creation they received this divine determination, having made it their own. But as creaturely entities, they could not escape the condition of preliminary creaturely freedom as the presence of different possibili-

22. Apollinarius, who did not allow the union of two natures in Christ, divine and human, stumbled over the fact that human nature, as creaturely and of necessity *treptos*, necessarily introduces changeability into the divine-human entity. But Apollinarius completely ignored the fact that creaturely nature can and must become in itself *atreptos*, which took place in the sinless human nature of the Lord Jesus Christ.

23. This is the religious-philosophical argument of St. Gregory of Nyssa against the eternity of evil which has never lost its force: evil does not have in itself the material for eternal life, and in this sense it cannot be equated with the good in respect of eternity.

ties, the condition of potentiality; for them only free and definitive self-determination that removed this potentiality could be a way out.

The presence of such a condition of potentiality is completely and unquestionably clear from the possibility of the fall of angels "who sinned" (2 Peter 2:4), who "did not preserve their dignity, but abandoned their dwelling" (Jude 6). This same fall is ontologically possible only by virtue of creaturely freedom which bears witness to the presence of a spiritual incompleteness that leaves space for the fall or, more precisely, for the falling away from its own nature ("abandoning their dwelling"). This event occurred not primordially but in time, as can be concluded from the direct testimony of the Word of God ("I saw Satan who fell from heaven" [Luke 10:18]; cf. Revelation 12:7-9 about the war in the heavens waged by the archangel Michael against the dragon and his host, and the casting down of the dragon, one event in a chain of others). Before his fall Satan was the highest of the cherubim, appointed to look after the earth's creation.[24] Therefore his fall did not happen straightaway but already with a view to the creation of our world. Neither the time nor the form of this fall is revealed to us, and only some general considerations remain accessible.

For the angels who everlastingly see the face of God, the temptations of paganism, which is shielded from God by means of the world and falls into cosmism or atheism, are completely uncharacteristic. For them the possibility of religious doubt is excluded. God is for them the sole, dominating, self-evident reality. Therefore here the fall is free of the ignorance, error, or misunderstanding found among humans and it occurs in the pure guise of theomachy, which has as its single source the extinction of love. Love for God and the reciprocal love of angels, their collectivity, is that image of their being outside of which they cease to be themselves. But love can only be free, and God left His creation the possibility not

24. In Isaiah's prophecy about the king of Babylon they see an image of the daystar (14:9-25): "How you fell from heaven, daystar, son of the dawn. But he said in his heart, 'I will go up to heaven higher than the stars of God and will raise up my throne and sit on the mountain in the multitude of gods, on the edge of the north; I will go up to the cloudy heights, I will be like the Most High.'" The prophecy of Ezekiel about the king of Tyre has a similar meaning: "You *are the seal of perfection, the fullness of wisdom, the crown of beauty.* You were found in Eden, in the garden of God; your clothes were ornamented with every precious stone; ruby, topaz and diamond, chrysolite, onyx, jasper, sapphire, carbuncle, emerald and gold, all was skilfully set in your little settings and threaded on you, *prepared on the day of your creation. You were an anointed cherub in order to defend, and I placed you in it;* you were on the holy mountain of God, you walked among stones of fire. *You were perfect in your paths since the day of your creation until iniquity was found in you*" (28:12-15).

only to love but also not to love Him, because without this freedom love would be impossible. For angels to love means to be themselves. They share in the divine nature by virtue of their self-renouncing love for God, by their sacrificial self-immolation through immersion in the divine ocean, for they do not have their own nature. They surmount their individual incompleteness, they communicate in the whole of Divine Wisdom only in a loving, collective union with other angels. Self-love for angels is ontological suicide — not in the sense of the self-extinction of hypostatic being (which is impossible) but in the sense of their own devastation through separation from their own proper nature.

In ecclesiastical literature the fundamental motive for the angels' fall is understood in three ways: carnal lusting for the daughters of humankind (Genesis 6), pride in their desire to become equal to God, and envy because of their powerlessness to compare with God. But all these motives comprise but a series of consequences of the fundamental fall which is the sin against love, i.e., self-love. Angels can only live in love and by love; it is the most self-evident truth, the law of their life. How could love for God and fellow angels die out in the bright cherub, the daystar, the son of dawn? This is a dark secret of creaturely freedom which hides the insuperable depth of non-being in itself that is ready to gape open until it is definitively overcome and reduced to potency, to a ghostly shadow. For this there can be no explanation, no interpretation, because such freedom, creaturely freedom, is absolute arbitrariness, irrationality; but at the same time it comprises the core of the free I, until it outgrows it, having attained that spiritual maturity when this meonal freedom will cease to exist, being forever surpassed.

Prior to this surmounting, its reality — with all its possibilities concealed within it — is the reality of creation itself. With it is attested the sincerity of the Creator's intentions who utterly humbled Himself before His creation, having given it authentic reality. In this way this same reality is also given to the absolute arbitrariness of non-sense, one of the possibilities of creaturely freedom. Love can only be free, for if it is not free it is not love. And *free* love is not self-interested (conceiving self-interest in the highest possible sense as the possession of the blessings which accompany love). One can love *not for* these blessings or *for their sake,* for such circumspection is self-love and slavery, but not love. One can love only for the sake of love itself, for the sake of God Himself. And precisely such is angelic love — with such love do they love God. A negative confirmation of this is the fall of Satan owing to the extinction of love. It is mistaken and senseless in its metaphysical improvidence but precisely for that reason it is an absolutely arbitrary, despotic, free act testifying to the lofty nature of a love that once was. So too the angels who contended with him with Michael at the head "did not love their own soul even unto death" (Revelation 12:11), out of love for God; in other words, to the very end they displayed the freedom, disinterestedness, and sacrificial character of love. (That some sort of danger "even unto death" unknown to us existed for Michael and the angels in their battle with the dragon and his angels arises from these mysterious words.)

Love's fading away has as its result the most terrifying spiritual egoism and isolation, which humankind cannot know, being for all that a generic entity and as such connected by natural threads with its own genus. Such natural links do not exist in the angelic world. They are connected by relations of *personal* love in which and through which their oneness in Divine Wisdom is revealed for them. In their love for God and in their mutual love they realize their collective oneness which crumbles with the loss of love, being replaced by lonely, cold individualism. Owing to this property of angelic nature the fall of separate angels remains isolated and does not extend immediately to *the whole* angelic world in the way that sin entered the whole human race through the fall of one human — the first Adam, and through the resurrection of One the whole race is saved from death. In the angelic world division and "war" occurred for which there is no analogy in the history of humanity (war and division in the limits of the one human race, and the hostility of Christ and antichrist within its history, have a different, derivative meaning).

Although the fall of one prime-angel was not immediately extended to the *whole* angelic assembly, it still infected separate angels and attracted them by its example. In Revelation it is said of the dragon that "his tail pulled from heaven a third part of the stars and cast them onto the earth" (12:4), with a lie (the devil is "a liar and the father of lies" [John 8:44]) and slander ("cast down is the slanderer of our brothers who slandered them day and night before our God" [Revelation 12:10])[25] being the means of seduction. In the heavens the devil found an arena for his satanic energies and by his example and his slander "attracted" other angels, "a third part of the stars" (it is hard to say if this must refer directly to the number of fallen angels or if it has another hidden meaning). Spiritual communion between all the angels, obviously, was not terminated after the fall of Sa-

---

25. The mysterious tale of the prologue of the book of Job (1–2) about the appearance before God of the sons of God and "among them" Satan contains an indication that Satan is trying to calumniate Job.

tan and his minions, still remaining in heaven for some time until his overthrow. We have no indications about whether or not this fall of the angels occurred instantly or gradually. But the devil finds the first arena for his egoism and love of power in heaven, until his overthrow has occurred, and he falls from the sky like lightning (Luke 10:18). According to the testimony of the Word of God, his overthrow from heaven, out of the spiritual world, happened not through an almighty operation of the chastising right hand of God, but through "the war of the angels." God even here did not violate the freedom of creation, but let it self-determine itself in consciousness and action. Although only love truly unites, antagonism against it, hatred, consolidates those who bear malice by means of solidarity in evil and commonality of action and goal. The domain of Satan forms therefore a special kingdom with his legions that exists indivisibly as long as he has the power and the possibility of taking possession (cf. Matthew 12:25-26; Mark 3:24-25; Luke 11:17-18). It is impossible to say whether or not the structure of this kingdom corresponds to the former hierarchical situation of the angels, but it does have its foundation there. Of course, this solidarity in evil retains force only as long as a common field of operation remains.

The archangel Michael's victory over the dragon and the overthrow of the devil and his angels from heaven is the decisive event for the whole heavenly world. The voice in heaven (belonging, obviously, to one of the angels) proclaims, "Rejoice, you heavens and you that dwell therein" (Revelation 12:12). This overthrow is the definitive localization of evil in the angelic world, after which it remains free of it. According to the belief of the church, by passing through this trial and battle, the angels were finally confirmed in love for God and acquired steadfast fortitude in the good: "sanctified by the Holy Spirit the angelic assemblies *remain immovable against evil* and are divinized according to their first blessed ascent."[26] For them the spiritual age of freedom, as the presence of diverse possibilities and not yet manifested potentiality, has passed; they *have surpassed* creaturely freedom turned towards primordial *nothingness* with its chiaroscuro and now they are turned irrevocably towards the divine light, "divinized according to their first blessed ascent." The life of the holy angels is unceasing divinization in a mutual union. By analogy with humanity here one can speak about the angels' completed salvation not from sin, but from the possibility of falling, where this self-salvation was accomplished by the powers of the angels themselves, by their love for God, and

26. Canon for the Bodiless Spirits, tone 6, ode 4, tr. 3.

by virtue of the Blood of the Lamb pre-eternally poured out for the salvation of the world.

What can the life of fallen angels be like and in what do they become firmly established? After their fall, having been torn away from God, they lost the possibility of living by divine nature and uniting with the assembly of angels to be reciprocally completed in it. Their existence was devastated and became like a spiritual death, but personal immortality and thirst for life remained inalienably theirs. They kept the spiritual-psychic structure of life with all its possibilities: will, reason, the capacity for psychic movement, but all this became without nature and empty. But *up to a time* this emptiness is filled up parasitically; evil is nourished by good and hatred by love *through combat* with them, originally in the heavenly world and after their downfall from heaven in ours. "Woe to you living on earth and in the sea, because the devil has come down to you in powerful fury, knowing that not much time remains for him" (Revelation 12:12). The fall of Satan occurred, so to say, *with a view to* the human world in which he desired to become "the prince of this world," its god, to ravish it away from God and thus fill up the lack in his own life.

The existence of Satan and demons is parasitical; they are nourished by the fumes of this world; they strike at its sinful passions and strive to corrupt it, making of it their own nature which they are lacking. Therefore the seducer, "the ancient serpent," already appears in the garden of paradise gaining the victory over our ancestors; so too in the desert he endeavors to tempt the Lord already as master of the world, by showing to Him in visions all his dependent kingdoms. And further he will lead an uncompromising, last struggle with the true King of the world. He enters Judas after the morsel is given to him (John 13:27) in order to destroy the Lord through him ("the prince of this world comes" [John 14:30]), but it turns out that he is "judged" (16:11) and "driven out of there" (12:31), and that "the powers are removed from the principalities and authorities" (Colossians 2:15). But until this definitive expulsion from the world and casting down "into the lake of fire" (Revelation 19:20; 20:10), the devil will wage a tireless struggle for this world, right up to the last rebellion of Gog and Magog which he will stir up (Revelation 20:7-8) and to the final attempt to become human in "the man of sin, the son of perdition" (2 Thessalonians 2:3-4). In this manner, although Satan and his angels have shut themselves off from the possibility of spiritual growth and knowledge, being separated from God, still in their parasitic existence they display a certain progress in evil and the work of evil; their metaphysical egoism becomes dynamic out of its stasis; their emptiness crosses over into efficacy.

But after the final division, when the world will become the Kingdom of God, Satan and his angels will be left again definitively without nature; they will be submerged in the state of metaphysical emptiness: a hypostasis thirsting for natural life and not having it — the fire that does not go out and the worm that does not sleep — "the eternal fire prepared for the devil and his angels" through his expulsion from the world. This state of naked subjectivity without any possibility of being freed from it and of slaking it, which people who have devastated themselves also share, represents the hellish fire of ultimate metaphysical suffering, the state of hypostatic life without nature. It has as its source the cold of egoism, freedom in non-love. God leaves Satan in his own wilfulness, in that spiritual blind alley to which he led himself. Can this experience of emptiness, of the definitive bankruptcy of rebelling creatureliness remain fruitless and is there no longer any path of repentance? The church keeps this question under the ban, as one that cannot be accommodated to our current consciousness.

The good angels, by surpassing creaturely freedom with the changeableness flowing out of it, have been forever firmly established in life in God; for them eternal life has already begun. The time of free self-determination and struggle with the fallen angels represents in the angelic world a certain likeness to our age, as a time of trial, after which the life of the future age enters, eternal life. But all the same the angels remain creaturely spirits with creaturely limitations. Communicating in divine life, they do not receive the properties of Divinity itself: omniscience, omnipotence, immutability, self-sufficiency, supertemporality, superspatiality, hypercosmicity, in general, absoluteness.

The creaturely limitedness of angels is expressed, first of all, in their metaphysical finiteness or formed state. Angels necessarily have their own internal form, a definite mode of being. Their spiritual or bodiless condition does not contradict this. Conformation holds for both corporeal and spiritual being, signifying simultaneously the power of being that is inherent in its reality, and limitedness. Only God is free from all limitedness, and thus from being formed. He is *above* form. This does not mean that in God the power of conformation is absent, that formlessness reigns. No, He has in His Wisdom the totality of all forms, which were spent by Him in creating the world. He is the form of forms, their absolute foundation. But although God unites in Himself all forms, He himself remains unconstrained by them. He is not determined by any form. On the contrary, everything creaturely has above all its own interior form — the creaturely idea, which then is disclosed also in the outside. But the formed state of angels is already a metaphysical limitedness by which is set for them an impassable distance from God. At the same time their being is qualified by it; they receive the power to differentiate each other and to have mutual relations.

Angels belong to one *assembly* and consequently have a common spiritual form; at the same time they differentiate among themselves, from which arises the possibility for their mutual relations, their "collectivity." For, entities which are entirely foreign to each other as well as those which are completely identical and mutually repeat themselves are likewise incapable of "forming an assembly." With respect to God the life of angels is an unceasing divine cognition through divine life, an ascent having no limit. With respect to themselves the life of angels is the *mutuality* of graced illumination and knowledge of one another in the manner of hierarchical correlation, where, however, the lowest ranks keep their independent meaning for the highest, for all angels are *individually* provided with qualities and enter into the fullness of the angelic world (after the manner of the structure of the church's body which consists of many different members whose differences are equally necessary — 1 Corinthians 12:12-27). And this mutual knowledge and common life of the angels has for itself its own *language*, which differs from human language of course by its intuitiveness.

But this difference can touch only the external cover of language — similar to the distinction of various human languages,[27] but not the Word itself which remains one for all creation, as the Word itself is one, through

27. The Apostle Paul does not speak about language but about angelic and human *languages* in his hymn of love (1 Corinthians 13:1): "If I speak with the languages of angels and men and have not love, I am clanking copper or sounding cymbal." The very construction of the phrase, where angel languages are placed in one bracket with human, is evidence that language here is understood as parlance, not interior but exterior word, dialect. It is scarcely even possible to add to this expression a dogmatic meaning and not only rhetorical significance in view of the fact that the supposition made here is out of place in the life of the angelic world, namely, the absence of love. We have an analogous expression, also having only a rhetorical and not a dogmatic meaning, in the letter to the Galatians 1:8: "But if we or an angel from heaven were to begin preaching to you what we had not preached, let him be anathema." It is clear that this very condition, as well as the presumed anathematization of the angel from heaven, is completely inadmissible and is taken here only for its more colorful expression of thought. Romans 8:38 has a similar non-dogmatic, rhetorical significance: "I am sure that neither death not life, nor angels, nor principalities, nor powers, nor the present nor the future nor the height nor the depth nor any other creature can separate us from the love of God in Christ Jesus, our Lord." Obviously, angels, principalities, and powers — willingly or unwillingly — can never separate from the love of God, and this whole series is only a rhetorical expression of the general idea that *nothing*, no power, can accomplish this.

whom all things came to be (John 1:1-3). Language is from words, but words in various languages have as their own content a common interior word of the things themselves, and these words-meanings-essences are from the Divine Word, by which God uttered the whole world. And this general truth is confirmed by the fact that angelic words are at the same time human. For the angelic hymn is made known to us by the prophet (Isaiah 6) and the evangelist (Luke 2) in human language, and the speeches of angels to humans are also spoken in human language, and — what is here decisive — in this human language the very Godhuman Himself spoke; and besides this He spoke not only to humans but also to His Father, who likewise responded to Him in human language. All this obviously confirms that the interior language is one, for the Word is one.[28] That angels speak in a special way or in their own language (which is self-evident) is therefore not of decisive importance; what is significant is that they *speak*, they master the word. It is the mode of their mutual illumination and at the same time their means of praising God. It is of no use to head off into further speculations about the particular properties of angelic language. Of course, the language of bodiless spirits differs from human language by its immediacy or intuitiveness. "The interior word" or the sense of a word will appear here as non-incarnated in an exterior cover, which the angelic word receives only on its encounter with the human word. In this sense one can say that angelic language contains in itself the ideal, semantic prototype of human language.

No matter how high on the ladder of divine wisdom and mutual cognition the holy angels are found, because they remain creaturely-limited entities, they are limited in their *knowledge*, which therefore can be continually enriched and broadened. This refers both to their general penetration in the life of the Holy Trinity and comprehension of the Wisdom of God, as well as to *events* in the life of the world, in which the creative will of God is revealed, in the plan of salvation of the human race (e.g., the angels rejoice over one repentant sinner [Luke 15:10]). Of course the relation of the holy angels to the mystery of divine incarnation which was foretold to humans by God as far back as paradise cannot be consid-

---

28. I have developed these ideas in my manuscript on the philosophy of the name as an introduction to *imiaslavie* and completed them in a speech to the special commission of a section of the All-Russian Church Council 1917-1918. *Imiaslavie* or "name praising" refers to the veneration of the divine name Jesus suspected of being idolatrous by church authorities. Bulgakov's text was published posthumously as S. N. Bulgakov, *Filosofiia imeni*, ed. L. Zander (Paris: YMCA Press, 1953). Translator's note.

ered complete ignorance, but for the fullness of this knowledge "even the angels desire to penetrate"[29] into this mystery, which is revealed in the Church. In a similar manner, although they know about the second coming of the Lord with his holy angels and about the Dread Judgment, they "do not know about that day" (Matthew 24:36; Mark 10:32). In a similar manner, according to the evidence of the church hymn, angels "wonder" when they see the accomplishment of the events of our salvation (see the invocations in the services for the twelve Dominical and Marian feasts). Of course this "wonderment" must be understood not so much in the sense of being dumbfounded by the new and unknown as in the sense of fathoming an accomplishment that is thoroughly disclosed.[30] One must believe that with respect to the general life of the world and the composition of creation, angels, who are inseparably linked with it, increase their knowledge of it by the same measure as they know themselves better. (One can compare this with the gradual human cognition of the world and the self: while it is darkened and impeded by sinfulness, it already contains in its creaturely nature the principle of limitedness.)

In this manner one can establish development and growth in the life of angels, the presence of a real filling of time; this is generally characteristic of creaturely existence which is limited in every moment of time. But together with this there is present the potential for becoming unlimited in the fullness of time. The thresholds of this development and its ages lie beyond human discerning, except those to which the doctrine of the Church directly points (in particular the time of the angels' testing).

$$*\qquad*\qquad*$$

Angels, who stand before the throne of God, give themselves up to divine knowledge, divine contemplation, theology. Being turned one to the other they gain cognition of the forms of everything that exists, what we in our human language call love of wisdom (philosophy) and knowledge of the world (science). Besides, they not only contemplate and come to know, they also *glorify* God and respond to His command with the creative movement of their spirit, like living mirrors of the Uncreated Light. The holy Church in her prayers and canticles constantly bears witness to the

---

29. 1 Peter 1:12; cf. Ephesians 3:10; 1 Timothy 3:16.

30. The philosophical meaning of the Greek *thaumazein*, which signifies precisely philosophical wonderment, reflection, corresponds to this. (Cf. p. 65, note 9.)

fact that the holy angels stand before the throne of God, "singing the triumphal hymn, shouting, crying and saying" (these four expressions describe the singing of angels in various respects). The *singing* of angels is the prototype of any singing, and in particular of our own; the doxology of the angels is the foundation of our human doxology, in which, as the Church puts it, the holy angels also participate. We have direct testimony about the doxology of the angels in Isaiah 6:3 concerning the seraphim: "and they called out one to another and said, 'Holy, holy, holy, the Lord Sabbaoth! All the earth is full of His glory.'" This Trisagion of the angels is praise of the Holy Trinity, which the seraphim, while flying, *call out one to another.* This is an important indication that the doxology contains not only each angel's personal address to God but also forms the beginning of their mutual communion, common life, and collectivity: it is not only prayer, but also common, mutual, creative inspiration, which in human language we call *art.*

Ezekiel's vision (chapter 1), which contains in a certain respect an image of the angelic world, occurs without a sound (except for the noise of wings). The words and sounds here are replaced by light and color: the rims of the wheels, full of eyes, the sparkling of the angels' feet, their appearance like burning coals or lamps, and the radiance from fire and lightning, the likeness of a throne above their heads as if of sapphire and the blazing metal as if of fire inside the likeness of a human, a certain fire and radiance around him like a rainbow on the clouds during a fire. This appearance of the angelic world, "the radiance of the Lord's glory" (10:4), is *luminous*[31] (and only the prophet hears in conjunction with the vision "behind me a mighty thunderous voice: blessed is the glory of the Lord from its place" [Ezekiel 3:12], i.e., he hears the doxology). The doxology of the angels occurs here not through word and sound but through light and color, images and forms. In the language of human art the name for this is painting, the art of form and paint, light and chiaroscuro.

The doxology of the angels was revealed to humankind as long ago as the Nativity of Christ, in the appearance "of a multitude of the heavenly host praising God and shouting out: 'Glory to God in the highest and on earth peace, favor among humans'" (Luke 2:13-14). This doxology, in contrast to the vision of Isaiah, has as its subject a definite *event* in the life of the world — the divine incarnation. It contains the glorification not

31. The Marian aspect of this vision is explained by me in *The Burning Bush,* in an excursus.

only of God in the heavens but also of the world on earth and of the favor shown to humans, i.e., it embraces in itself heaven and earth, the life of the whole universe. This is also significant for the angels themselves who include in their doxology the destinies of creation. In the vision of the Seer (Revelation 4:6-8) the four living creatures, filled with eyes in the front and the back and inside, resemble what Ezekiel saw: "Neither by day nor by night do they take rest, crying, 'Holy, holy, holy, the Lord God Almighty, who was, who is, and who will come,'" a doxology similar to that heard by Isaiah. This is a hymn to the greatness of God in eternity. But in Revelation 5:8-12 we already have the doxology for the expiatory Lamb: four living creatures together with twenty-four elders "sing a new hymn, saying: 'Worthy are You to take the book and remove the seals from it; for You were slain and with Your blood You have purchased us for God. . . .' And I saw and heard a voice of many angels around the throne, and living creatures and elders, and their number was myriads of myriads and thousands of thousands, and they spoke with a loud voice: 'Worthy is the Lamb who was slain to receive power and riches and wisdom and gentleness and honor and glory and favor.'" Here the doxology is performed for the slaughtered Lamb, i.e., for God the Savior and Redeemer, God in creation. And a remarkable peculiarity of this doxology of the angels is that with them is united in doxology "all creation, that is found in heaven and on earth and under the earth and in the sea, and all that is in them, I heard, and it said: 'Worship and honor and glory and authority to the one seated on the throne and to the Lamb for the ages of ages'" (5:13). In this way, the angelic and human world, all of creation, are united in *one* doxology *with one and the same content.*

The above-mentioned forms of doxology, of course, do not exhaust all the forms of the angels' praise of God. And as if testifying to this inexhaustibility of theirs, the psalmist cries out to the holy angels:

"Bless the Lord, all His angels, mighty in strength, who do His word" (Psalm 102/103:20).

"Praise the Lord from the heavens, praise Him in the heights. Praise Him, all His angels, praise Him, all His powers" (Psalm 148:1-2). Then with the same summons the psalmist addresses the whole creation.

Likewise in the song of the three youths in the fiery furnace (Daniel 3:58): "Bless the Lord, angels of the Lord, sing and exalt Him for ever" (Then follows a similar summons to all creation and to human offspring.)

Also relevant are such testimonies of the Church as, e.g., "The angels in heaven sing your resurrection, O Christ our Savior; make us on earth worthy," etc.

The doxology and hymnody of the angels has, first of all, as we learn from revelation, a divinely visual and mental content which refers to God in Himself — to the mysteries of the Holy Trinity, to God's holiness surpassing comprehension (the Trisagion), to the triune hypostases separately, to the mysteries of the divine incarnation and economy, to God — the Creator and to the greatness of His creation. Knowledge of God is here united with knowledge of the world. Doxology is testimony about God as Truth in itself and as the truth of all things. In our human language we must name doxology in *this* respect divine sapience or theology, love of sapience or philosophy, and world sapience or cosmology. The Divine Logos is also the Logos of the creaturely world, its truth, meaning, and inherent law, and cognition of the logic of things is united with knowledge of the Logos, just as the reflection of the sun is united, and in a certain sense identified according to content with the sun itself. Elevated to the comprehension of the Logos of the world, the cognizing mind itself becomes a logos in virtue of participation in it; it is the self-consciousness of the Logos in its creaturely otherness.[32] The Divine Logos is one in all creation. He is one and the same in the angelic world and in the human world. Therefore we are right to bring together not by degree but qualitatively angelic knowledge and human knowledge and to see in the first the prototype of the second.

It is further incumbent upon us to recall anew that the seraphim, in Isaiah's vision, *cry out* the thrice-holy hymn *one to another.* This means that hymnody by its content is the general and mutual work of the whole angelic world. It is first of all the proper life of the angels for their very selves, their cognition which by the power and truth of things becomes doxology. And thus, in the angels' doxology we must single out their *cognition* of God and the world, the power of thought and knowledge, as the creative element of their proper life. And one must not understand doxology statically, as an immovable contemplation of the unalterably given, shown or seen, but one must grasp it dynamically, as a continual creative work in cognition, an ever deepening knowledge of the Creator in Himself and in creation. And this knowledge unites the angelic world with the human, as the Word of God directly attests in Revelation 5:13, Psalm 102/103 and 142,[33] in the song of the youths, Daniel 3:58ff.: humankind is summoned together with the angels to sing praise. And of course, this refers to doxology

32. In the history of philosophy this was sensed with the greatest force by Hegel.

33. Bulgakov's reference seems erroneous; perhaps he is thinking of Psalm 148 again. Translator's note.

in general and to its content in particular, i.e., to intelligence of God. Here, however, one can establish a distinction in the forms of cognition, angelic and human, the indisputable unity of their divine root notwithstanding.

There exists, first of all, an enormous distinction in divine cognition on the side of clarity of comprehension which is proper to the bodiless spirits and those clothed with human flesh. From this arises the intuitive character of angelic cognition in contrast to discursive human cognition. The distinction in cognition of the world is determined, further, by the fact that one can call it *the disinterestedness* of angelic cognition in contrast to the unwillingly selfish, pragmatic, economic-technical relation to cognition among humans, for whom the world is the arena of struggle for existence, of labor in the sweat of one's brow. This imposes on human cognition the stamp of dependency, self-interest. On the contrary, angelic cognition possesses freedom, generally inherent only in art; it is cognition as creative work, as mental painting.[34] But human cognition, with all its pragmatism, likewise cannot fully renounce a lovingly contemplative, freely disinterested relation to its subject; herein lie the pathos of cognition, its angel wings. (The reckless and unreserved pragmatism or economism in the concept of cognition, which has its ultimate expression in contemporary economic materialism, is a slander against humankind.) But these wings are always bound, inasmuch as the human in cognition is not only the contemplator — the artist, free seeker of truth, but also a master who is at the same time a slave. For him practical half-truths prove to be more needful and important than truth, and the criterion of utility invariably argues with the criterion of truthfulness. Therefore the angels' cognition is invariably doxology, whereas in the human world — alas — this is not the rule but rather the exception. In addition the being of God is not so obvious a truth for humankind as for the angelic world, whereas the being of the world has for humankind a natural, forced obviousness such as the being of God does not have. From this one can understand the sad phenomenon that for humankind knowledge of the world and knowledge of God not only do not merge into one, as in the world of angels, but often are mutually opposed. The world hides itself from God, and knowledge of the world not only is not theology and doxology as in the angelic world, but they ordinarily contradict each other.

The angels' doxology is contemplation and praise not only of Truth but also of Beauty. In this sense it is in essence an artistic creative work, art

34. Philosophy is sometimes called *the art of comprehension* in order to express its freely contemplative, disinterested creativity in cognition.

in the precise meaning of this word. That such is its character is manifestly clear from the fact that doxology is sung, is called a song. In this way it is imprinted like a creative covering for the ideas of truth in the forms of beauty, as the creativity of beauty in the image of Beauty. "Song" is here the general designation for art — for artwork in general. Song unites in itself the art of word and sound, versification and music in their oneness, and also, of course, in their separateness. What does the art of the word represent — the word, clothed in the form of beauty, versification in relation to the word itself, to meaning? Here the meaningful word and its link with all other meaningful words is not abolished — logos and logic, for they are indissoluble because they have their foundation in the Logos through whom all things came to be. Everyone in the world and all things are words-meanings in their mutual connection, and they speak themselves in a word (indifferently — angelic or human). But above logos and logic there is still something in the element of a word that is not contained in the word-meaning and logical connection, although it does not abrogate them. This is the form, rhythm, aural covering, through which a word is dressed in beauty, begins to burn with a new light, is illuminated from within, and becomes not simply a word but a song, hymnody, logology. In contemporary language this art of the word is called poetry, and hymnody is called versification, poetic speech, which includes not only speech in verse form in the narrow sense but also rhythmic speech in general, speech winnowed by the beauty of form (in contrast to prosaic speech as dryly semantic, logical). In general one can say that speech is never separated from artistic, poetic form, that it always has a form, while the beauty of a word is inseparable from meaning, just as the life of the hypostasis of the Word is indivisible from the life of the Holy Spirit who rests on Him.

But in human usage, along with general utilitarian pragmatism there encroaches prosaic expression, insensitivity to the beauty of the word which becomes vapid. Words, when they are deprived of life and beauty, wither and as it were turn into bank-notes which replace coinage of full weight (so now new words are being formed in our homeland). They are dry leaves, rustling like paper but not ringing sonorously. In the Church the life of a word in beauty becomes the inheritance of sacred, liturgical hymnody, but in the worldly sphere, it is the lot of a special artistic creation, poetry. An element of the beauty in a word is laid bare; the word is exposed not only as divine meaning but also as divine form. The relation to this form unites but at the same time divides the human and angelic worlds. Angels are continually singing, "taking no rest day or night," like the four living creatures of Revelation 4:8. Not knowing human exhaustion, they also do not know human prosaic expression. Their word is a song, their knowledge is artwork, the rhapsody of the world in angelic song-creation.[35]

But there exists a single Beauty that penetrates heaven and earth with its rays, known to both angels and humans. Human art has its prototype in angelic art; human artistry becomes related to angelic artistry where it has its own foundation and ascends along with it to the prime source, to God, to Beauty. "The Lord reigns, he is clothed in loveliness." The clothing in beauty is the Kingdom of God coming in power. A word, clothed in the form of beauty, ceases to be itself even as it preserves all its force of meaning: it is already a super-word, a metalogos, not only meaning but also beauty, beauty in meaning. Therefore in hymnody a human song is united with an angelic one and is in a certain sense homogeneous. For that reason the possibility of the joint service of humans and angels becomes comprehensible. It follows that the distinction of human and angelic language is not a divisive obstacle. This is confirmed by the fact that the song of angels, which is humanly audible, finds direct access to the human soul, and is apprehended or translated into human language. Isaiah speaks about the song of the seraphim which he heard and the Seer joins with him here. (According to tradition, the Trisagion, which was sung by the angels, was heard by a youth, lifted up in the air.) All this says that an angelic song is akin to a human canticle. But here it is necessary to bring to attention all that difference which exists between human and angelic life. That which in our life comprises a rare festival among wearisome workaday routine — a song, the light of poetry, beauty — is the element that fills the whole life of the holy angels, who know no rest either by day or by night in their hymnody. Another even more important difference consists in the fact that thanks to the angels' holiness, all their singing is a doxology for God, whereas in human singing only a small portion is immediate doxology. In the enormous majority of cases a greater or lesser share of human, passionate, and sinful nature is alloyed to it, and in general it is darkened and burdened by the flesh and sin. But in itself the power of beauty and creative work, even independent of the subject, raises humankind towards the heights of the angelic world, from where invocatory doxology is heard.

In addition to the beauty of the poetic word, a song and a doxology contain another element as well, the beauty of sound, music. Sound in music is obtained from its natural source, the human organ of speech,

---

35. In Russian Bulgakov has created a rhythmic, poetic sentence as if to illustrate the point he has been explaining. Translator's note.

and then from musical instruments. On this basis musical accompaniment is possible, the union of song and music, which is imprinted by the psalmist: "Praise Him with the sound of trumpet, praise Him on the psaltery and harp. Praise him in tympanum and chorus, praise him on strings and organ" (Psalm 150:3-4). This bears witness to a certain unity of human and instrumental, i.e., non-human, sound in music and in hymnody, very significant and important.

In nature everything has not only weight, form, mass, and color but also sound even though the latter cannot always be extracted or made accessible to our ear ("the harmony of the celestial spheres!") This universal fact is realized differently. Nature is full of unmusical sounds, noises, from which we distinguish musical sounds and weave them into music. If we set aside the physical-acoustic and musical-theoretical aspect of sound, we can say that if sound is a certain self-disclosure, self-evidence of the existent, then musical sound and music are the clothing of sound by beauty, by form, which has force both for a separate sound and for their connection. Music as such is the beauty of sound, independently of word-meaning. Musical sound is something else, greater and higher than a simple sounding. Sound, as the sounding of substance, is a property or state of matter, and musical sound is already meta-matter having substance as its own substrate; it ascends above substance to the world of bodiless spirits. The genius of language bears witness to this when we involuntarily speak of sweet sounds: angelic sounds, angelic song. And in truth, music and song are audible news from the other, higher, angelic world, news that unites the celestial and terrestrial worlds. Everything alive sings, blessing the Lord, and to this song the whole creation is summoned (in psalms and in the song of the three youths).

It is remarkable that the capacity for song and in general musicality comprises the property not only of the human world but also of the animal world, especially of birds and certain insects. In humankind music becomes a conscious creative work, art. In *song* humankind and all creation truly unite with the song of angels as such, despite all the difference in its perfection and quality. The difference here remains both quantitative and qualitative. Song and music in the human world gild only the surface of sound, the life of which consists of unmusical and even anti-musical featureless and ugly noises and cacophonies. Natural sound, heavy and inert, is impenetrable for music like that matter whose property it is. On the contrary, angelic sounds, the prototype of earthly sounding, musically limpid through and through, are already music and song. Likewise in accord with its vital significance, human and all the more so animal sound serves, first of all, for the expression of material, lewd, and carnal life, passions and desires. And human music and song serve for clothing the passions, both noble and mean, if not with beauty, then with prettiness. Even that pragmatism, which we have already noted in the field of thought and cognition, manifests itself here, subordinating the musical life of humankind to the necessities of its mortal, carnal existence, to the events of its temporal life. One can say that only a certain participation in song and music, which fill the angelic life as doxology, is accessible to humankind and the human world. This is one of the multiform expressions of the reality of Jacob's Ladder, along which the angels of God ascend and descend from heaven to earth. And in times of inspiration the human soul remembers these angelic sounds: "her tedious songs of earth could not replace the sounds of the heavens."[36] The foundation for the art of sound is found in the angelic world, in its harmonies. This is the authentic music of the heavenly spheres which the ancient Pythagoreans glimpsed in the motion of the heavenly bodies.

There exists yet another field in human creative work — the art of light, color, and form, pictorial art. It receives its ecclesiastical consecration alongside of the art of sound in church architecture, in murals and iconography. The art of visual (in painting) and tactile forms (in sculpture and architecture) reveals Beauty in the world, alongside of the beauty of nature. It likewise has its prototype in angelic doxology. But there is no direct evidence about this and one can only reach a conclusion on the basis of the data of Revelation. Does not the creative work of forms and paints, so to say their song, enter together with verbal song into angelic doxology? It cannot but enter, for it has its basis in the angelic world, in the region of pure forms and color.

Angels are second lights, mirrors of Uncreated Light, in which there is no place for any shadow and which surpasses forms. But second lights, being creaturely, called out of non-being into life, contain in themselves the possibility of chiaroscuro and the necessity of a boundary, and consequently a form. The white ray of the Divine Sun is transcendent to color; it is without color, for it is beyond color, it embraces all possible colors and tints in itself. But second lights already enter the region of color and tints. The angelic world has in its chiaroscuro, which corresponds to the creatureliness of what is created out of nothing, all the fullness and richness of form and color for both the heavenly and the whole earthly world. These forms and tints bedeck the world with color, creatively mirrored in

36. A quotation from Mikhail Lermontov's poem, "Angel." Translator's note.

figurative art. It anchors in the forms of earthly life these heavenly visions, and it sees the supernatural in nature. Forms and tints, like musical sounds, are immediately linked with substance, but they likewise overcome it. They are meta-matter in matter; in them matter surpasses its very self, ascends beyond itself. Beauty in the world and in art is for us a perceptible ladder between heaven and earth.[37]

But can one limit the being of angels, as the prototypes of all forms and of color, by means of a passive state which has in itself no creative principle, or rather is their being a kind of self-creativity, a creative self-determination? It is enough to pose this question in order to recognize only one possible answer, namely, that angelic nature possesses itself in actuality, determines itself efficaciously. This is applicable to angelic doxology, which occurs not only in song and word but also in form and color. One can obliquely confirm this with the consideration that angelic doxology cannot be more meagre than human doxology. In human doxology (temple liturgy) *all* arts participate, not only verbal-musical, but also figurative, not only word and sound but also gesture and color, form and fragrance. The correspondence to all of this is found in angelic doxology, where it has its primary basis.

It is not out of place here to recall once more that in the doxologies of the psalms of praise and in the song of the three youths an appeal to glorify God is addressed to all creation ("bless the Lord, all you works of the Lord, sing and exalt Him for ever"), and then all its forms are enumerated together, with the angels at the head: elements and forces of nature, fish and animals, and finally servants of the Lord. What does this unity mean? How can the sun and moon, the stars of heaven, every rain and dew, all winds, fire and heat, cold and sultriness, dews and hoarfrosts, nights and days, light and darkness, ice and frost, hoarfrost and snow, lightning and clouds, earth, mountains and hills, the sea and rivers, whales and all moving things in the waters, all birds of the sky, wild beasts and all livestock together with human offspring praise, sing, and extol the Lord together with the angels (Daniel 3:58-82)? It is obvious that together with the angels and in the angels, the whole universe with all of its attributes sings and praises the Lord: with color, light, form, resonance, sparkling, transparency, fragrance, tactility. Surely the angels of fire, winds,

37. Here it is appropriate to recall the words of God to Bezalel which bear witness to the divine inspiration of true art: "And the Lord God spoke to Moses, saying, 'See, I have called Bezalel, son of Uri, son of Hur, from the tribe of Judah. And I have filled him with the Spirit of God, with wisdom, understanding and every art'" (Exodus 31:1-3).

waters, and other elements about which Revelation speaks have in the form of their being something corresponding precisely to these elements? If beauty is poured out in all of them, in various forms and colors, then all this enters into the angels' doxology like a kind of artwork. Iconography hints at this; it dresses angels not only in resurrection robes "that dazzle" but in different, variegated colors. Such is the doxology of angels, their life of prayer, and creative work, a manifestation of themselves and of their essence to the glory of God.

But their life of prayer is not exhausted by doxology and gratitude. It includes the work of their love for the world, their prayer on behalf of the human race, their constant intercession on its behalf, about which the holy Church bears witness.[38] Angels have no need to pray for themselves or their fellow angels, for in their life that fullness and perfection is already realized which will be attained for the world only in the life of the future age, when "God will be all things and in all." Among them the sole prayer for their own selves is doxology and gratitude. But as long as our world goes through the pangs of birth, as long as "the whole creation together groans and is tormented until now," "awaiting the revelation of the children of God," and we "ourselves groan, waiting for adoption as children and the redemption of our body" (Romans 8:19-23), the angels assist the world, in addition to their direct service, by their incessant prayer on its behalf. Thereby they not only serve the world, but also satisfy the requirements of their own proper life, for they are created by the God of love for love. But in contrast to their proper life in doxology, here they are linked with the life of our world, with its changeable condition. Through this they themselves are drawn to a certain degree into the life of our world, which they serve; they live with it a common life in all of its incompleteness; and they take part in its historical process, as the Revelation of St. John the Theologian graphically shows us.

38. "O Word without Beginning, by the sacred prayers of the cherubim, seraphim, powers, thrones and divine forces, of the angels, archangels, principalities, lordships, bestow on us the riches of Your mercy, for You are a lover of humankind" (Canon for the Heavenly Powers and all the Saints, ode 1, tr. 1). "Your noetic powers do now beseech You, merciful Lord, the powers, thrones, seraphim, lordships, angels and archangels and principalities: be merciful to Your people and save us, for You are merciful of heart" (ode 5, tr. 1). Cf. also ode 6, tr. 1; ode 8, tr. 9; ode 9, tr. 1. Service for the Bodiless Powers, tone 1, the kathisma verses and canon, ode 9, tr. 2, etc. One can say that the testimonies of the Church about the prayer of the angelic powers for our sake, as well as appeals to them with a request for prayerful assistance, are innumerable. They prove the possibility and power of such an appeal to angels, as well as the fact of their incessant prayer for us.

CHAPTER 6

Theophanies and Angelophanies

One of the most important features of the theophanies in the Old Testament is that God appears to people in the form of an angel, or, the other way around, that an angel represents the person of God. First of all, we shall establish this very fact in general terms on the basis of biblical narratives.

Genesis 16: The appearance of an angel of the Lord to Hagar in the desert, where this angel speaks to her immediately in the person of God: "by multiplying I will multiply your offspring" (v. 10). "And Hagar called the Lord who was speaking with her by this name: You are the God who sees me" (v. 13), and the spring there also received that designation.

Genesis 18-19: The appearance of the three angels to Abraham by the oak of Mamre, in which the Church generally sees a revelation of the Holy Trinity. The conversation of one of the angels with Abraham and Sarah goes this way: "and the Lord said" (18:13, 17, 20, 26, 33).

Genesis 31:11, 13: Jacob relates, "The angel of God spoke to me in a dream: 'Jacob, I am God who appeared to you at Bethel where you poured oil on the monument and where you made a vow to me.'"

Genesis 22: The sacrifice of Isaac. The angel of the Lord, who appeared to Abraham, speaks here in the person of God: "I know that you fear God, and that you have not spared your son, your only one, for me" (22:12, 15-18).

Exodus 3: The appearance of the burning bush to Moses. "And the angel of the Lord appeared to him in the flames of fire out of the midst of the thorn bush" (v. 3). "And God called to him out of the midst of the bush ... and said: 'I am the God of Abraham, the God of Isaac, and the God of Jacob'" (vv. 6ff. to the very revelation of the divine name Yahweh). The very same is confirmed in the speech of the protomartyr Stephen: "an angel of the Lord appeared to Moses in the desert of Mount Sinai in the burning flame of the thorn bush" (Acts 7:30), and at the same time it is said here, "but when he approached to look, *the voice of the Lord* came to him" (v. 31). And then more expressively, "This Moses . . . God sent as leader and deliverer through the angel who appeared to him in the thorn bush" (v. 35).

Concerning the giving of the law on Mount Sinai Exodus 19:3 says only that "Moses went up to God [on the mountain], and *the Lord called to him* from the mountain, saying" (and further on chapter 19 speaks all the time about the commandments of the same Lord, the revelation of His Glory and so on up to the end of the book of Exodus). Nevertheless this theophany is explained in the New Testament as an angelophany, namely, in Stephen's speech it is said directly about Moses, "This is he who was in the congregation in the wilderness *with the angel who spoke to him on Mount Sinai.*" And it is said so definitely in the letter to the Galatians 3:19 that the law "was given through *angels*" (already the plural number in contrast to the singular by Stephen). Hebrews 2:2-4 also refers to this: "For, if the word *proclaimed through angels* (likewise in the plural) was firm," then how will we not be anxious about salvation "which having first been preached by the Lord" was firmly established by God through signs and wonders and gifts of the Holy Spirit.[1]

Exodus 13:21-14: The Lord himself walks before Israel at its exodus out of Egypt (cf. Numbers 14:14; Deuteronomy 1:33; 4:37; Nehemiah 9:19), about which, however, it is said: "and the angel of God moved, going before the camp" (14:19). Cf. Numbers 20:16 likewise.[2]

---

1. From our perspective the indifferent usage of singular and plural number, angel and angels is meant here to indicate not so much a definite angel as the angelic world in general in contrast to Divinity. But of course this excludes the possibility of seeing here "the angel of great counsel," that is, the Word of God (as one sometimes understands). This is especially clear from the direct *contrasting* of the angel and Christ in the letter to the Hebrews, chapter 2. In Exodus 33:2-3 there is a unique but characteristic Old Testament contrasting of an angel and God Himself which is difficult to interpret: "and the Lord said to Moses, 'I will send before you *an angel* . . . [and he will lead you] into the land where milk and honey flow, for *I myself will not go among you* lest I destroy you on the way, because you are a stiff-necked people.'" As we already know, Exodus 13:21-14 and its parallels say straightforwardly that the Lord went before Israel at its exodus from Egypt. This seeming contradiction must be understood according to the sense of the general doctrine about angelophanies as theophanies: here appearances of the power of God happen in place of a hypostatic appearance of the Lord Himself, which takes place only in the divine incarnation, when God appeared in the flesh.

2. On the contrary, Exodus 12:23, 29 speaks about the Very Lord where one could have expected an angel — in the story about the slaying of the firstborn of Egypt. A simi-

Exodus 23:20-23: The Lord says to Israel, "Behold I am sending an angel to guard you on the way. . . . Attend to yourself before his person and listen to his voice, do not be obstinate against him, because he will not forgive your sin, for *my name is in him*."

Numbers 22:23f. The story about the prophet Balaam where an angel of the Lord appears who speaks (vv. 32-33) directly from the person of the Lord (similarly Judges 2:1-4).

Judges 6:11-24 speaks of an appearance of an angel of the Lord to Gideon, and then it speaks directly about the angel: "the Lord, having looked on him, said" (vv. 14, 16, also 23), and then again it speaks of "the angel of God." Similarly Judges 13 narrates the appearance of God's angel to Manoah; when Manoah asked the angel his name he replied, "Why are you asking about my name? It is wonderful" (13:18). (The words "Why are you inquiring about my name?" are said word for word at God's appearance to Jacob when he wrestled with God.)

And finally, the naming of "the angel of great counsel" in Isaiah 9:6 (Slavonic) also refers to this.

On the basis of the adduced comparisons one can see that the identification of the appearance of God with that of an angel, theophanies and angelophanies, runs like a red thread through the whole Old Testament revelation. And this is so clear that for rationalist understanding it only remains to see here the traces of original polytheism. For believing comprehension this fact demands a purposeful explanation. The Old Testament does not know an *unmediated* revelation of God. God is inaccessible (transcendent) to humankind. "No one has ever seen God" (Exodus 19:1-18; 1 Timothy 6:16); only in Christ, in the Divine Human, has a theophany occurred: "the only-begotten Son, being in the bosom of the Father, he has made him known" (John 1:18). The servant of the Word bears witness about this theophany: "Concerning that which was from the beginning, what we heard and what we saw with our own eyes, what we examined and what our hands touched, concerning the Word of life — for life has appeared and we saw and bear witness and proclaim to you this eternal life which was with the Father and appeared to us" (1 John 1:1-2). Christ coming into the world, His becoming human, was a single, authentic, perfect theophany which forever has abrogated all preliminary theophanies.

But perhaps some will say that the Old Testament also knows its

---

lar case is Numbers 23:3-4, 16, in the story about Balaam. These exceptions, it seems to us, only confirm the general rule with respect to the deliberate indifference of this word usage, in which it is necessary to see not archaic primitivism but a profound revelation.

own theophanies. Does not Israel say after his night-time wrestling with God, "I saw God face to face and my soul was preserved" (Genesis 32:30)? But of course this is only said about the reality of the theophany, not about its immediacy. We will recall that Jacob does not even know with whom he was wrestling. Further, is it not said of Moses that the Lord spoke with him face to face "as someone would speak with his friend" (Exodus 33:11; cf. Deuteronomy 34:10)? "Mouth to mouth I speak with him, and plainly, not in riddles, and he sees an image of the Lord" (Numbers 12:8). But this too must be understood only in a relative sense, as evidence of the greatness of Moses in comparison with other prophets, which is manifestly clear from the words of the Lord Himself (in the same chapter, Exodus 33:20, 23): "you cannot see my face because a human cannot see me and remain among the living," "you will see me from behind, but my face will not be visible," and the Lord shows Moses only the glory of God. Likewise the words of God about Moses' vision "of an image of God" (Numbers 12:8) are spoken by God "who came down in a fiery pillar" (v. 5; cf. 11:25).[3] In a similar manner the theophany to the prophet Elijah (1 Kings 19:11-13) in "the breathing of thin fresh air" was not a personal theophany. This preliminary theophany of both Old Testament God-seers, Elijah and Moses, is contrasted with an authentic vision of God, the appearance of the very Son of God in the flesh, whom they were made worthy to see on the Mount of Transfiguration. There remains the appearance of God to the prophet Isaiah — Isaiah 6:1-6. Here it is said that he saw "the Lord who was sitting on a high and exalted throne, and His glory filled the whole temple" (v. 1), "my eyes saw the Lord Sabbaoth" (v. 5). But this vision is explained by the Lord himself not as a theophany but as a vision of glory, a doxophany: "Isaiah said this when he saw his glory" (John 12:40-41), where this doxophany unites with an angelophany. Ezekiel's vision was also the appearance of glory. The vision of the prophet Daniel (Daniel 7) of the

---

3. All the more must the text of Exodus 24:10 be understood in conformity with Exodus 33:20, 23 concerning how Moses and Aaron, Nadab and Abihu, and seventy of the elders of Israel on the mountain "saw the God of Israel and under His feet something like a work of pure sapphire and clear like the very heaven. And he did not stretch His hand against these chosen from the sons of Israel. They saw God and ate and drank." Without a doubt, these words about the vision of God cannot be related to a personal immediate divine appearance, but to the vision of God's glory, to a theophany as a doxophany. This understanding is confirmed by the parallel account of Deuteronomy in Moses' speech to the people where it is said, "See, the Lord our God showed us His glory and His greatness, and we heard His voice from the middle of the fire; today we have seen that God speaks with a man who remains alive" (Deuteronomy 5:24).

Ancient of Days, sitting on a throne, was not so much a theophany as it was an eschatological dream in connection with other images (as the prophet himself calls it at the beginning of the chapter containing the entry "the dream and the prophetic visions of his head as he lay on his couch").

And so we definitely have in the Old Testament one group of theophanies as doxophanies (we have explained them in another place)[4] and a second group as angelophanies which are now subject to our efforts to comprehend them. In the Old Testament we distinguish *general* theophanies, about which it is simply said "the Lord appeared to Abraham" (Genesis 12:7; 17:1; 18:1; 26:2, 24; Exodus 6:3), to Solomon in a dream at night (1 Kings 3:5; 2 Chronicles 1:7) and also not in a dream (1 Kings 9:2; 11:9). Then, there are *prophetic* theophanies about which it is said "the Lord said to me" (Exodus 8:1, 5; Jeremiah 15:1; 19:1; 22:1), "and the word of the Lord came to me" (Jeremiah 1:4; 2:1; Ezekiel 1:3f., etc. in almost all the prophetic books), "and the hand of the Lord was upon me" (Ezekiel 1:3; 8:1). Finally there are *deliberate* theophanies especially marked out as such — to Abraham ("and the Lord appeared to him when he was sitting at the entrance of his tent, during the heat of the day. He lifted up his eyes and looked, and there three men were standing opposite him" (Genesis 18:1-2), to Moses, Elijah, Isaiah, and Ezekiel. All the theophanic angelophanies listed above are relevant here.

The first group of theophanies (general and prophetic) are more correctly reckoned to be *revelations of God*, mysteriously and ineffably communicated to a human being. This is the *divine presence*, immediately or intuitively accessible to a human as an inner hearing of the word and knowing of the will of God. The anthropomorphism of verbal expression does not alter the purely inner and spiritual character of these theophanies. From them are distinguished theophanies in the strict sense, which are accompanied not only by a spiritual but also by a certain sensible, physical perception by the whole human being, as an integrally pneumatosomatic entity. Here not only does a passive hearing and feeling of God take place but also a certain *encounter* with Divinity. It can be a personal, "face to face" encounter with a divine hypostasis, or else it is an encounter with Divinity as divine power, glory, and wisdom, but not hypostasis. In a final way God appears in his glory in a cloud,[5] which not only reveals but

---

4. *The Burning Bush*, excursus on the Glory of God.

5. The Marian sense of the appearance of a cloud is explained in *The Burning Bush*, excursus on the Glory of God.

also conceals the face of God. In the narrative of God's appearance to Moses the vision of God's face, inaccessible to a human being, *is directly contrasted with* the vision of His glory, which is accessible to a human (Exodus 33:19-23).The divine presence in Moses' tabernacle in the guise of a pillar of cloud (Exodus 33:9-11) has that same meaning, as it does in Solomon's temple in the guise of a cloud (I Kings 8:11; Chronicles 5:13-14) as well as "in the breathing of the thin voice" in the theophany to Elijah and even in the vision of Isaiah where likewise "the house is full of His glory" (Isaiah 6:1). This tangible revelation of God's presence, His glory, the Shining of Divinity, is the light of Tabor on earth prior to the Lord's Transfiguration. But in contrast to the non-hypostatic theophanies in the Old Testament, revelations of the Ever-Eternal Light, its revelation in the New Testament was substantially *hypostatic* for it was the revelation of Divine Glory of the God who became human and thereby drew near to humankind, the Son of God who showed the Father to us and revealed the Holy Spirit resting on Him — our Lord Jesus Christ, the Godhuman.

However, the Old Testament too knows *hypostatic* theophanies, human *encounters* with God, reciprocal communication, conversation. But such encounters, as is already well known to us, happen only through theophanic angelophanies. God appears through an angel and an angel speaks in the person of God; the angelic hypostasis is endowed with divine power. The mission of the angels, their service in the world, receives here a completely exceptional significance — it presents God Himself in the world, it appears to the world *in place of* God. How is this possible? First of all, it is necessary to take into account the whole inaccessibility (transcendence) of Divinity for fallen humankind even in the womb of the Old Testament church. Since the cherub's weapon has barred access to the gates of Eden, where God came to converse with humankind (even God's judgment on the fall represents a still uninterrupted conversation), the possibility of *direct* divine communication has been removed. But God's love found a possibility for encounter with humankind through the medium of angels. The latter, being creatures, can be within the reach of humankind but at the same time, living by the life of divine nature, they are completely transparent for God. God made the creaturely hypostases of the angels, which are united with divine life, the personal medium for communicating with humankind,[6] with His image.

---

6. As it is said in the book of the prophet Ezekiel: "and the noise from the wings of the cherubim was heard even in the outer court, *as if it were the voice of God Omnipotent when He speaks*" (Ezekiel 10:5).

Angels are the creaturely-hypostatic countenances of the Divine Wisdom-Glory, which is hypostatized in them by God in order for Him to appear to humankind until this Glory will be revealed by the incarnate Word himself, by the hypostasis of Divine Wisdom and Glory, by Christ. An angel, as a creaturely ray of Divine Wisdom, possessing life in God, is a creaturely God, not only by grace like humankind but also by participation, although not according to its creaturely hypostasis. But it is precisely this creatureliness of an angelic hypostasis that makes it possible for humans to withstand the unbearable fire of theophany. This is the measure in which humankind can receive an appearance of God before His becoming human. But of course such a theophany has force only in the bounds of a definite purpose and is exhausted by it. In other words, it is completely lacking in that power which the sole true theophany has, i.e., the divine incarnation, in which it is not a creaturely hypostasis, even that of an angel clothed in the Glory of Divinity that appears, but rather the Second Person of the Holy Trinity Himself. This theophany has universal, pan-human and cosmic meaning. It abolishes the preliminary prototypical Old Testament theophanies through angels and renders them superfluous and no longer possible. The Lord Himself, the Angel of Great Counsel, is sent by the Father to earth.

And so, theophanic angelophanies are Old Testament appearances which pass away in the New Testament as the stars of night fade in the light of the rising sun. But their possibility must be explained on the basis of angelic nature. The very highest and ultimate possibility of angelic service is manifested here: mediating between God and the world, uniting heaven with earth. The meaning of the vision of Jacob's ladder is disclosed thereby in a special sense. "And he dreamt: behold a ladder *is standing on earth and its top touches heaven.* And behold the angels of God are ascending and descending on it. And behold the *Lord stands on it* and says: 'I am the Lord, the God of Abraham, your father, and the God of Isaac'" (Genesis 28:12-13). God speaks to the patriarch as the angels descend and ascend. Although this is not *directly* stated, it is clear in the light of all the remaining Old Testament theophanies that here too He speaks to humankind in and through angels. Therefore in essence we have only a theophanic angelophany there as well.

A question remains. The angels through whom God speaks in theophanic angelophanies are nowhere given names and they are not defined in their hierarchical position — they are simply called "angels." On the other hand, God who appears to humans and speaks with them is likewise not defined in relation to the three hypostases. The mystery of the

Holy Trinity, although contained in the Old Testament, remains covered over, which is why one cannot expect such a definition. In ecclesiastical literature this question is posed and resolved in the sense that the Logos speaks and appears and acts in the Old Testament prior to His incarnation. From this one can perhaps conclude that an angel who speaks in the person of God in theophanic angelophanies belongs to the Second hypostasis. Apart from other arguments such an opinion can be supported by the fact that since a theophany is accompanied by a word, it thereby belongs to the Word. But this consideration loses its force by the general fact that it is not God Himself who is the one speaking here but an angel who speaks to a human in human language for the sake of comprehension. Therefore the presence of the word in and of itself does not attest that the one speaking it is an angel of the Word, announcing the hypostasis of the Word. Therefore in each remaining case one needs to determine essentially if a given revelation refers to one definite hypostasis or to the entire Holy Trinity in its indivisibility.

First of all one ought to dwell on the appearance of the Lord to Abraham in which the Church sees a mysterious appearance of the Holy Trinity. The three angels, obviously, belong to the realm of the three divine hypostases, where the First naturally stands out, who speaks in the person of all and is called Lord (Genesis 18:13, 17, 20, 22, 33), while the remaining two angels (Michael and Gabriel?) are not defined in their hypostatic attributes. Perhaps this corresponds to the content of the theophany in which only a general and preliminary revelation of the Holy Trinity is given. Only the "monarchy of the Father" is deliberately disclosed here, the sense of which is that the entire Holy Trinity is the self-revelation of the Father in the Son and Holy Spirit. "Personal properties of the separate hypostases are generally speaking not disclosed."[7] The appearance of God to Abraham in the guise of three angels is the only one in which a theophany has the externally manifested features of tri-hypostaseity; in all other cases we have the appearance of only one angel.

With very good reason it is possible to see the revelation of the First hypostasis, and hence of an angel that refers precisely to Its domain, in the theophany to Moses on Mount Horeb, "in the flame of fire out of the

---

7. In the text of Genesis 18–19 the distinction between "the Lord" and "the two angels" arises so seldom that it is possible to see in them, really, only angels who accompany the Lord. But such an understanding is rejected by the Church, which sees here an appearance of the Holy Trinity and therefore does not make a distinction between the angels in the degree of their divinity (Rublev's icon of the Holy Trinity).

midst of the thorn bush" (Exodus 3:2). One can think this on the basis of the revelation of God's name, *Jehovah-Yahweh*, i.e., the One who is ("I am who I am" — Exodus 3:14). This Name of God in which the hypostatic character of Divinity is revealed as the absolute I corresponds most of all to the First hypostasis which out of itself begins the Holy Trinity.[8] There is a basis too for seeing in the angel who appeared to Abraham at the sacrifice of Isaac the envoy of the First hypostasis, for here we have a prototype of the sacrificial sending of the Son by the Father, and the testing of Abraham's faith, which God sends him, consists precisely in the sacrifice of the son. "God said to him: 'Take your son, your only one, whom you love, Isaac and . . . offer him as a holocaust'" (Genesis 22:2). When Abraham had already raised the knife to stab his son, "the angel of the Lord said to him, now I know that you fear God and did not spare your son, your only one, for Me" (22:12). This sacrifice is pre-eternally predetermined by the Father who so loved the world that He gave up His only-begotten Son for its salvation (John 3:16). He does not require it of a human being to whom however it is given to complete its human prototype after having shown obedience to God. It is far more complicated to say in the person of which of the hypostases the angel speaks and acts, who at first appeared to Hagar alone and then with Ishmael (Genesis 16:7-13; 21:17-19); however, according to the character of his words ("multiplying I shall multiply your offspring" — 16:10, "I shall raise up from him a great nation" — 21:18), it is possible to see here as well a manifestation of the First hypostasis, "the Almighty."

One can see the angel of the Second hypostasis in Jacob's wrestling at night. (He is called "someone" in Genesis 32:34 but in the prophet Hosea he is defined as God and as an angel.)[9] This wrestling with God is already an early forecasting of the approaching divine incarnation in which "indivisibly and without confusion" divine and human natures are united in Christ. Does not the angel who led the Israelites out of Egypt refer to the Second hypostasis? See Numbers 20:16.[10]

---

8. See my "Chapters on Trinitarity," now published in S. N. Bulgakov, *Trudy o Troichnosti*, ed. Anna Reznichenko (Moscow: OGI, 2001), pp. 54-180. Translator's note.

9. "Having taken courage [Jacob] wrestled with God. He fought with an angel and overcoming him he wept and entreated him" (Hosea 12:3-4).

10. In Exodus 13:21, it is said about the exodus of Israel out of Egypt: "The Lord went before them in a pillar of cloud, showing them the way, and by night in a fiery pillar, shining for them." On the contrary Exodus 14:19: "and the angel of God moved, walking before the camp of Israel and he went before them; and the pillar of cloud moved from their face and stood in their midst." Cf. also Judges 2:1 where we read, "I brought you out of Egypt and led you into the land."

In theophanies of a prophetic character one can see the angel of the Third hypostasis, who speaks through the prophets. Numbers 22:20-25, 23:4-5 refers to this, the story with Balaam, his donkey and the prophesying, as does the appearance of the angel to Gideon (Judges 6:11-24) and to Manoah (Judges 13:3-22). Here an appearance of an angel is related, and then Manoah tells his wife, "we saw God" (13:22f.) in view of the prophetic character of both appearances. With the greatest probability the appearance of the angel in Ezekiel's vision, Ezekiel 8ff., must also be understood in such a sense.

In this manner we come to the conclusion that theophanic angelophanies in the Old Testament cannot be fixed only to the one hypostasis of the Logos but refer to all three divine hypostases, both in their tri-unity and individually.

CHAPTER 7

The Incorporeality of Angels

The incorporeal spirits are created as angels, ministering spirits *(pneumata leitourgika)* (Hebrews 1:14). This angelic ministry possesses an ontological foundation in the inner mutual relations of the angelic and human world, and is rooted in this indissoluble, essential bond.[1] Angels are sent for service to the world because their proper life is connected with it, and if one is to keep in mind that the world, headed by humankind, is essentially a human world, one can best express the angels' bond with the world as their co-humanity. This definition in no way obliterates the impassable barrier between the assembly of incorporeal powers and the human world, but expresses their inner, primordial bond since the moment of creation. In its general fundamentals this bond was disclosed above, whereas here it is fitting to touch upon only one of its aspects, namely, the relation of angels to corporeality.

The fundamental ontological difference between angelic nature and human nature is not that angels are spiritual entities, for the human soul is also a spiritual entity. But the human is an incarnated spirit, possessing a body through which it is connected naturally with the whole world; the whole world is in the human, who is a cosmic entity. Angels are incorporeal spirits which do not have their own world or nature. Their proximity to God, which flows out of their lack of nature and their immersion in di-

---

1. Therefore it is erroneous to distinguish excessively and contrast in angelic nature their nature and ministry as we find in blessed Augustine: "Angels are spirits; although they are spirits, they are not angels; since they are sent, they become angels. For angel is the name of a ministry, not of a nature. If you seek the name of this nature, it is spirit; it is angel from what it does" (*In psalmis Enarratio* I:15, in *Patrologia Latina*, 37:1348).

vine life, determines their humanly inaccessible eminence; but their lack of a nature makes their existence depend on the human world which supplies for them their creaturely natural essence, and is for them, in a certain sense, a necessary suppletion. (St. Gregory Palamas expressly noted that the possession of a body marks the ontological superiority of humankind in comparison with angels, even though it is the source of weakness and of the peculiar discursive quality of human existence.)

Only in the human world does creation attain its culmination as the realm of human dominion, its ontological focus. God created the world in order to be all in all in it (1 Corinthians 15:28), depending on the world's readiness to receive it. Angels simply stand before God, illumined by His light; this divine participation is their life, and generally speaking the only one possible for them (aside from that spiritual suicide which the fallen angels committed). Before their fall, God came to humans in their own world to converse with them (according to the evidence of Genesis 3:8, "they heard — Adam and Eve — the voice of the Lord God who was walking in paradise in the cool of the day"). God comes into the world in order to take human nature upon Himself, without division and without confusion, and to raise it to the heavens to reside eternally in the Godhuman, in Whom God makes Himself co-human by virtue of His condescension towards creation. God "does not take upon Himself the angels, but the seed of Abraham" (Hebrews 2:16), not because humans proved to be holier than the angels and more worthy than they. On the contrary, the fall of humankind is one of the causes of the divine incarnation. The assumption of angelic nature by God is ontologically impossible because angels are missing a proper nature of their own. But the greater fullness and ontological independence of the human being, in comparison with the angels, is clearly expressed in the most holy humanity of the Mother of God which proves to be higher than the angels by virtue of the union with Divinity, divinization. For, the Theotokos is "more honorable than the cherubim and more glorious *beyond compare* (i.e., ontologically, naturally) than the seraphim." And closest to Christ after her comes the holy humanity of the Forerunner and Baptizer of the Lord, the angel-man. These facts are sufficient in order to establish the fundamental ontological correlation between the angelic and human world, according to which humankind is the fundamental and central axis of the universe, and is autotelic ("God did not subject the future universe to angels" [Hebrews 2:5]), whereas angels by their essence are destined for service to the world. Such service in and of itself, of course, is not humiliation; on the contrary, it even presupposes the hierarchical superiority of angels over humans. But hierarchical superiority is at the same time not ontological superiority in every case.

In any case the life of the angelic and the human world must be understood not as the separate existence of two ontologically independent worlds, but as the single, joint life "of heaven and earth" in which the hierarchical superiority of eminence and divine participation belongs to the angelic world, while the superiority of fullness and autotelicity belongs to the human world.[2]

The co-humanity of the angels is metaphysically expressed in that correlation of the angelic and human world in virtue of which the first contains the ideational prototypes of the second in hypostatic angelic collective existence, and the second realizes them in natural human existence. This co-humanity finds expression in the fact that the whole angelic world has a ministerial-protective relation to the human, as separate angels are guardians of separate humans, in their personal life. The world is created for the human and in accordance with the human, but it is preformed in the angelic world. From this flows the fundamental axiom of angelology and anthropology which is expressed in the words of Revelation: "by human measure, which [measure] is also the angel's" (21:17). This correlation is expressed in the heavenly Jerusalem, coming down to earth, which "has twelve gates and on them twelve angels; on the gates are written the names of the twelve tribes of the sons of Israel" (21:12). Here the twelve tribes express the fullness of the human race together with which is supposed the fullness of the angelic world so that it expresses the crown

2. Precisely in this sense the ontological correlation of humankind and angels becomes the subject of a deliberate elucidation in Hebrews 1–2. In the first chapter a general explanation of the superiority of the Son of God over the angels is made on the basis of a series of comparisons of prophetic texts, definitely pointing to the ministerial significance of spirits (1:14). In the second chapter the exaltation of the Son of God is woven together with the exaltation of humankind, which is united with Him according to nature. Here we find the following comparisons: "*For God did not subject the future universe to the angels,* about which we are speaking; on the contrary someone has testified somewhere, 'What do humans mean that You remember them; or human offspring that You care for them? You made them lower before the angels for a short time, and You crowned them with glory and honor, and placed them over the works of Your hands; You subjected everything beneath their feet' [Psalm 8:5-7]. 'When you subjected everything to him, you did not leave him anything that was not subjected to him' [Psalm 2:5-8]. So too Jesus in His humiliation was humbled not for long before the angels, so that by the grace of God He could taste death on account of all" (Hebrews 2:5-9). And then it is even deliberately underscored that "He does not take angels upon Himself but He takes the seed of Abraham."

and fullness of creation, in the heavenly city, where God will live with humans.

From the general co-humanity of the angels arises the important consequence that angels assume a human likeness in their relations to humankind; they appear to humans in human form (although with necessary distinctive features). This conformity to humankind is the condition of communication itself, as there is abundant evidence for this in the Word of God and sacred tradition.

This is first of all evident in the fact that angels speak with humans in *human* language, as was already noted above: the angels' song, their prayer, and their verbal appeals — all of this becomes accessible to humans inasmuch as it is made in human language. This signifies first of all the fundamental unity of the word, as that which proceeds from the Word, among angels and humans. And even in theophanic angelophanies the word of God, spoken by angels, is a human word. This further signifies the unity of the angelic and human word according to content, inasmuch as the earth in itself reflects heaven, and all that is on earth exists as an ideal form in heaven, the angelic world. "Heaven and earth" constitute one creation and have in themselves and about themselves one word, for it is about one thing. The idea is one, the word is one, the knowledge is one, although it is realized in different degrees.

The most important evidence of the co-humanity of the angels is that when they appear to humans they have *a bodily* form, human or even animal. Let us recall that the three angels in the theophany to Abraham stood before him like "three men" (Genesis 18:2). Joshua son of Nun saw the chief commander of the Lord's army as "a man" (Joshua 5:13), the prophet Daniel saw the archangel Gabriel as "a man clothed in a linen robe" (Daniel 10:5), and the New Testament appearances of the angels of the resurrection were likewise in the form "of a youth clothed in a white garment" (Mark 16:5), or "two men in glistening garments" (Luke 24:4). Further, in Ezekiel's vision the cherubim have the form of animals with four faces: human, lion, calf, and eagle (Ezekiel 1:10); "their appearance was like that of humans" (1:5). In this manner it is the developed human form as a pan-animal. In Revelation the four animals individually resemble a lion, a calf, a human, and an angel (the four symbols of the different evangelists). To this human dimension of the angels' appearances is added their subjection to the limits of space and time. They come to a definite place where they are sent for a definite time, and when it passes they depart. In general they enter into the life of our world without ceasing to be alien for us, although not strangers. In its dogma concerning the veneration of icons the Seventh Ecumenical Council established that the Divinity manifested in the divine incarnation could be depicted, and consequently, that it was co-human; it affirmed that the holy angels could be represented on icons; and by that very fact it confirmed the angels' co-humanity.

Both patristic writings and theological literature pose the question of whether or not angels have a body, even though it may be subtle when compared with the human body. Opinions are usually divided. Some fathers hold that "every creature — an angel, a soul, a demon — is a body by nature; because although they are subtle, in their essence and their particular properties as well as in their form, corresponding to the subtlety of their nature, they are subtle bodies, whereas our body is heavy."[3] Sometimes they define this subtlety of the body of spirits in terms of natural science or occultism as ethereal or gaseous bodies, so that the degree "of heaviness" of the body of incorporeal spirits and humans only comes down to a difference in the density of matter.[4] The opposite opinion predominates among the majority of the fathers. In the sessions of the Seventh Ecumenical Council no objection was raised against the opinion of Bishop John of Thessalonica that angels are not entirely incorporeal, but have thin bodies. St. Tarasius, Patriarch of Constantinople, confirmed the opinion that "one ought to depict angels, for they are circumscribable, *tous de aggelous graphesthai oti perigraptoi eisin* and the council concurred with this" (Mansi XIII, 164-65). Prologues and vitae abound with evidence about the appearances of angels and souls in a transparent luminous envelope (abundant material is collected by Bishop Ignaty Brianchaninov).

And so, on the one hand angels are incorporeal spirits, and by nature they are free from a bond with a body — whether heavy or subtle makes no difference; on the other hand they can be painted, and consequently, they have a form, which under certain conditions can be perceived by humans, and this form is human. How can one unite both of these seemingly contradictory propositions, each of which must be preserved in its full force? It is impossible by any measure to shake or limit

3. St. Makary of Egypt, *Works*, 4th ed., pp. 27-28, discourse 4 §9.

4. This point of view is expressed in the compositions of Bishop Ignaty Brianchaninov (Sermon on Death and the addenda). The views of Bishop Ignatii provoked a decisive reproof for being materialistic and out of step with orthodox doctrine from Bishop Theophanes the Recluse in his work: "The soul and an angel are not bodies but spirits." Justly denying any materiality for the soul, Bishop Theophanes nonetheless leaves open the question of whether or not the spiritual essence of angels and souls is clothed in "a thin, substantial envelope," "by a thin ethereal body," or is free of it. "If anyone wishes to hold either of these two opinions, let him do so."

the truth about the spiritual quality and incorporeality of the essence of angels and souls, and hence it is completely impossible to allow (without falling into materialism or occultism) for any sort of body whatsoever, even the most subtle, that would be indissolubly bound to an angelic spirit and clothe it. But at the same time one cannot reject the authenticity of angels appearing in human form, and it is impossible to see here only an accommodation to the limitedness of human perception, an illusion, a type of hallucination.[5] Angelic essence is *incorporeal* but the appearance of angels in human form *is authentic.*

This question is solved on the basis of the general doctrine about the nature of angels in their relation to the world, their co-humanity. Angels are appointed or sent for service to the world not as to a region alien to them but one familiar and even inseparably bound with their own. The angelic world, having in itself the prototype of creation, contains all its ideal-spiritual forms, which in their realization receive bodily existence, are clothed with a body, and become bodies. The body has not only a material existence, but also an inner ideal form that shapes it, its entelechy, and this ideal form of the body, which possesses the entire fullness of reality, is precisely its first reality. The embodiment of the soul is not a physical union or the insertion of the soul into a body as into a case; it is the inner bond of the spiritual creative principle, of the metaphysical energy or form, with the pliable material given shape by it. Through the power placed in it by God, the soul shapes for itself a body in its image and lives in it. If one were to examine the soul outside the body and independent of the body, it would not differ from an angelic incorporeal spirit (and this is confirmed by the fact that both angels and souls of the dead have been visible in similar luminous modes, having the form of the body). The (ontological) difference between them is that the soul contains in itself the image of its own body as a corporeal form (and in this sense is already ideally clothed with it), whereas an angel has in itself only the inner prototype of that image. With respect to this ideal prototype they are akin and similar; with respect to the spirit becoming a body, they are opposites. The inner ideal images are proper to angels only on the basis of their relation to the world; they correspond to the human image if they are received by a human, or, rather, it is the reverse: the human realizes the angelic pro-

---

5. In separate cases of angels' appearance separate features are especially noted which are not authentic, in contrast to the authenticity of the whole appearance. Thus in the story of Tobit, the archangel Gabriel directly says to Tobias and Tobit, "I was visible to you every day, but I did not eat or drink — you only imagined seeing this" (Tobit 12:19).

totypes for itself. One can say it this way too: the ideal form of the body is proper to angels, which really comes to be only in a human.

The only question is, *can* these ideal forms be perceived through their becoming a reality for our world too? This is obviously impossible for our *corporeal* perception, for which the spiritual world simply does not exist. If we allow that spirits and souls have a certain very subtle envelope, i.e., corporeality (the degree of its fleshiness is of no substantive significance), we thereby introduce them into our world, the domain of the bodily senses, although their perception would require a special refinement of organs similar to how refined states of matter are discerned only by special instruments and how the world of small entities is visible only through a microscope. (Occultism calls for the development of such organs of occult perception.) With this the chief difference between incorporeal and incarnate spirits is removed and they all indifferently enter into the region of our corporealized world.

Forms or images do not have corporeal being even of the most subtle kind, but rather ideal being. They are not envelopes, but ideal inner energy as a defining power. A form is not material (and it is not "an envelope") but ideal, super-material, spiritual. The body is the product of this power, which the spirit has as its own inner form, entelechy.[6] The vision of

---

6. In connection with this the following question is raised: ideal forms are inherent not only in human bodies, belonging to a rational, conscious spirit with its energies, but also to plants and animals. In a kernel the plant already pre-exists by entelechy as does an animal in the seed. How is this forming principle to be understood here; to whom does it belong? Occultists answer this question with the doctrine of the multiple planes of being, different principles of being existing in different planes: thus, to the kernel of a plant in the ethereal plane corresponds its "spiritual" (in fact, its refined-corporeal) form, and images of the animal kingdom belong to the astral plane. A system of universal corporeality of ever more refined degrees is obtained, in which the principal distinction between soul and body, form and matter (the primordial "earth") is obliterated. But if this distinction is to be maintained in all clarity, a question necessarily arises: to whom does the ideal form in a plant and an animal belong, since here there is no spirit, the true subject and bearer of ideal corporeality? These forms are implanted by the word of God, spoken on the fifth and sixth days of creation, but they could not be heard and perceived "by the earth," soulless and meonal matter, but only by the corresponding angels of the creature who fulfill the word of God. Angels are the souls of the plant and animal kingdoms, of the extra-human world; the ideal forms belong to them, the images of its being. The plant and animal kingdoms are human, having their focus in humankind, and the angelic world watching over creation is also focused on humankind. And in this sense one can say that the ideal forms of the whole extra-human, mineral, plant, and animal world belong to the human spirit in its ontological depth, although this be-

this form, if it is possible, is only spiritual, i.e., by the same intuitive perception by which spiritual entities, angels (and likewise, demons) see and know one another. We see and hear and smell and touch not with the body but with the soul, through the medium of the body. The soul has senses — vision, hearing, smell, touch, taste — and it is only for this reason that the body has corresponding organs, fashioned by the soul. But in a human who is a spiritual and corporeal entity, this inner sensation is *inseparably* united with the corporeal, so that all our images are pneumatosomatic, ideal-sensory. It is as equally impossible to remove the ideal form from them, because deprived of it they are extinguished, they lose meaning and content, as it is to separate it from corporeal incarnation. In this are the character, power, and fullness of human pneumato-somatic being.

But despite the unity and integrity of the human being, it remains complex, composed out of body and soul, principles of both worlds. This complexity allows their partial division for which there is no place in a simple angelic being. Death is such a division of soul and body, but certain states of frenzy (ecstasy) resemble it, when the soul is partially liberated from its bond with the body, and then sees immediately, spiritually, after the manner of angelic being. In this division the soul sees the spiritual world, which is closed for it by the curtain of the body. When humans die, the first thing that is presented to them is the world of spiritual entities encircling them, angels and demons. Some pious people, thanks to the special regard of God's mercy, receive this faculty for spiritual vision before their death, as in angelophanies. But for all people it naturally arrives with death, and once it has appeared, it is no longer lost even after the resurrection, since the life of a human in the future age will be in communion with the holy angels. To fabricate some sort of luminous envelopes or gaseous bodies as an explanation for the possibility of this vision is a misunderstanding. The very *forms in themselves* simply become visible, as ideal forms. The real spiritual world is seen that exists before the material world, beyond it and above it, as it is in its immediate being, by virtue of spiritual intuition, which has no need of any intermediaries and does not allow any explanation. Of course, in any description of such a vision *translation* into the language of our sensible forms becomes unavoidable, which coarsen and even materialize the phenomenon. Otherwise it is impossible to talk about this, to bring it close to earthly consciousness. But this is only a translation, and not the original.

---

longing is realized through the medium of angels, because if all creation is Sophianic in its foundation, only humankind has in itself the image of Divine Sophia in its fullness.

And so, when a human sees angels it is in their own form and not in one that conforms to our corporeality. Like is known only by like, spirit is known only by spirit, and this very vision is evidence of the original bond and kinship of the angelic and human worlds, of the angels' co-humanity. This does not diminish the eminence and sanctity which distinguishes angels from humans and that is expressed in the special luminescence of their winged forms, but their essential co-humanity is not diminished by this division. On this is based their representation on icons, which can be given meaning dogmatically only by taking their co-humanity as the point of departure. In the iconoclast disputes the question of the representation of God, who is Spirit, provoked the chief altercations. The basis of the dogma of icon veneration is the divine incarnation in which God became a human being and therefore able to be depicted. As a Spirit, God cannot be depicted. But here the distinction of the absolute Divine Spirit and the creaturely, relative spirit comes forward. Absolute Spirit surpasses all images and forms although it contains in Itself the foundation of them all: the Form of Forms itself cannot have any particular form at all. But we know that God appeared in the Old Testament to humankind in theophanic angelophanies through the medium of angels. This signifies that although it is a spirit, an angel has an inner form or image which is accessible to spiritual vision. Therefore it can be depicted, although the depiction of an angel is all the same only the translation of the supersensible into the language of sensible images. Usually when contrasting God as absolute Spirit and angels as creaturely spirits in order to distinguish them, a certain corporeality is attributed to angels, in view of the fact that God is incorporeal Spirit. But in reality this distinction does not pertain to corporeality and incorporeality; rather it must refer to the fact that creaturely spirits, angels, have a form but absolute Spirit is beyond both form and image. The creatureliness of the angelic spirit in and of itself does not make it corporeal, in any sense whatsoever, but it does make it limited, with a definite form or image, and hence able to be depicted. Therefore the dogma of icon veneration in relation to icons of the Lord Jesus Christ, and with Him, of the Holy Trinity, has its foundation in the divine incarnation, whereas in relation to the holy angels, the dogma is based on their co-humanity. The latter, of course, is distinct from and even in a certain sense contrary to hominization, which remains impossible for angels.

The distinction between the relation to the corporeality of absolute Divine Spirit and creaturely angelic spirit can be expressed from yet another aspect. One can call God incorporeal in the sense that a material body formed out of "earth" and constituting the ontological property of humankind with its whole world is completely foreign to Him as well as to angels. But one should not understand this freedom from a body as applied to Divinity in a restrictive, negative sense, which would deny any positive foundation of creaturely corporeality in God. Where could it have arisen from otherwise? God is incorporeal Spirit, free in His being from bodily limitedness; but being free from corporeality God possesses it in His divine world as the fullness of the ideas, the forms of every being. This ideal corporeality is the divine world before its creation, i.e., Divine Sophia who in this sense can be defined as the spiritual "body of God." The world, created on the foundation of Divine Sophia, carries the forms of this body in its creaturely, earthly corporeality. And since the world is humankind (Adam-Kadmon) in its totality, the materiality of the world is human, receiving in the human body its perfect fullness.

The human body, as the organ of the spirit, bears its seal and is its revelation. The human spirit has the image of God which is extended to its corporeality. Therefore the Word of God speaks about God in anthropomorphic corporeal images. A false anthropomorphism, condemned by the Church and consisting in the assimilation to God of an earthly human body, must not be an obstacle to true anthropology, which has an indestructible basis in the divine incarnation. For, if Christ united a Divine and a human nature in Himself, without division and without confusion, if He assumed a true and not a spectral body, this means that between His divinity and His humanity there exists a *positive* correlation, which alone makes the divine incarnation possible. If God were alien to any corporeality, He would be limited by it. How then could He become incarnate, take a body, which on the mountain of Transfiguration showed the perfect image of Divinity? And so the foundations of creaturely, earthly corporeality are contained in the pre-eternal Wisdom of God, the perfect organism of divine ideas, but, to be sure, fully free from earthly corporeality, from meonal matter. The human in its earthly corporeality has the creaturely image of divine corporeality in its Sophianic fullness. In this it differs from the angels who are alien to the fullness of ideal corporeality because they do not have their own nature or world. In its individually qualified being each angel contains a definite aspect of Divine Sophia whose fullness is inherent only in the whole angelic assembly. In this way we come to the conclusion that the incorporeality of the angels, as creaturely spirits, has another meaning besides the incorporeality of Divinity. God, as absolute Spirit, is free of a body, but He possesses perfect spiritual corporeality in Divine Sophia as the organism of ideas, and according to her image the earthly world is created and in it the human body. Angels taken separately do not possess corporeality, even in a spiritual sense, except for the particular form of it inherent to and intended for each angel. Therein is expressed the true ontological limitedness of angelic nature as that which does not have a body. Nevertheless and in the measure of the Sophianicity of being which is inherent in each of the angels, they have in themselves their own ideal forms, and these forms are co-human, for the Sophianicity of angelic and human being is one. All the same, the *"joy"* of the Wisdom of God, i.e., its fullness, is in human sons and daughters.

A spirit can become perceptible for another spirit in various and diverse ways. We know this from the experience of human relations: people are always found in a spiritual give-and-take with each other, and the influence of one spirit on another has different degrees and forms. But in human interrelations this give-and-take never remains purely spiritual because it takes place through the medium of a body. Human relations with the angelic world occur apart from any corporeality and are purely spiritual, which is why they are so fine and elusive, so tender and difficult to notice. We sometimes feel in us a certain inspiration of love for God, a surge of good desires, without pondering over whence and why this sudden and unusual inspiration, these or other good thoughts and yearnings have appeared. So it is sometimes that in the presence of a person who stands on a spiritual height we feel ourselves to be different, we become better from this sole presence and from its immediate influence. But this presence is visible to us and in general can be noticed by our bodily senses.

But the presence around us of a luminous spirit, which we experience on ourselves, remains unknown to us, although effective. This explains that without knowing it we are always found in the region of influence and interaction with the angelic world, insofar as we do not counteract it or block the path by our sins. We need not think that the influence of the angelic world on us is restricted to direct angelophanies and does not exist outside of them. On the contrary, these appearances of angels are only manifestations of that which is continually going on with us and around us that have become for us spiritually observable and perceptible.[7] These appearances of the angels have a basis in a special divine

---

7. This is disclosed with great clarity in the book of Tobit. The archangel Raphael speaks here to the devout Tobias before he takes leave of him through his removal to heaven: "'when you and your bride Sarah prayed, I brought the memory of your prayer before the Holy One, and when you buried the dead I also was with you. And when you were not hindered by laziness to get up and leave your dinner in order to go and dispose of the dead one, your charity was not hidden from me, but I was with you. And now God

regard, in the mission intended for each angel. But of themselves they do not contain anything whatever that corresponds to the nature of the mutual relations of the angelic and human world, supernatural or contrary to nature. The unusual and extraordinary can be just as natural as the routine and constant. (Similarly miracles represent an unusual testimony of the omnipotence of the Creator and His providence for the world, which, however, is always manifested in the order of the universe that God established. We always are surrounded by the spiritual world and are found in immediate communion and interaction with it,[8] and the appearances of the angels are only testimonies about this.)

And so, the appearances of angels have a spiritual character; it is not the body but rather the soul that sees them, although in the act of perception it involuntarily gives them a corporeal form. Thus the idea that angels have a body similar to ours, although refined, or that a particular body or even bodies of a soul exist, as occultism teaches, represents at least a misunderstanding. Sometimes this idea is expressed in this way: an angel, being itself free of a body, nevertheless can fashion for itself a body as a temporary envelope or a means of communication in order to appear to a human being. But this idea likewise contains in itself a misunderstanding. It is true that the holy angels have the possibility of direct influence on the life of the world, as this is sufficiently disclosed in Revelation, without speaking of other biblical testimonies (an angel strikes 185,000 Assyrians, subdues the flame of fire in the burning oven, rolls the stone away from the grave, frees the apostle Peter from prison, and others besides). It is necessary not only to support this idea with all its force but also to give it the broadest application in the sense that the angelic world is the ideal spirit-energy basis of this world which exists only on condition of the angels' constant service.

But this power of the angels does not belong to the number of natural *powers of this world* in any sense whatsoever (even if through the assumption of a temporary body). This power is not physical but metaphysical; it is spiritual energy which operates from within on the very foundations of being. For God performs miracles in the world not by en-

---

has sent me to heal you and your bride Sarah . . . I came not by my own choosing but according to the will of our God. . . . I am ascending to the One who sent me.' And they stood up and saw him no longer" (Tobit 12:12-21).

8. "O Lord of all, you clearly save the human race by your appointed angels, for you have appointed them for all the faithful" (Service for Bodiless Spirits, tone 1, canon, ode 7, tr. 2). "Wanting all humans to be saved, you appointed the holy angels as mentors and guides into the light" (Canon of the Guardian Angels, ode 1, tr. 2).

tering among its physical forces — God is absolute Spirit — but by influencing the metaphysical structure of creation. Therefore the action of the angels is so irresistible and mighty that the destruction of the metaphysical atoms of the world and its metaphysical structure has an incommensurately greater effect than the corresponding physical processes, no matter how powerful they might be. For that reason angels are expressly entrusted with bringing about the end of the world, the last harvest, the burning up of the darnel and the final separation. At the voice of the archangel and the trumpets of God the resurrection from the dead is accomplished (1 Thessalonians 4:16). "And he will send His angels with a thundering trumpet and they will gather His elect from the four winds and from one end of heaven to the other" (Matthew 24:31). This metaphysical action has a corresponding expression in the natural world. While difficult to comprehend in the manner of its execution, it is comprehensible in its essence which consists in the fact that *our world is not closed in on itself*. It is opened to the action of spiritual powers so that its life and inherent laws are not only immanent-physical but also transcendent-metaphysical. The creation has two inherent laws and two faces, one turned to the natural world, the other to the spiritual, angelic world. Examined in itself the world is a mechanism and organism of natural forces, but it has its spiritual or metaphysical basis in the angelic world.[9]

On this is founded both the common correlation of the worlds determining the inherent laws of our life as well as direct interaction of the worlds. The angelic world is not merely the sum total of ideal prototypes; rather, it consists of hypostatic spirits which have personal activity and

---

9. In his doctrine on the cognition of angels, blessed Augustine outlines this bond and unity of the angelic and human world which have a common foundation in Divine Wisdom, though he does not carry it through to the end. According to his doctrine (developed primarily in *De Genesi ad litteram libri XII.*, partially in *De civitate Dei*), the angels grasp the foundations of creation in God and this is the true *day* of creation, diurnal cognition. (Blessed Augustine does not draw from this the further conclusion that angels, cognizing the fundamental principle of creation in the Wisdom of God, are thereby its creaturely prototype, for to cognize metaphysically means already *to be* — by participation.) Then, contemplating these prototypes in their earthly realization, they come to know by a darkened, *evening* cognition: "and it was evening," *cognitio vespertina*. But turning to the very Wisdom of God, they clearly see them — "and it was morning," *cognitio matutina*. From this union of evening and morning arises the *day* of creation, in keeping with the characteristic word usage of the book of Genesis: "and it was evening and it was morning, the day was one" (Genesis 1:5f.), with *night*, that corresponds to non-being and ignorance, being quite absent in this calculation of metaphysical time (*De Gen. ad lit.* V. 18; IV, 31).

are capable of manifesting it in the world, without merging with it or ever being separated from it; perhaps they exercise it both from the outside and from the inside. In this manner there is neither any necessity nor metaphysical possibility for the angels to become cosmic entities, to take root in our world by ceasing to be themselves for the sake of appearing in the world or exerting influence on the world. Therefore the idea that in order to make their appearance angels fashion for themselves a substantial body belonging to our world must be rejected on this account. It can be accepted only in the general sense that angels, while remaining what they are, extra-cosmic entities, have power in this world to influence its elements. For example, the story about the angel who rolled the stone away from the door of the tomb and sat on it should be understood in this sense: the angel does not become like a strong man who is able to accomplish an action that is not within human power to do (although it happens freely by means of a hoisting crane). No, this means that the stone rolled itself away under the metaphysical influence of the angel, which is not subject to any physical reckoning in this world. The world is not closed in itself for a single moment, at any point of its existence, but is always opened to the influence of spiritual forces, which is determined and limited only by the will of God.

But there remain still some misunderstood instances of deliberate anthropomorphism in the appearance of angels. In particular, how is one to understand, for example, the three angels' eating of food in their appearance to Abraham ("and they ate" Genesis 18:8)? How is one to understand Jacob's night-time struggle, after which his hip proved to be injured (Genesis 32:31-32)? Of course, it is impossible to give an exact answer to such questions; it is only possible to indicate a general possibility of their solution. In the book of Tobit, the archangel Raphael directly explains that he merely assumed the appearance of eating food; consequently, his fellow travellers were left in a certain illusion. For the sake of sense perception, the realism of an angel's presence in his co-humanity is automatically expressed in features such as correspond not to angelic but to human nature. But sometimes such features are absent, as for example in the appearance to Gideon and Manoah (Judges 6:20-21; 13:15-16). One thing is beyond question, that the angels who represented God Himself in their appearance to Abraham obviously could not eat earthly food, because they did not have earthly bodies.[10] But precisely how those standing nearby could see them

10. What appears to contradict this is that these two angels later become the object of the sinful desires of the Sodomites (Genesis 19). But this speaks not about their corpore-

eating is not known to us. As for Jacob's night-time struggle, it too must be understood first of all as the spiritual state of theomachy; inherent in all his heirs, it was already pre-formed in the patriarch. In keeping with the spiritual and corporeal nature of humankind, this spiritual state was accompanied by a feeling of physical combat to such a degree that it was expressed even in physical injury. In a case such as this, where a theophanic angelophany takes place, one must completely refrain from attributing to the One being revealed any sort of corporeality prior to His incarnation. But at the same time it is impossible here not to see a kind of spiritual prefiguration and anticipation, although unattainable for us.

Thus the appearances of angels in human form must be explained on the basis of the angels' general co-humanity, while fully dismissing the natural corporeality of this appearance in any sense whatsoever.

The co-humanity of angels is deliberately manifested in the exclusive relation of the guardian angel to humankind. In this relation there is one feature that deserves special attention. Christians, on receiving a Christian name at baptism, enter into special relations with that *saint* whose name they bear, the saint usually being called their "angel" (and the name day, "the angel's day"). There are different ways to define this relation between a name and its bearer, but it is beyond question that the one bearing the

---

ality but only about the sensual depravity of the residents of Sodom, for whom spiritual eyes were opened for the vision of the angels in human form, but whose sinful blindness prevented them from proving themselves worthy of this vision. This case shows, by the way, that the vision of the spiritual world can be accessible to humankind outside a direct correspondence to its spiritual condition (for example, after he sinned and even though he repented David saw the Lord's destroying angel with a naked sword drawn against Jerusalem [1 Chronicles 21:16]). Even an irrational creature, Balaam's donkey, by the special providence of God, could see an angel blocking its path (Numbers 22:23-33).

The exegesis of Genesis 6:2, 4, the story about the "sons of God" (and in some manuscripts, precisely "angels of God") taking wives and going in to them, presents an exceptional difficulty. Besides the general doubtfulness of interpreting this passage with reference to angels, even if it really is to be understood about angels who are of course fallen, it is necessary to understand this text in keeping with the general doctrine of angels' nature, who cannot have bodily intercourse because they are incorporeal. But fallen spirits can desire it, and they can delight in it with humans and arouse them, which is what demons of fornication do. One can understand this passage in the sense of a spiritual and not a carnal arousal or co-sharing in the carnal life of people, although it is necessary to admit that this is not directly indicated. The generation of giants, i.e., when humanity became excessively carnal ("since they are flesh" [Genesis 6:3]) resulted when the fallen angels, who so perverted their essence that they lost the desire to be themselves, but wanted to live a corporeal life, became spiritually carnal.

name of the saint stands in exceptional personal proximity to the saint, becomes a member of the saint's spiritual family, and in some measure is imprinted with the saint's nature. The spiritual countenance of this saint is for them simultaneously the spiritual basis and ideal, the given and the proposed as some sort of spiritual entelechy. There really exists here a parallel with the guardian angel and thus it is not by accident that the saint is also called an angel. In this manner it is shown that every Christian has in the heavens *two* protectors — a saint and a guardian angel who intercede on their behalf in prayer. The difference between them, however, is that an angel stands immediately before the throne of God and in the fullness of its life there is no longer room for change or increase. Angels have achieved already the ultimate perfection after the trial and victory over Satan, whereas saints, no matter how great their present glory, remain in a preliminary state, for they are waiting for the resurrection in a glorified body and their proximity to God is not yet definitive and final. In addition, a guardian angel has one immediately protected human, and is its prototype in the heavens, whereas the "angel" saint has many who bear his name and constitute so to speak a spiritual nest. Between the angelic and the human world in the glorified church special interwoven interrelations arise in the *common* work of guarding and protecting the human race. And in this is manifested once again the co-humanity of the angels.

A name is not an alias, but a power: *nomen omen*. The name of a saint which one receives is already one's idea and entelechic power, and naming is spiritual sowing. This is clear in the relation of a human with the baptismal name, taken from any saint at all. But in relations between humans and their guardian angel? Is not the heavenly name of a human contained here, which is unknown to us, insofar as this is an angelic name, and yet is real and effective? It is known that angels have their own names. This could have been supposed already a priori but it is established a posteriori too, for the names of the highest angels who stand before the throne (the biblical names among them are Michael, Gabriel, Raphael) are revealed to us. There is absolutely no basis for thinking that they constituted an exception in this, and that the remaining angels were left nameless. On the contrary, to each angel is inherent its own individual place in the hierarchies and its proper ideal basis or Sophianic theme of its being, but the idea is at the same time a word, for everything participates in a word. A word — its own proper one, is already a name. Thus angels are our heavenly homonyms, similar to how saints are our "angels." In this a new interaction between the names of angels and humans begins to take shape. But we lack straightforward facts for disclosing this interaction further.

CHAPTER 8

The Angelic World and Divine Incarnation

The relation of angels to God is established by means of their creation and is confirmed by their free self-determination in their testing and the division which ensued. After this it is definitively accomplished and in itself the being of angels has no need of suppletion and does not allow substantial change. The angelic rank is in itself perfect, *apart from* any relation to the redemptive sacrifice of Golgotha which saves the human race. The relation of angels to the Word and to the whole Holy Trinity is direct and immediate: "You have made the bodiless intelligences participants, O Savior, of your inexpressible glory,"[1] "theophoric coals kindled by the dawn of your essence."[2] The angels' relation to the world and to humankind likewise is fully established by means of their creation in conjunction with the world and for its service, the presence of a direct and substantial bond between the celestial and the terrestrial world being its ontological foundation. This bond is indestructible, for it is based on something more than affinity; it is based on the ideal identity of both worlds. It constitutes the very condition of our world's existence, without which — outside the custody of the angels — it loses its being. But this interrelation of both worlds, although it is not interrupted, it is disturbed by the fall of our ancestors, which entailed the sickness of the whole universe. That this bond is not utterly torn asunder by the fall is made clear first of all from the angelophanies in the

1. Service for the Bodiless Spirits, tone 1, canon, ode 9, tr. 1.
2. Ode 1, tr. 1: "The seraphim who approach the theurgic light in unmediated fashion and are abundantly satisfied with it appear as first created by first-given flashes and they are like second lights, divinized by divinity" (Ode 2, tr. 1).

Old Testament, and also from other evidence that angels keep watch over the human world in the fates of individuals, independent nations, and the whole natural essence.

A clear vision of this bond was given to the patriarch Jacob in a dream when he saw a ladder uniting heaven and earth: "and behold angels of God ascend and descend on it" (Genesis 28:12). Although Jacob's ladder is interpreted by the Church as a prototype of the Mother of God, and consequently is understood in the light of the divine incarnation now accomplished, its meaning expands into the Old Testament to which this very vision belongs. But the fall, which disturbed the relation of humankind with God and through this with the world, and above all, with itself, changed this relation to the angelic world too. The path for direct communion of angels with humans was cut off, after Eve and, through her, Adam entered into communion with the serpent, who had become the prince of this world and spread his hellish influence on the whole human race. Corresponding to how humankind distanced itself from God and immersed itself in its corporeal world, it distanced itself also from the angels of God. But the estrangement of humankind from God was not unconditional and final, for the world cannot exist outside of God. In a similar way the estrangement from the angelic world could not be a complete separation, for this would not correspond to their original and fundamental correlation.

Although remaining transcendent, God is revealed to Old Testament humanity in angelophanies, appearances of Glory (doxophanies), and prophetic aureoles, patent and clear in the bounds of the Old Testament church, dim and veiled beyond its bounds, in paganism. Likewise the angels who are deliberately sent by God draw near to humankind, but they are not absent at any point in human life, although they are deprived of that concord which was pre-established for them. The co-humanity of the angels does not reach its fullness, for the heavy shadow of humankind's original sin lay on the angelic world as well. Not only in keeping with the co-suffering love for fallen humanity, but also according to their own nature for which life in union with the human race was pre-established, the holy angels hoped for our salvation. Although they did not know fully the form of its achievement, they did know its path, for they themselves took part in smoothing it out. The history of the world's salvation through the divine incarnation already begins in paradise with the proclamation of the so-called Protoevangelium about the Woman's Seed, and it is accomplished as a living genealogy of the Savior through the whole history of humanity. And in this the holy angels operate "as petitioners of your becoming human and honorable rising."[3]

In all the decisive moments of the life of the Hebrew nation the holy angels, keeping watch over the world, draw near to its leaders and prophets. Their closeness, although not manifest but dim, is sensed already by the whole pagan world, for it is full of presentiment and of visions of gods, genies, demons, Fravashi,[4] etc., who animate the world and enlighten humankind, being the guardians of souls and bodies. In their ignorance of the true God, pagans were being led and taught by angels, as is obvious from the story of Cornelius (Acts 11:13) and the prophecy of Daniel. But through heaven's bending down to earth and the Son of God's coming down from the heavens and becoming human, the path to that perfect union with humanity has been revealed to the angels of God and as such corresponds to their co-humanity. This is not the merging or mixing of both natures, for angels and humans remain themselves. Neither is it the angels' becoming human, for along that false path only Satan goes, seeking ultimately to become human in the antichrist. Rather, this is the perfect union of angels and humans in Christ and His Church. "The earthly having wedded with the heavenly, O Christ, you have made one church for angels and humans, and we unceasingly extol you,"[5] testifies the Church.

The divine incarnation in this respect has a double meaning: on the one hand, together with the Logos in His divine incarnation the angelic world draws near to earth and comes to humankind as His servants. "Angelic companies precede Him with every principle and power." The gospel story witnesses to the service of the angels to Christ over the course of the whole history of the divine incarnation; in the annunciation, in His nativity, baptism, and temptation, in the sufferings and resurrection and in the glorious second coming. At the same time the power of redemption opens to the angels an access to fallen but rehabilitated humankind. Therein lie the meaning and power of that testimony of the Church that a guardian angel is given to us at our baptism, and as a result, in a real sense draws near only to the baptized. In this manner the union of the angelic world

3. Service for the Archangels, tone 1, canon, ode 3, tr. 2. About the archangel Gabriel the Church sings, "you are pre-eminent among the bodiless servants, and to you alone, Gabriel, is gloriously entrusted the primordially commanded dread mystery, the ineffable birth of the holy Virgin" (Service for the Synaxis of the Archangel Gabriel, 3 July, kathisma verse).

4. A Fravashi is the guardian spirit of an individual in Zoroastrianism. Translator's note.

5. Service for the Archangels, ode 9, tr. 1.

with the human world is accomplished by virtue of both natures of Christ
— divine and human — by virtue of divine condescension and salvific redemption. Strictly speaking, only the latter is connected integrally with
the fall of Adam, whereas the former can be examined independently although in fact they both are indivisibly united for fallen humankind.
Even if Adam had not fallen, the incarnation, according to the opinion of
some theologians, would all the same have occurred for the sake of the
complete divinization of humankind and in it the angelic world would be
completely and finally reunited with the human. Thanks to the fall the incarnation becomes redemption as well. Therefore it is necessary to distinguish these two aspects of the significance of the incarnation for the angelic world. The incarnation as redemption benefits only fallen humanity
and in itself has no power for the angels. On the contrary, as the
divinization of humans, which is possible after their rehabilitation, it has
power for the angelic world as well because without this divine means it
remains deprived of the power finally to fasten the golden chain of creation, which joins *heaven and earth*. In this manner the divine incarnation
has meaning not for angelic nature itself, as such, but for its relation to
humanity. "All power *in heaven and on earth* has been given to Me" (Matthew 28:19). With these solemn words the Risen Lord bears witness to the
accomplishment of His salvific work. The circle of the universe, which begins through "in the beginning God created heaven and earth," is closed
by this last uniting of heaven and earth under the authority of Him by
Whom all things came to be (cf. Hebrews 12:22-24).

The meaning of the incarnation for the reunion of the angelic and
human world is solemnly attested by the Lord Himself in his conversation
with Nathaniel. "Truly, truly I say to you, from now on you will see heaven
opened and the angels of God ascending and descending upon the Son of
Man" (John 1:51). This text has paramount importance for understanding
the meaning which belongs to the incarnation in the establishment of relations between the angelic and human world. It is naturally brought in
connection with the prototypical vision of Jacob's ladder (Genesis 28:12).
In it the Lord stands above the ladder and from there he gives a promise
to the forefather, in whose loins is already sown the human flesh of the
Divine Human, from Whom the descending angels are sent below and to
Whom the ascending angels are lifted up. Here the Lord Himself is found
on earth; the descending and ascending angels come to Him on earth, and
heaven remains open. That the Old Testament knows only angelophanic
theophanies which are completely unknown in the New Testament corresponds to this. Here on earth God Himself has appeared in the flesh and

"He lived with humans," and that is why the angels draw near to Him in their own rank for the service of God and humankind together and for the full reunion in Him with the human race. In this way the incarnation and the redemptive sacrifice have meaning first of all for the reconciliation of humankind with God, but in it for the union with the angelic world as well. "It was pleasing to God [the Father] that [in Jesus Christ] all fullness should dwell and that by means of Him to reconcile everything with Himself, *both on earth and in heaven,* having made peace through Him, by the blood of His cross" (Colossians 1:19-20).[6]

Connected with the incarnation is also the glorification of human nature which has its personal expression in the Most Holy Theotokos, "more honorable than the cherubim and more glorious beyond compare than the seraphim." United according to the flesh with the One born of her, the Mother of God stands in such proximity to God that it surpasses the angels' proximity. She herself heads *in fullness* the whole creation, which the angels represent only ideally, not each angel separately but only all angels in their assembly. Hence in her is realized the ultimate goal of creation, which the angels themselves serve. But, obviously, the very possibility of the appearance of such a human being, who in herself unites all the power, holiness, purity, and fullness of the angelic world with all the reality of human nature, is the result of the elevation of humankind through the divine incarnation. It was accomplished through the descent of the Holy Spirit upon the Mother of God at the annunciation, by the divine conception and birth. In the Spirit and the Word the Mother of God received and reunited with human nature all that the holy angels have.

St. John the Forerunner comes after the Mother of God in proximity to God. According to the witness of the Church, although he does not surpass the angels as does the Mother of God, he is united with them in their station before the throne of God. But being above all a human, he exceeds them by the fullness and complexity of his angelo-human nature. This very union represents the mystery of the future age, and we can only approximate an understanding of it. The Forerunner, as the human being who is "greater than all born of women," and as the baptizer who is placed by his ministry higher than the angels, becomes a participant in the angelic world too. The mode of angelic being consists in their immediate

6. The words of Revelation concerning the struggle of the archangel Michael and his angels with the dragon have this general meaning of the redemptive sacrifice for the reconciliation and reunion of humankind with God: "They defeated him *by the blood of the Lamb* and by the word of their testimony" (Revelation 12:11).

participation in divine life, since they do not have their own world and nature, whereas for humans such participation is accessible only through the divinization of their nature by virtue of the incarnation. In the Theotokos, by virtue of her Divine Motherhood, both the immediate participation in the divine and the perfect divinization of her humanity are realized. But in the Forerunner too his immediate proximity to Christ, equal to the angels, is united with his human nature which is of course inalienable. This establishes the life of the Forerunner in both worlds or, rather, the twofold form of his relation to God: angelic and human.[7] The Mother of God and the Forerunner are themselves at the head of humanity that is saved and united with God.

Owing to the redemptive work of Christ the angels receive a new possibility for active love towards the human race and for sharing in the common work of the universe. Redemption from original sin for an individual human is realized in baptism and that is why a guardian angel, attendant to us from creation, receives the possibility to draw near interiorly, and not only externally, and to serve us from holy baptism. In this sense sometimes it is said that the guardian angel is given at baptism.[8]

The participation of the angels in the accomplishment of the end, in the final reckoning, in the separating of the wheat from the darnel and the burning of the latter, deserves particular attention. The historical and metaphysical participation of angels in the destinies of the human race is expressed by these images. And this participation, this common life and common work, is concluded *by the encounter* of the whole human race and the whole angelic assembly in the last hour of the life of the world at the Dread Judgment. This encounter, which for each one is anticipated by the encounter beyond the grave, will no longer be interrupted by a severing, except for the outcast whose lot will be communion with Satan and the fallen angels in "the eternal fire prepared for the devil and his angels" (Matthew 25:41). This will be the inseparability and commonality of the life of humankind with the angelic world. It contains the source of those unearthly joys which we in our present existence can neither see nor imagine and for which we cannot even make room. And yet foreknowledge and

---

7. The result of this is that the Forerunner is his own angel, and this is why for his human essence there is no prototype in the angelic world. He is "the friend of the Bridegroom" and thus in Christ he has his Friend, similar to how the Divine Bride and Mother has her heavenly prototype in the hypostasis of the Holy Spirit indwelling in her.

8. In the order of catechesis that is performed before baptism, in the fourth prayer one reads "pair the life of his bright angel who delivered him from all perfidy," etc.

presentiment of them is given to us all the same. It is nourished and warmed in us by our love for the holy angels, our prayer to them and our common praise and prayer to God. . . .

Thy will be done on earth as it is in heaven — the Lord teaches us to pray for this as for a higher, ultimate accomplishment. The Lord created the world as *heaven and earth,* which look at themselves one in the other. In the heavens the will of God is performed without fail by angelic companies; in its condition the angelic world corresponds to God's plan for it. Not so is the earthly, human world in its present being. But humankind must become conformed to Christ, so that everything earthly and heavenly finds its head in Christ. And through the fulfillment of the will of God, through the correspondence of creation to God's plan for it, that harmony and unity of the angelic and human worlds, heaven and earth, is naturally established, which is placed at the foundation of the universe: "in the beginning God created heaven and earth." The power of these words is mysteriously inserted in the Lord's Prayer.[9]

The last revelation which is given by the Word of God about the disclosure of the co-humanity of the angels together with the union of angels and humans is contained in the last vision of the last book of the New Testament, the Revelation of St. John (21:12-17). The Seer sees the Holy City coming down from heaven in order to be the eternal dwelling of God with humans. This city has twelve gates and on them twelve angels, and on the gates are written the names of the twelve tribes of the sons of Israel. "And he measured its wall as one hundred and forty-four cubits (12 x 12) with a human measure, which is also the angel's measure." Both measures, identical from the very beginning, have coincided in the final accomplishment. *The human measure which is also the angel's measure* — the exposition of these mysterious words of Revelation constitutes the chief task of the present work, and in them is expressed its fundamental and sole idea.

9. The significance of the petition being examined is explained also from the place that it occupies in the general composition of the Lord's Prayer. The mysterious meaning of its first part refers to the Holy Trinity as a whole: "Our Father who art in heaven" is the First hypostasis. "Hallowed be Thy name" is the Second hypostasis of the Word-Name. "Thy kingdom come" (the older variant in St. Gregory of Nyssa, "May the Holy Spirit come") is the Third hypostasis. In this part is attested the participation of the whole Holy Trinity in the production of the world. And in the fulfillment of this world-building and world-producing activity of the Holy Spirit the world is shown its ultimate goal: "Thy will be done on earth as it is in heaven," let God be all in all. The following and further petitions refer to our present life on earth (for daily bread, for forgiveness of sins, for not being led into temptation, and for deliverance from the evil one).

CONCLUSION

About Angels

The holy angels have their name not from themselves (as do humans) but from their service. Their purpose is to mediate between God and the world. This service is not only God's will for them but by virtue of their freedom it is their own self-determination, the form of angelic love. The power of love consists in its sacrificial quality and its form is the form of selflessness. The particular form of angelic love consists in the fact that their personal love for God and the whole human race (for any love, first of all, is personal) is accompanied by a natural, metaphysical kenosis. In it is accomplished a repudiation of possessing their own, proper independent nature and the co-assumption of the life of another creature, that of a human being. Angels, as incorporeal spirits, are also without nature. They live by divine participation, as second lights, and by co-humanity, as guardians of our human nature. For all their supernal loftiness they abase themselves with measureless humility in their love for God, who has willed them to serve, and in love for the human world which could not have received being and lived its own life without that service. "Love does not seek its own" (1 Corinthians 13), and in truth, angelic love does not have or know anything that is its own. Incorporeal spirits, pure hypostases, in their voluntary love they renounce *being in themselves:* they live only outside themselves, not *their own* life, in metaphysical self-kenosis. By nature they are *only* angels, hypostatic *metaxu*. Such a form of being can seem to be a state of poverty and emptiness, a kind of half-being, a not-full-being. And yet, in reality, the superabundance of being takes place here, for in it is revealed the triumphant power of superabundant love.

The mystery of love and its power consist in dying for the sake of res-

162

urrection, in life through death, for love is selflessness. Creaturely love demands empirical selflessness, the sacrifice of one's possessions or wealth, as this is symbolically shown in the Savior's words to the rich young man, "who placed his hope in his wealth." But angelic love is metaphysical selflessness, not only rejecting its own "wealth," but also and in general all *of its own.* This characteristic of angelic love is illustrated *negatively* in the image of the fall of the fallen spirits who desired precisely their own, by soliciting the others to find their kingdom with "the prince of this world." But this solicitation was rejected by the good angels, "who did not love their own souls to the point of death" (Revelation 12:11). Such self-kenosis in angelic love, voluntary because moved by love, is the form of divine love. The life of the Holy Trinity is defined by the mutual self-kenosis of the divine hypostases, which have Their own Selves and Their own life not in Themselves, but in the Others: the Father in the Son and Spirit, the Son in the Father and Spirit, and the Spirit in the Father and the Son. Similarly, angels have their life in God and in the human world, retaining for themselves only an "incorporeal" being, i.e., one without nature even though hypostatic. They have only the possibility of being, without its power, and in a certain sense they potentialize themselves.

Furthermore divine love for the world, revealed in its creation, is hypostatic; it is another form of the self-draining of Divinity, which by voluntarily limiting Itself, places the relative being of the world alongside of Itself, and provides it with reality. God gives everything to this creation, while receiving nothing from it for Himself, being all-sufficient, all-blessed, and self-sufficing. Angelic love for our world is similar: it does not have its own, it only gives to it, "serves," it helps humankind become itself for the sake of its very self. But in the self-renunciation of angelic love is contained an endless wealth which is found by love. By virtue of their love for God the holy angels communicate in the life of Divinity Itself, and by virtue of their love for the world they communicate in the life of our world, they live by it, while remaining naturally outside its limits. By this they unite in themselves all the fullness of life as only can be accessible to creation: life in God and in the creaturely human world. In angels the worldly *all* is placed at their creation, but by themselves they acquire this *all* through their service. The life of angels, as created spirits, differs from divine life; it is divine by the gift of participation. It differs also from the life of the human world, but participates in the world by virtue of angelic service. But, above all, it is *personal* love, which finds for itself a Friend and friends in God and humankind. For the Lord too in His creation, in giving everything for it and taking nothing from it, wants one thing from

His creation — love, and in an angel and a human He wants to have for Himself another, a friend.

The world is sheltered by angel wings. Angel eyes keep watch without rest over us. Between heaven and earth the holy angels ascend and descend unceasingly. They join with us in our prayers. Angel hosts unceasingly glorify the Creator of the worlds. Angels, standing before the throne of God, live a common life with us, and are united by the bonds of love. How great is the joy bestowed on humankind knowing this!

> Praise Him, all His angels, praise Him, all His powers!
> Holy archangels and angels, pray to God for us!
> Holy guardian angel, pray to God for us!

Index

Abraham, 106; angelophany to, 152; theophany to, 129, 133, 136, 137

Adam: creation of, 69; fall of, 156; as male, 92

Ahab, 61

Ambrose of Milan, 23

Angelophanies: and angelic forms, 146-47; and corporeality, 142-43; as divine revelation, 156; instances of, 130-31; as manifestations, 149-50; and theophanies, 131-33, 135-38

Angels, 16-17, 26-29, 33-34, 151-52; appearance of, 12, 146-47, 152-54; co-humanity of, 141-43, 153-54; as contemplative, 118-19; creation of, 22-23; divination of, 101-3; domain of, 23-25, 34-35; and eschatology, 58-59; fall of, 48-49, 110-14; form of, 36-38, 116, 142-43, 145-46; freedom of, 64-65, 68-70, 78, 109-10; and gender, 87, 89, 94-100; and God, 15-16, 81-87; hierarchy of, 77-81; hosts of, 21, 44; and humans, 34-38, 61-66; image of God in, 66-68, 75; immortality of, 103-6; and incarnation, 155-61; incorporeality of, 139-41, 143-48; individuality of, 75-78; influence of, 149-51; life of, 115-18; and love, 162-64; and music, 126; Old Testament on, 59-61; and paganism, 25-26; personhood of, 74-75; and prayer, 128; Revelation on, 53-58; as second lights, 73-74; and theophanies, 129-38; and wisdom of God, 30-33; worship of, 119-28

Annunciation, 50, 62; and Gabriel, 45

Anthropomorphism: and angelophanies, 152-54; and corporeality, 148

Antichrist, 157

Apostles, 3

Arius, 102n.4

Art, 126-27. *See also* Iconography

Ascension, 52

Athanasius the Great, 102n.4

Augustine, 5, 23

Babylon, 56, 57

Balaam, 131, 138

Balthazar, 60

Baptism, 39-40

Basil the Great, 23, 40

Beauty, 84-87; in art, 126-27; praise of, 122-24; primacy of, 87

Birth, 70-71

Brianchaninov, Ignaty, 42, 143

"Canon for the Heavenly Powers and all the Saints," 128n.38

Chastity, 100